Ke

Mom

IN THE WAKE OF
LEWIS AND CLARK

IN THE WAKE OF LEWIS AND CLARK

The Expedition and the Making of Antebellum America

Larry E. Morris

ROWMAN & LITTLEFIELD
Lanham • Boulder • New York • London

Published by Rowman & Littlefield
An imprint of The Rowman & Littlefield Publishing Group, Inc.
4501 Forbes Boulevard, Suite 200, Lanham, Maryland 20706
www.rowman.com

Unit A, Whitacre Mews, 26-34 Stannary Street, London SE11 4AB

British Library Cataloguing in Publication Information Available

Library of Congress Cataloging-in-Publication Data

Names: Morris, Larry E., 1951– author.
Title: In the wake of Lewis and Clark : the expedition and the making of antebellum America /
    Larry E. Morris.
Description: Lanham : Rowman & Littlefield, [2019] | Includes bibliographical references and
    index.
Identifiers: LCCN 2018030652 (print) | LCCN 2018045043 (ebook) | ISBN 9781442266117 (elec-
    tronic) | ISBN 9781442266100 | ISBN 9781442266100 (cloth : alk. paper)
Subjects: LCSH: Lewis and Clark Expedition (1804–1806) | West (U.S.)—Discovery and explora-
    tion. | United States—History—1783–1815. | United States—History—1815–1861.
Classification: LCC F592.7 (ebook) | LCC F592.7 .M686 2019 (print) | DDC 917.804/2—dc23
LC record available at https://lccn.loc.gov/2018030652

∞ ™ The paper used in this publication meets the minimum requirements of
American National Standard for Information Sciences Permanence of Paper
for Printed Library Materials, ANSI/NISO Z39.48-1992.

Printed in the United States of America

Thus the Seer,
With vision clear,
Sees forms appear and disappear,
In the perpetual round of strange,
Mysterious change
From birth to death, from death to birth,
From earth to heaven, from heaven to earth;
Till glimpses more sublime
Of things, unseen before,
Unto his wondering eyes reveal
The Universe, as an immeasurable wheel
Turning forevermore
In the rapid and rushing river of Time.

—Henry Wadsworth Longfellow,
"Rain in Summer," 1845

CONTENTS

INTRODUCTION

On Sunday, June 29, 1806, Meriwether Lewis and William Clark and their party of twenty-nine men, one woman, and one child "pursued the hights of the ridge on which [they] had been passing for several days" and, five miles farther on, "decended from [the] ridge [and] bid adieu to the snow." Later called Lolo Pass, at the present Idaho-Montana border, this was hardly foreign territory to the captains—they had followed the same Indian trail in the opposite direction the previous September. So it was not by accident that after a supper of venison, they "continued [their] march seven miles further to the warm springs."

The principal hot spring was "about the temperature of the warmest baths used at the hot springs in Virginia," wrote Lewis, who spent nineteen minutes in the water but only "with difficulty." Then he looked on as "both the men and indians amused themseves with the use of a bath." After staying in the hot pool "as long as they could bear it," the Indians "ran and plunged themselves into the creek the water of which is now as cold as ice can make it; after remaining here a few minutes they returned again to the warm bath, repeating this transition several times but always ending with the warm bath."[1]

The next day, "a little before sunset," they arrived at their "old encampment on the south side of the creek a little above it's entrance into Clark's river." This was the Travelers' Rest camp of September 9–11, 1805, just south of present Lolo, Montana (twelve miles south-southwest of Missoula).[2]

Deer were plentiful in the area, and over the next few days the hunters brought in a good supply of venison. Others in the party packed supplies and repaired guns while the horses got a well-deserved rest. There was even time for some of the men to run footraces against the "hardy strong athletic" Indians, the sole annoyance being the "musque-toes," which were "excessively troublesome." By July 2, Lewis and Clark and their band of explorers were ready to depart the next day with ambitious plans to split into five different groups and explore a good deal of present Montana. That peaceful night, as he had done on many nights, Lewis recorded botanical details in his journal, noting that "the wild rose, servise berry, white berryed honeysuckle, seven bark, elder, alder aspin, choke cherry and the broad and narrow leafed willow are natives of this valley."[3]

In many ways, that July day was the last "normal" day of the expedition for the captains, the last time they were both in good health and traveling together, the last time Clark would draw on Lewis's journal entry to write his own, the last day of traveling together that neither of them had seen any Europeans, other than the expedition members, since departing Fort Mandan.

Forty days and more than six hundred miles later, on August 12, the various troops of the Corps of Discovery reunited in present North Dakota, just above the confluence of the Missouri and Little Missouri Rivers. "At meridian Capt Lewis hove in Sight with the party which went by way of the Missouri as well as that which accompanied him from Travelllers rest," wrote Clark. The joy of the reunion, however, was quickly tempered: "I was alarmed on the landing of the Canoes," continued Clark, "to be informed that Capt. Lewis was wounded by accident—. I found him lying in the Perogue."[4]

Although on July 27 Lewis, George Drouillard, and the Field brothers had escaped unharmed—but had killed two Blackfoot Indians—in the sole violent encounter of the entire expedition, on August 11, Lewis had been accidentally shot by boatman and fiddler (and one-eyed) Pierre Cruzatte as the two were hunting elk. "As wrighting in my present situation is extremely painfull to me I shall desist untill I recover and leave to my frind Capt. C. the continuation of our journal,"[5] Lewis wrote on August 12. It was his final entry.

Just as Lewis's gunshot wound and his leaving the journals to Clark were portents of things to come, the captains' first meeting with Europeans was likewise a signal of the future. "At 8 A. M. the bowsman informed me that there was a canoe and a camp he believed of white-men on the N. E. shore," Lewis had also recorded on August 12. "I directed the peroque and canoes to come too at this place." Lewis found "two hunters from the Illinois by name Joseph Dickson and Forrest Hancock. these men informed me that Capt. C. had passed them about noon the day before." Dickson and Hancock had ascended the Missouri in the summer of 1804, just weeks after Lewis and Clark, and had been "hunting and trapping beaver"[6] for two years, the first of a host of frontiersmen the captains would meet over the next six weeks, all of them going upriver before learning of the corps' successful return.

Clearly, Lewis and Clark can hardly be credited with igniting this trapping frenzy—especially since rumors abounded the same summer that the entire Corps of Discovery had been lost or slaughtered by Indians—but John Colter's going westward with Dickson and Hancock, with Clark's enthusiastic approval, was another sign, this one a harbinger that Lewis and Clark veterans would play key roles in the most successful trading and exploration ventures, with an unbroken line leading from Lewis and Clark, Manuel Lisa, Andrew Henry, and William Ashley to Jedediah Smith, Thomas Fitzpatrick, Kit Carson, and John C. Frémont.

As Lewis and Clark rushed home to St. Louis, sometimes making eighty miles a day, other portents followed—they met one trader destined to become Clark's bitter enemy in the War of 1812 and quite likely met another destined to help discover key western landmarks and also become "the most important fur merchant in the history of the American fur trade during its period of greatest eminence."[7]

On September 23, 1806, Lewis wrote to Thomas Jefferson and announced "the safe arrival of myself and party at 12 Oclk. today at this place [St. Louis] with our papers and baggage." Knowing that finding a water route from Atlantic to Pacific had been Jefferson's top priority for the expedition, Lewis got right to the point, stating "with confidence" that he and Clark had "discovered the most practicable rout which dose exist across the continent by means of the navigable branches of the Missouri and Columbia Rivers."[8]

Trappers, soldiers, and explorers would find out soon enough, however, that treacherous mountains and unnavigable rapids made a truly "practicable" water route impossible. In that regard, Lewis and Clark could not fulfill Jefferson's lofty objective. Nevertheless, the captains had provided crucial information on the rivers that tens of thousands of Oregon Trail pioneers would follow from east to west: the Missouri, the Platte, the Snake, and the Columbia. Not only that, but Lewis and Clark had kept meticulous geographical and cartographical records, with Clark producing an amazingly accurate map of the West; they had made significant diplomatic contact with several Indian nations, including some who had never seen Europeans before, keeping detailed records of Indian culture and language; they had discovered and described "178 plant and 122 animal species previously unknown to science, compiling one of the best records on natural history ever produced."[9]

In short, writes Albert Furtwangler, the Corps of Discovery was "the first party of Americans to cross the Rockies, the first to link American claims in the Columbia River country to the newly acquired realm of Louisiana, . . . the first citizens to know the territory of the United States in its full continental dimensions."[10]

Henry Nash Smith concurs, noting that although the concrete plans of an east-to-west water route that Jefferson announced to Congress in 1803 "proved unworkable when brought to the test of practice," such "practical difficulties were of minor consequence beside Jefferson's continental breadth of vision. The importance of the Lewis and Clark expedition lay on the level of imagination: it was drama, it was the enactment of a myth that embodied the future." This vision "gave tangible substance to what had been merely an idea, and established the image of a highway across the continent so firmly in the minds of Americans that repeated failures could not shake it."[11]

In 1845, a journalist by the name of John L. O'Sullivan, born seven years after Lewis and Clark's safe return to St. Louis, coined a new term that reaffirmed and added to Jefferson's vision: *manifest destiny*.

I

"WHAT WILL BE THE CONSEQUENCE?"

A very cold winter's day," Mahlon Dickerson wrote in his diary on November 22, 1809. "Read the horrible account of Capt. Meriwether Lewis's death on the 10th Oct. I think he was the most sincere friend I ever had."[1]

The thirty-nine-year-old Dickerson, a prominent lawyer and commissioner of bankruptcy in Philadelphia, had known Lewis for seven years. Earlier that day, he had thumbed through the November 13 issue of the *Democratic Press*. At first glance, the four-page newspaper had simply looked like more of the same, with news from London, New York, and Boston; stories about wars and disasters in far-off places; and finally, amid the advertisements for theater tickets, worm-destroying lozenges, large brass wash kettles, squirrel and fowling guns and ammunition, and German silk, fleecy petticoats, and "fancy ribbons of every description," were the notices inevitably seen every week:

- reward for securing mulatto boy guilty of absconding from the service of his master;
- request of anyone having demands against estate of man recently deceased;
- plea to owner of stray cow to prove property, pay charges, and take animal away.

Dickerson easily could have missed the inconspicuous two lines in the middle of the second page introducing a new article:

Lexington, (Ken.) Oct. 28.
Governor M. Lewis

In the wire service—or social network—of the day, a widely re-printed story announced the death of the thirty-five-year-old governor of upper Louisiana by merging extracts from three different sources: an unnamed Kentucky gentleman's letter, a Nashville newspaper article, and the commentary of an unnamed editor of yet another newspaper.[2]

"A gentleman from Nashville informs me that he conversed with a person who had seen governor Meriwether Lewis buried on the 12th inst. about 40 miles beyond Nashville on the Natchez road," read the article. Lewis reportedly arrived at a house quite weak from a recent illness "and showed signs of mental derangement. After a stay of a few hours at the above house, he took his pistols and shot himself twice, and then cut his throat."[3]

Lewis had apparently "drawn bills to a considerable amount on the government . . . which came back protested," reported the unnamed editor. "We can hardly suppose, however, that an incident of this kind could have produced such deplorable consequences."

According to the Nashville paper, Lewis, "on his way to Washington City, came to the house of a Mr. Grinder near the Indian Line, . . . Mr. Grinder not being home." After Lewis and his servants partook of din-ner and some spirits, "Mrs. Grinder retired to the kitchen with the children, and the servants (after the Governor went to bed, which he did in good order) went to a stable about three hundred yards distant to sleep—no one in the house with the governor." Then, sometime before midnight, "Mrs. Grinder was alarmed by the firing of two pistols in the house—she called to the servants without effect—and at the appear-ance of daylight the servants came to the house when the Governor said he had done for himself—they asked what and he said he had shot himself and would die."

Lewis asked the servants to bring him water. "He then laying on the floor where he expired about 7 o'clock in the morning of the 11th—he had shot a ball that grazed the top of his head and another through his intestines, and cut his neck and arm and ham with a razor. When in his best senses he spoke about a trunk of papers which he said would be of great value to our government."

The editor again interjected: "During the few leisure moments [Lewis] had from his official duties, he was employed in writing the particulars of his celebrated tour up the Missouri—to complete which appears to have been the wish nearest his heart." Fortunately, "we have it from a source which can be depended upon, that he had accomplished the work in three very large volumes, with an immense number of paintings," all of which was ready for the press.

The thoughtful and well-read Dickerson would have appreciated the lines from Thomas Gray's "Elegy Written in a Country Churchyard" that concluded the article:

> The boast of heraldry, the pomp of pow'r
> And all that beauty, all that wealth e'er gave,
> Awaits alike th' inevitable hour.
> The paths of glory lead but to the grave. [4]

On that cold winter's night of November 22—154 years to the day before the death of John F. Kennedy—with the weather matching his somber mood, Dickerson recorded his reaction to his dear friend's death and then turned back to earlier entries in his diary. At the end of his original mundane notes of Tuesday, October 10, he added: "Poor Meriwether Lewis killd. Himself this night." Then he scanned back to 1807, the year he had last seen Lewis, to the entries of June 15, when he "walked till late with Capt. Lewis—round the Centre Square"; July 2, when he and Lewis had visited a mutual friend, spending "the day very pleasantly in eating drinking and shooting at the trees"; and July 13, when he wrote, "my Friend Capt. L in trouble"—apparently a reference to Lewis's unsuccessful attempts to find a wife. "Busy all day at my office," Dickerson had written on Monday, July 20, shortly before Lewis left for St. Louis. "Walkd. at evg. with Capt. Lewis, round the Centre Square—perhaps for the last time." Now, acknowledging the finality of his loss, Dickerson underlined the last sentence and added: "Saw him no more."

The same day that Dickerson paid this private tribute to Lewis, Thomas Jefferson, the man who had appointed Dickerson commissioner of bankruptcy and his departed friend governor of Louisiana, arrived back at his Monticello home after two weeks away on business. Now sixty-six, Jefferson was several months removed from his two-term presidency. As he warmed himself near one of Monticello's eight fireplaces, he shuffled through the letters, newspapers, and other items received during his absence, and a letter from Tennessee caught his eye. Brushing aside other correspondence and newspapers (both of which, he would soon learn, contained news of Lewis's death), he made himself comfortable—likely in his New Orleans Campeachy chair—and opened the letter from James Neelly, the US Indian agent to the Chickasaw nation, written in Nashville on October 18.[5]

"It is with extreme pain," opened Neelly's seven-hundred-odd-word epistle, "that I have to inform you of the death of His Excellency Meriwether Lewis, Governor of upper Louisiana who died on the morning of 11th Instant and I am sorry to say by suicide."

Correctly surmising that Jefferson would want details, Neelly provided them. "I arrived at the Chickasaw Bluffs [site of present Memphis] on or about the 18th of September," he wrote, "where I found the Governor (who had reached there two days before me from St. Louis) in very bad health." Lewis had been on his way to Washington via New Orleans, but thinking war with England probable and not wanting his valuable papers, which included his journals of the expedition, to fall into British hands, he decided instead to go overland through the Chickasaw nation (which included parts of western Tennessee and northern Mississippi). "I furnished him with a horse . . . and a man to attend them; having recovered his health to some degree at the Chickasaw Bluffs, we set out together. And on our arrival at the Chickasaw nation I discovered that he appeared at times deranged in mind." They rested for two days, then crossed the Tennessee River, but then lost two horses. "I remained behind to hunt them & the Governor proceeded on, with a promise to wait for me at the first house he came to that was inhabited by white people."

This was the Grinder house, and Neelly's account of Lewis's death is quite similar to the Nashville newspaper version discussed above (raising the possibility that Neelly was a key source for the article). Neelly closed with three additional points: he had had Lewis "as decently Buried as [he] could in that place"; he had in his "possession two trunks of papers (amongst which is said to be his travels to the pacific Ocean)"; and he had given fifteen dollars to Lewis's servant, a free mulatto named John Pernier, on his way to visit Lewis's mother and Jefferson in Virginia.[6]

We have no record of how Jefferson, whose only son died weeks after his birth, reacted to the shocking news about Lewis, who lost his father at age five. Still, almost four years later, Jefferson offered a glimpse of his feelings in a memorable eulogy for his surrogate son, honoring Lewis's "courage undaunted" and "firmness & perseverance of purpose" and adding that the events of October 10–11, 1809, along the Natchez Trace "plunged his friends into affliction and deprived his country of one of her most valued citizens."[7]

For the time being, however, Jefferson did what he could to wrap up the loose ends of Lewis's business. Pernier arrived as expected, and Jefferson interviewed him and, finding him trustworthy, sent him on his way to President Madison with Neelly's letter as well as one for Madison himself. The former and current president assisted William Meriwether (Lewis's cousin) and John Marks (Lewis's half brother) in their attempts to retrieve Lewis's property from Chickasaw Bluffs and the Chickasaw nation and settle the estate. Of particular concern to Jefferson, of course, was the status of the expedition journals.

In his November 23 letter to John Conrad of C. and A. Conrad and Company, the publisher that had contracted with Lewis to publish his history of the expedition, Jefferson wrote that he was "waiting the arrival of Genl. Clarke, expected here in a few days, to consult with him on the subject [of the expedition history]. His aid & his interest in the publication of the work may render him the proper depository to have it prepared & delivered over to you."[8]

Jefferson's claim that William Clark was on his way east was accurate: On September 21—three or four weeks after Lewis and Pernier boarded a Missouri River keelboat and voyaged south—Clark, his wife, Julia, their eight-month-old son, Meriwether Lewis Clark, and a slave couple, Scott and Chloe, trekked overland into Illinois via carriage and horseback, with plans to go to Virginia, where Julia could visit her family and Clark could visit Jefferson, and then on to Washington, where Clark, like Lewis, had matters to take up with Secretary of War William Eustis.[9]

By October 28, Clark and his company had traveled some three hundred miles from St. Louis and were in Kentucky. That night, after getting his family settled, Clark sat down in a tavern owned by a Mr. Shannon (but not George Shannon of the Lewis and Clark Expedition), and, amid the revelry of drink and laughter, penned a mournful letter to his brother Jonathan. "When at Shelbyville [twenty-two miles west of Frankfort] to day I Saw in a Frankfort paper called the Arguss [*Argus of*

Western America] a report which givs me much Concern," he wrote, "it Says that Govr. Lewis killed himself by Cutting his Throat with a Knife, on his way between the Chickaw Saw Bluffs and Nashville, I fear this report has too much truth, tho' hope it may have no foundation . . . I fear O! I fear the waight of his mind has over come him, what will be the Consequence?" Clark closed the letter with a touching apology: "I hope you will excuse me, and parden this hasty Scraul which is written in a room Crouded with different descriptions of people. Some drunk."[10]

Two days later, after confirming Lewis's death in a conversation with his brother-in-law Dennis Fitzhugh, Clark wrote to Jonathan: "I have herd of the Certainty of the death of Govr. Lewis which givs us much uneasiness."[11] Another letter, composed a week later at Bean Station, Tennessee, was particularly heartfelt: "You have heard of that unfortunate end of Govr. Lewis, and probably more than I have heard, I was in hopes of hearing more perticular[s] at this place, but have not. . . . I am at a loss to know what to be at his death is a turble Stoke to me, in every respect. I wish I could talk a little with you just now."[12]

Clark's party arrived at Fincastle, Virginia, on November 21, Julia's eighteenth birthday, and she had a joyous reunion with her parents. A few days later, Clark wrote to Jonathan that he did not know what to do about the history of the expedition. He knew he needed to talk to Jefferson as soon as possible and was glad that Monticello was only a hundred miles away. Around the first of December, Clark left on horseback on his way to visit Lewis's family at Locust Hill, Jefferson at Monticello, and President Madison and others in Washington.

On Thursday, December 7, Clark reached Monticello, where he was greeted first by a well-dressed male slave (though called a "servant") and not long after that by Jefferson's daughter, Martha "Patsy" Randolph, who at thirty-seven was two years' Clark's junior. Eventually Jefferson himself appeared, typically dressed in "corduroy small clothes, grey worsted stockings, blue waistcoat, and a rather stiff home-spun jacket badly made from the wool of his prized merino sheep."[13]

Jefferson invited the man he had appointed militia brigadier general and principal Indian agent west of the Mississippi to dine and stay the night. Unfortunately, Clark left the details of the meeting unrecorded, simply saying that he and the former president (and former minister to France, secretary of state, and vice president) "spoke much on the afs of

Gov. Lewis &c&c&c."[14] Lewis's death must have been the first topic of serious conversation, and while both men had a genuine affection for Lewis and mourned his loss, both also thought Lewis capable of suicide. That topic was naturally followed by the question, as Clark had put it to Jonathan, of "what [to] do about the publication of the Book."[15] Clark did not feel capable of producing the history himself and no doubt expressed that. Jefferson apparently suggested that a qualified writer and editor be asked to assist. According to a letter Jefferson wrote a few days later, Clark "desired the trunks [containing the expedition journals] to be sent on to Washington under the care of Mr. [Jenkin] Whiteside, the newly elected Senator from Tennessee."[16]

Neither Jefferson nor Clark offered any other details on their meeting, but it is easy to imagine the two men admiring the artifacts in Monticello's Entrance Hall—"the head and horns of an elk, a deer, and a buffalo"; "a fine painting of the Repentance of Saint Peter" oddly paired with "an Indian map on leather, of the southern waters of the Missouri, and an Indian representation of a bloody battle, handed down in their tradition."[17] Among the Indian clothing, utensils, weapons, ornaments, and other odds and ends on display, Clark recognized several items from the expedition, especially a Mandan eagle-bone whistle and a Sauk tobacco pouch.

Both Jefferson and Clark had a deep appreciation for and interest in American Indian culture. In his letter outlining the objectives of the expedition, Jefferson had instructed Lewis to discover the "names of the [Indian] nations & their numbers; the extent & limits of their possessions; their relations with other tribes of nations; their language, traditions, monuments; [and] their ordinary occupations in agriculture, fishing, hunting, war, arts, & the implements for these." While such observations would certainly be important for strategic or imperialistic reasons, Jefferson also revealed his personal and academic curiosity by requesting information on Indian "food, clothing, & domestic accomodations," the diseases prevalent among them and remedies used, their "moral and physical circumstances," and "peculiarities in their laws, customs & dispositions."[18]

In all interactions with Indians, Jefferson had counseled, "treat them in the most friendly & conciliatory manner" and "make them acquainted with . . . our wish to be neighborly, friendly & useful to them, & our dispositions to a commercial intercourse with them." Nor was

Jefferson's expression of goodwill perfunctory—he also gave instructions intended to spare Indians the horrors of smallpox.[19]

Lewis and Clark responded just as Jefferson had hoped, treating Indians with diplomacy and dutifully recording countless details about everything from appearance, clothing, food, tipis and lodges, villages, customs, and languages to use of tobacco, hunting practices, weapons, warrior societies, and skill with horses. As Clay Jenkinson has written, "The fact that Clark went into considerable detail about the origin and migrations of Mandan and Hidatsa culture . . . indicates how seriously the captains took Jefferson's ethnographic instructions."[20]

Again, Clark's interest in and respect for Indian tradition was evident when he recorded Mandan chief Sheheke's account of the origin of his people: "He told me his nation first Came out of the ground where they had a great village. a grape vine grew down through the Earth to their village and they Saw light Some of their people . . . Saw Buffalow and every kind of animal also Grapes . . . [and] they gathered Some grapes & took down the vine to the village, and they tasted and found them good." As Gary Moulton notes, "Clark's Biblical phrasing here suggests that he recognized the religious nature of this origin story, and its kinship to Genesis."[21]

Still, any image of Jefferson and Clark sipping wine while admiring a Mandan eagle-bone whistle or a Sauk tobacco pouch offers a skewed and distorted picture because these two men played key roles in the displacement of tens of thousands of American Indians and the subsequent destruction of their culture. As James Ronda has written, "The fascination with things Indian had a more ominous side. Nothing attracted Jefferson and his contemporaries more than the prospect of acquiring tribal lands. . . . As president, Jefferson took the passion for land and made it the central feature of federal Indian policy; all other considerations were subordinated to the drive to acquire the tribal estate."[22]

Anthony F. C. Wallace takes a more strident tone: "There was a degree of ruthlessness in Jefferson's dealings with the Indians, the ruthlessness of a benevolent zealot who would do virtually anything to ensure that his new, free American republic survived and grew." According to Wallace, Jefferson's attempt to convince Indians to sell their land actually consisted of five smaller steps: first, run the Indians into debt and "threaten to cut off their supplies"; second, bribe chiefs with money and other incentives; third, invite friendly chiefs to Washington to visit, and negotiate; fourth, "permit white trespassers on Indian lands to remain long enough to provoke the Indian owners to harass intruding families, steal horses, and murder a few hunters"; and, fifth, wage war against the "hostile" offenders.[23]

In his important work *Native America Discovered and Conquered: Thomas Jefferson, Lewis and Clark, and Manifest Destiny*, Robert Miller argues that from the fifteenth century on, when European countries set out to colonize the New World, they acted under widely accepted international law now known as the Doctrine of Discovery. "The Doctrine provided . . . that newly arrived Europeans immediately and automatically acquired property rights in native lands and gained governmental, political, and commercial rights over the inhabitants without the knowledge nor the consent of the indigenous peoples."[24]

This is not to say that the non-Caucasian, non-Christian inhabitants of the "discovered" country were presumed to have no rights at all. As Henry Dearborn, appointed US marshal for the District of Maine by George Washington (and later secretary of war by Jefferson), wrote, "The Indians being the prior occupants, possess the right to the soil. It cannot be taken from them unless by their free consent, or by the right of conquest in case of a just war. To dispossess them on any other principle, would be a gross violation of the fundamental laws of nature, and of that distributive justice which is the glory of a nation."[25]

Given the attitudes of the age, Dearborn's ethical concerns were admirable, but the problem, of course, was that even in the best of circumstances, it was up to the European "conquerors" to decide what constituted "free consent" or "just war." Not only that, but a key feature of the doctrine held that "the discovering European country gained . . . the sole right to buy the land from the native people"—meaning the Indians had *no right* to sell to any other country or individual.[26]

But even these points miss the heart of the matter: The European notion of dividing land into parcels that could be bought and sold was completely foreign to the Indian way of life. Indians migrated because of climate, disease, famine, or war—or to find better lands for farming or hunting—but talk of latitude and longitude and artificial boundaries and "property" made no sense in that world, no sense at all to the Comanche, who, after obtaining horses, migrated to the southern plains, with their mounted nomads eventually "circulating within a territory that was 500–700 miles in diameter," and "supported 7 or 8 million buffalo and 2 million wild mustangs."[27] Little wonder that the young Cherokee chief Dragging Canoe protested in 1775 when fellow chiefs agreed to sell hundreds of thousands of acres in present Tennessee and Kentucky to Richard Henderson, Daniel Boone, and others. Dragging Canoe accurately prophesied that "new cessions would be applied for, and finally the country which the Cherokees and their forefathers had so long occupied would be called for; and a small remnant which may then exist of this nation, once so great and formidable, will be compelled to seek a retreat in some far distant wilderness"; his warning that the land called *Kanta-ke* by the Iroquois had a "dark cloud"—later liberally paraphrased as "dark and bloody ground"[28]— proved tragically prescient, not only for the Cherokee nation but also for the Apache, Lakota, Nez Perce, Kiowa, Choctaw, Cheyenne, Navajo, Blackfoot, and all the others.

As Ronda points out, when push came to shove, Jefferson's eloquent thoughts about American Indians and their cultures were "quietly left behind" in the face of what Jefferson called "our final consolidation," or a vision of one American empire, stretching from sea to sea, and inhabited by one people speaking one language. "Throughout the nineteenth century, the consolidation policy had many faces, none of them promising much good to native peoples."[29]

Shortly before noon on Friday, December 8, 1809, eight weeks and two days after Lewis's death at Grinder's Stand, Jefferson offered his best wishes and farewells as Clark mounted his horse, pulled his coat closer for a long day in the cold, and rode down the hill from Monticello. Jefferson, who had already written a letter that morning to Virginia congressman John Wayles Eppes and asked Clark to deliver it, now went to his desk and wrote another letter, this one to his younger (and only surviving) brother, Randolph. "Dear Brother," he wrote, "I send to you by Squire the Gigg harness [which Randolph had asked to borrow] and shall be very happy if after your return, instead of sending it you would avail yourself of it to pay us a visit here with my sister [Randolph's wife, Mitchie Pryor Jefferson]."[30] (A gig was a two-person carriage that could be pulled by a single horse.)

Keeping up with his correspondence, the retired president often wrote multiple letters on the same day. That was true on Monday, December 11, when he wrote three, informing John Conrad in one of them that the expedition journals and William Clark were both expected soon in Washington. On December 14, Jefferson received a letter from James Madison, which discussed, among other subjects, the disposition of Lewis's papers. Three days later, a letter arrived from Nicholas Biddle, a Philadelphia native and "acknowledged genius who attended the University of Philadelphia at age ten"—and graduated from the College of New Jersey at fifteen—"and became one of the country's foremost litterateurs, scholars, and financiers of his day."[31] Biddle, who had just been admitted to the Pennsylvania bar, had served successively as secretary to the US ministers to France and Great Britain from 1804 to 1807. He was writing to inquire about a land grant that Jefferson had supposedly awarded in 1783 to a French citizen who had served in the American Revolution. Biddle's letter had nothing to do with Lewis and Clark, but he would soon play a pivotal role in the story of the expedition.[32]

How Biddle and William Clark first met is not clear. From Monticello, Clark had first gone to Richmond, Virginia, where he and William Meriwether, executor of Lewis's estate, shared their feelings about Lewis's death and agreed that Clark would divide Lewis's papers into three categories upon their safe arrival in Washington: government documents—to be sent to the appropriate department; expedition journals—to be kept by Clark; and personal letters, receipts, and so on—to be sent to Jefferson, who would examine and forward them to Meriwether. While in Richmond, Clark also met with prominent attorney (and future attorney general of the US and candidate for president in 1832) William Wirt and asked him to assist with the writing and editing of the expedition journals. Wirt said he would consider the matter.

In Washington, Clark found that Senator Whiteside had done his job well—the trunks containing Lewis's belongings, including the expedition journals, had arrived in good condition. Early in January, Clark met with Madison's secretary Isaac Coles and divided the papers as he and William Meriwether had agreed.[33] Clark wrote Jonathan on January 12 that certain influential people in Washington—not identified by name—expressed a desire for Clark to be nominated to succeed Lewis as governor of the territory. No such nomination was forthcoming, quite possibly because Clark had told those same parties what he told Jonathan: "I am afraid, and Cannot Consent if I was [appointed], no doubt would remain—I do not think myself Calculated to meet the Storms which might be expected."[34]

With the expedition journals—described as "sixteen Note books bound in red morocco with clasps"—in hand, Clark rode 130 miles northeast to Philadelphia, where he had several meetings planned, including one with John Conrad, Lewis's publisher, and another with Benjamin Rush, the physician (and signer of the Declaration of Independence) who had tutored Lewis before the expedition. Biddle, a frequent contributor to the highly respected periodical *Port Folio*, was well known among Philadelphia printers—Conrad was quite possibly the one who introduced him to Clark. Neither Clark nor Biddle reported details of their first conversation, which took place late in January, but they obviously took a liking to each other. Biddle was especially interested in the history of the expedition Clark was producing and learned that Clark was still waiting for Wirt's decision. Even so, there is every indication that Clark was so impressed with Biddle that he began to think him the right man for the job and even mentioned the possibility of Biddle somehow getting involved.[35]

Clark left Philadelphia around January 28, stopped in Baltimore, and was back in Washington by February 2. A letter from Meriwether was waiting for him. Wirt, reported Meriwether, would be available to "look over the journal of your travels," but only to correct grammatical errors and delete minutia. More extensive work would require more time than Wirt could spare (probably because Wirt was already working on a biography of Patrick Henry).[36]

"Am sorry to find that Mr. Wort Cant write our naritive," Clark wrote in his response to Meriwether. "I shall be obliged to get a gentleman in Philadelphia to write it, whom I would have engaged when in that place had I known that Mr. Wert would or could not write it."[37] Although Clark may not have "engaged" Biddle's involvement in the history, his subsequent letter to Biddle made it clear that he had at least broached the subject. Writing from Fincastle on February 20, Clark said he had expected to hear from Biddle before leaving Philadelphia. After explaining that Wirt would not be writing the narrative, he said he had calculated on Biddle writing for him and added: "If you will undertake this work, Cant you Come to this place where I have my Books & memorandoms and stay with me a week or two; read over & make yourself thirily acquainted with every thing which may not be explained in the Journals?"[38]

On March 3, Biddle wrote Clark a short note expressing his regret at having to decline Clark's invitation and explaining that he had neither the health nor the free time to devote to such an undertaking.[39] Luckily—for Clark and a generation of readers—Biddle changed his mind two weeks later, saying he now had "a prospect of better health & more time than [he] had originally expected" and that he would leave in a few days to meet with Clark at Fincastle.[40]

"How paradoxical that the role of preparing for publication the Lewis and Clark journals," writes Paul Russell Cutright, "should fall to a man who had never traveled farther west than the Susquehanna River, had never heard the eerie wail of a coyote, had never seen the vast herds of bellowing bison in the days of their abundance, had never scented the pungency of sagebrush."[41] Still, Clark could not have chosen a better compiler, editor, and writer, not to mention friend. Biddle arrived late in March, and the two men spent almost three memorable weeks examining the journals and talking about the grand tour of the West, closer to Clark's heart than ever with Captain Lewis now gone. Clark's mention that Biddle had taken "such Notes as will enable him with the explanations made on such parts of the journals as required it" was classic Clark understatement: Biddle's "notes" totaled well over twenty thousand words and covered everything from Sioux medicine bags to polygamy among the Mandan, Indian languages along the Columbia River, and the quality of soil near the Platte River.

Biddle took to his new vocation with boyish enthusiasm. In July he wrote to Clark (by then back in St. Louis): "Ever since my return to Philadelphia, I have been engaged seven or eight and even more hours a day on our work," adding that he could scarcely bring himself to devote half an hour to any of his friends. Even though the project was more difficult and occupied more of his time than expected, wrote Biddle, "I am by no means discouraged. I rise habitually at 5 O'Clock every morning & by constant exertion feel myself advancing in it."[42]

On his return to St. Louis, Clark had stopped in Kentucky to visit expedition veteran George Shannon. Just as Biddle had gone to Europe on government assignments as a teenager, Shannon had gone west with Lewis and Clark as an eighteen-year-old. (Sacagawea, about three years younger than Shannon, had been the only other teenager in the group.)

Clark took a special interest in the young man, especially after he was wounded in the leg (which was eventually amputated) during an aborted 1807 attempt to return Mandan chief Sheheke and his family to their North Dakota home. Led by expedition member Nathaniel Pryor, the group had returned to Fort Bellefontaine, northwest of St. Louis, after an attack by Arikara warriors in present South Dakota. Two men had been killed on the spot; one other died nine days later; and three men beside Shannon had also been wounded. After a long recovery, Shannon had slowly returned to "normal" life, not easy in the manual-labor world of the early 1800s. Luckily, he had an aptitude for study, and in October of 1808—one year after losing his leg—he headed east from St. Louis to attend Transylvania University in Lexington, Kentucky. Although Shannon lacked the wealth and pedigree—and youth— of most of his classmates, he carried with him letters of recommendation from both Lewis and Clark.[43]

Shannon had done well in his first year and a half of studies; he had also made the acquaintance of a fellow student later hailed as "the Father of Texas," Stephen F. Austin (fifteen when he met Shannon), and was befriended by the rising star of Lexington: Henry Clay. Born in 1777 in Virginia, Clay was licensed to practice law in Kentucky at age twenty-one and named professor of law and politics at Transylvania at twenty-eight. By 1810 he was serving in the US Senate for the second time. Shannon and his comrades had been enraptured both by Clay's eloquent lectures and the gossip about his drinking and gambling.

In his personal experience the previous six years, the unlikely Shannon had thus seen remarkable portents of what would follow the next four decades:

- As one of Lewis and Clark's recruits, he had crossed the Continental Divide and explored the West for the "purposes of commerce."
- As one of Pryor's men, he had seen how an apparently friendly Indian nation—in this case the Arikara—could suddenly grow hostile when their own "commerce" was threatened.
- In Austin, he had met a man whose Texas experience would illustrate Andrés Reséndez's thesis about national identities: "At the frontier, choosing one's identity could constitute an exciting busi-

ness opportunity, a bold political statement, and at times it was quite simply a matter of survival."[44]

- Clay, who would plead for Shannon's disability pension, would also soon stand as one of the leading advocates for the conquest of Canada "to extinguish the torch that lights up savage warfare."[45] He would also unwittingly help make Andrew Jackson the most powerful man of the era.

To what extent the Lewis and Clark Expedition *caused* western exploration and expansion, trade wars, Indian conflicts, war with Britain, the rise of Jackson, or the colonization of Texas—and the subsequent combat with Mexico—is a complex and problematic question (more to the point, the *wrong* question)—but there is little doubt that the captains' "tour of the Pacific" *hastened* the astounding series of events about to unfold.

Now, through Clark's influence, Shannon was about to get well acquainted with another rising star who, like Clay, would figure prominently in the history of antebellum America (and, again like Clay, would be bitterly opposed by Andrew Jackson): Nicholas Biddle.

Clark had stayed in contact with Shannon and had made sure he received regular government checks for his disability, so Shannon likely assumed that Clark's stopping (in May of 1810) on his return to St. Louis was a typical visit. Instead, Clark revealed his special interest— and trust—in Shannon by asking him, among the dozen and a half surviving expedition veterans, to assist Biddle in producing the history of the Voyage of Discovery, quite an honor for the soldier who had been best known as a greenhorn for either getting lost or forgetting tools or weapons on the trail.

Clark's dynamic meetings with Biddle had made it clear that the journals left many questions unanswered and that Biddle would ask all of them and many more. Clark's responsibilities as a husband, father, brother, general, and Indian agent—as well as the distance between St. Louis and Philadelphia—made an extensive correspondence impractical and ineffective. There was no substitute for having a firsthand witness work alongside Biddle, filling in details and answering both queries and follow-up queries. Clark brought up Shannon's name during one of his and Biddle's hours-long dialogues, and Biddle voiced his support for having Shannon come to Philadelphia for as long as necessary.

Shannon eagerly accepted Clark's invitation and left for Philadelphia on June 12, 1810, delivering a letter from Clark to Biddle upon his arrival in August. "This will be handed to you by Mr. George Shannon the young man I spoke to you about. . . . [He] possesses a sincere and undisguised heart," Clark had written, "he is highly spoken of by all his acquaintance and much respected at the Lexington University where he has been for the last two years. Any advice and friendly attentions which you may show to [him] will be greatfully acknowledged by him, and Confur an additional obligation on me."[46]

Twenty-four-year-old Biddle thus became the mentor of twenty-five-year-old Shannon. The two worked well together and worked hard; several months into the project, Biddle's initial enthusiasm—and presumably Shannon's—was tempered by the "most persevering & undivided attention" required by the "excessively troublesome" work.[47] Still, they "proceeded on," keeping up Biddle's strenuous schedule of rising early and working most of the day. Luckily, Biddle was independently wealthy—allowing the two of them to live comfortably, since neither was being paid for his labor. The details of how they collaborated are not clear, but Biddle reported to Clark that he had "derived much assistance from that gentleman [Shannon] who is very intelligent and sensible & whom it was worth your while to send here."[48] Shannon's university training (rare among Lewis and Clark's men) empowered him to handle any editing task required by Biddle, while his first-person accounts sometimes allowed Biddle to write a narrative more powerful and informative than anything contained in the journals. The perfect example is the Shannon/Biddle description of Sacagawea's experience when Lewis and Clark's party arrived at a camp of Shoshone Indians, her native people:

> We soon drew near the camp, and just as we approached it a woman made her way through the crowd toward Sacajawea; recognizing each other, they embraced with the most tender affection. The meeting of these two young women had in it something peculiarly touching, not only from the ardent manner in which their feelings were expressed, but also from the real interest of their situation. They had been companions in childhood; in the war with the Minnetarees [Hidatsa Indians] they had both been taken prisoners in the same battle; they had shared and softened the rigors of their captivity

till one had escaped from the Minnetarees, with scarce a hope of ever seeing her friend relieved from the hands of her enemies.[49]

Moments later, the captains met with a Shoshone chief, hoping to buy horses. After greeting, embraces, and the ceremonial smoking of a pipe, Clark called for Sacagawea to interpret. "She came into the tent, sat down, and was beginning to interpret," wrote Biddle, "when, in the person of Cameahwait, she recognized her brother. She instantly jumped up, and ran and embraced him, throwing over him her blanket, and weeping profusely. . . . After some conversation between them she resumed her seat and attempted to interpret for us; but her new situation seemed to overpower her, and she was frequently interrupted by her tears."[50]

Lewis, by contrast, offered a rather matter-of-fact summary of Sacagawea's reunion: "Shortly after Capt. Clark arrived with the Interpreter Charbono, and the Indian woman, who proved to be a sister of the Chif Cameahwait. the meeting of those people was really affecting, particularly between Sah cah-gar-we-ah and an Indian woman, who had been taken prisoner at the same time with her, and who had afterwards escaped from the Minnetares and rejoined her nation."[51]

By late June of 1811, only fifteen months after Clark and Biddle's first meeting and less than two years after Lewis's death, Biddle and Shannon had produced a four-hundred-thousand-word manuscript that was part compilation, part synthesis, and part original work, merging the expedition journals with Shannon's reminiscences and Biddle's notes—as well as his extensive study of Indian ethnography. Also included was what Clark called "a large Connected Map . . . much more Correct than any which has been before published."[52] Landon Jones has called it "a cartographic masterpiece, a remarkably accurate rendering of the inner continent of North America."[53] The monumental effort by the three men would have done Captain Lewis proud.

* * *

As Clark was taking care to leave a record of his and Lewis's trek for posterity, several veterans of the expedition were leaving a legacy of their own by pushing westward once again. In March of 1810, a band of trappers in present Montana were fighting a series of spring blizzards.

Hours after leaving Fort Raymond, near the confluence of the Yellow-stone and Bighorn Rivers (about fifty miles northeast of Billings), a man by the name of William Brown "became blind from the reflection of the sun on the snow," his eyes hurting him so much that he begged his companions to shoot him. "I watched him during that night for fear he commit the act himself," wrote Thomas James, a fellow trapper. "He complained that his eye balls had bursted, and moaned and groaned most piteously." The next morning, Brown was overjoyed when James examined his eyes and reported they were "whole and sound."[54]

These mountaineers were on their way to the prime beaver trapping territory near Three Forks—where the Gallatin, Madison, and Jeffer-son Rivers (all discovered and named by Lewis and Clark) converge to form the Missouri River. The coleaders of this trapping expedition were Pierre Menard and Andrew Henry, partners in the St. Louis Missouri Fur Company along with the likes of Manuel Lisa, William Morrison, Benjamin Wilkinson, Pierre Chouteau, Dennis Fitzhugh, Reuben Lew-is (younger brother of Meriwether), and William Clark.[55]

Menard and Henry had wisely chosen as their guide John Colter, "who thoroughly knew the road," wrote James, "having twice escaped over it from capture and death at the hands of Indians."[56] Destined to be the most famous member of the Lewis and Clark Expedition other than the captains themselves and Sacagawea, Colter had now spent six years in the wilderness. Not long after the captains and their company had reached present North Dakota on their return journey, Colter had requested permission to leave the group and join Joseph Dickson and Forrest Hancock, two westbound trappers. Colter had served well, es-pecially as a hunter and scout; permission was granted.[57]

So it was that on the cool morning of August 17, 1806, near the Hidatsa Indian villages at the mouth of the Knife River, the twenty-six adventurers who had served under Lewis and Clark "fitted [Colter] out with Powder lead and a great number of articles . . . for a trapping voiage of two years," said their farewells, and then stood on the bank of the Missouri and watched—some with envy—as Colter, Dickson, and Hancock climbed in a small canoe and paddled upstream toward the Montana country so rich with beaver and so full of peril.[58]

Colter and his companions had one objective—"to Stay until they make a fortune."[59] They hardly considered themselves empire builders, but in their own way, they were advancing the main mission assigned by

Jefferson to Lewis and Clark—"to explore . . . for the purposes of commerce."[60]

Now, three and a half years after departing with Dickson and Hancock—in a triumvirate that broke up within weeks—Colter was again going west, leading James and all the others along a path unknown to everyone but him, a path he had traveled when he made his famous escape from Blackfoot Indians.

James did not describe the group's route in detail, but he did offer some tantalizing clues, and when those clues are combined with others mentioned by his friend and fellow trapper John Dougherty, eighteen years old in March of 1810, certain facts are clear. As Mark W. Kelly has written, what is known is "that the route began on the Big Horn and ended at the Three Forks of the Missouri; . . . the Yellowstone River proper was not followed upstream; Bozeman Pass [between present Bozeman and Livingston, Montana] could not have been utilized; and lastly, the trek encompassed no fewer than three hundred miles in length, taking ten to twelve days to effect."[61]

All things being equal, the logical course would have been to ascend the Yellowstone River until it goes south (near present Livingston), cross Bozeman Pass, continue west, pick up the Gallatin River, and descend it to Three Forks. But all things were not equal—Colter had been running for his life when he followed this path in the late summer of 1808—and again in the subsequent winter—and the best evidence shows that he chose a route that would get him out of hostile Blackfoot country—and into friendly Absaroka (Crow) country—as fast as possible. According to Kelly's proposed route, which is consistent with the frustratingly spare accounts of both James and Dougherty, Colter led the four or five dozen other men southwest from the Bighorn River to Pryor's Creek and Pryor Gap (now on Montana's Crow Reservation), then continued southwest into present Wyoming, crossed over to Clark's Fork of the Yellowstone, ascended it back into Montana to a pass (now called Colter Pass), crossed (back into Wyoming) to Soda Butte Creek and the Lamar River (now in Yellowstone Park), and then descended the Yellowstone River (back into Montana) until they saw a breach in the Gallatin Range and turned west. They were likely near Tom Miner Creek when, wrote James, "it commenced snowing most violently and so continued all night. The morning showed us the heads and backs of our horses just visible above the snow which had crushed down all our tents."[62]

Battling enormous snowdrifts—and the prospect of freezing to death—the men forged their way west, with the strongest horses leading the way until they gave out and were replaced by "the ablest bodied pioneers." They finally reached the Gallatin River, which James forded, followed by Dougherty, William Weir (called "Ware" by James), and one other trapper. Colter led the larger group through an opening in the mountains, but James and his friends continued down the west bank of the river, stopping that night, where they camped (with wet clothes and wet bedding) and "supped" on a meager piece of buffalo meat "about the size of the two hands." Next came snow blindness again, first obscuring their vision like "a silk veil or handkerchief," but then leaving them unable to see the way at all and unable to hunt. For two days they teetered on the edge of starving or freezing. They were saved when they recovered "somewhat" from their blindness and one of them was able to kill a goose and make a soup that "stayed the gnawings of hunger."[63]

By going south into Absaroka country and then zigzagging westward along the Montana-Wyoming border, Colter stayed well clear of Blackfoot Indians, some of whom had seen him fighting with the enemy in an 1808 battle that pitted hundreds of Blackfoot warriors against a confederacy of hundreds of Absaroka and Salish allies. Now, in 1810, he led the Missouri Fur Company men into Blackfoot hunting grounds through the same back door that had provided his earlier escape—the Gallatin River and Gallatin Range. Thus it was that on April 3, 1810, about the same time that Clark and Biddle began meeting at Fincastle, the entire group of fur traders made it safely to Three Forks, an area that Lewis had said opened suddenly to "extensive and beautiful plains and meadows which appear to be surrounded in every direction with distant and lofty mountains."[64] Clark had noted the "emence number of beaver," with "maney thousand" inhabiting "the river & Creeks near the 3 forks."[65]

Lewis and Clark's entire contingent had seen Three Forks in July of 1805, going west, and most of them had seen the forks again, returning east, a year later. They had not encountered—or even seen—Blackfoot Indians either time. How many expedition veterans were now present is not clear, but two certainly were: Colter and George Drouillard. If the former had been one of the most valuable hunters and scouts in the group, Drouillard, born to a French Canadian father and Shawnee Indian mother in 1773, was *the* most valuable. And while Clark had chosen Colter as his right-hand man in reconnoitering the Salmon River in 1805, Lewis had selected Drouillard as his in ascending the Marias River in 1806. The one mention in the expedition journals of interaction between Colter and Drouillard noted that they quarreled when leading an unbroken horse together (in present northern Idaho, in May of 1806), likely indicating that neither wanted to take directions from the other.

Peter Weiser, who, like Colter, served as a private in the expedition, went up the Missouri with Lisa in 1807 and was apparently with Menard and Henry at Three Forks because Reuben Lewis mentioned him in an 1810 letter (discussed later in this chapter). Two other expedition members—Pierre Cruzatte and Richard Windsor—are known to have been on the upper Missouri in 1807 in Manuel Lisa's employ, but whether they were numbered among Menard and Henry's men at the headwaters of the Missouri is unknown. What is known, however, is that for the last year and a half, Colter had frequently recounted his tale of how expedition veteran John Potts had been "riddled" by Blackfoot arrows and then cut to pieces when he and Colter attempted to trap Three Forks in 1808 (after which Colter had made his famous run), but that reality had not deterred any trappers, whether previously associated with Lewis and Clark or not, from entering Blackfoot country themselves and making a fortune.[66]

Three other of Lisa's 1807 hands had definitely followed Colter to the forks during that unforgiving spring of 1810: Kentuckians John Hoback, Jacob Reznor, and Edward Robinson, destined, like Colter, to reject multiple opportunities to return home, escape multiple Indian attacks, and leave their names in the history books.

When such names are added to those of Menard and Henry, as well as Jean-Baptiste Champlain and Michael Immell, the list of those reaching the forks is impressive indeed. What no one could have prophesied, however, was that the man among them who would figure most prominently in the history of the upper Missouri in the next few decades would be the greenhorn befriended by James: John Dougherty.

Like his friends, Dougherty felt tremendously relieved to have survived the elements on the trek from Fort Raymond and pleased to finally get busy with the task at hand—trapping beaver. James, Dougherty, Weir, and Brown agreed to descend the Missouri toward the falls (now known as Great Falls) described by the Lewis and Clark men and find a good trapping spot. First, they labored—chopping down two sturdy trees and hollowing out good-sized portions of each trunk to fashion a canoe for each two-man team. They set off downstream on April 6 or 7. Meanwhile, a group of eighteen men ascended the Jefferson River to trap while the rest of the company stayed at the forks to construct a trading house and fort between the Jefferson and Madison Rivers.

As the foursome prepared to leave, a friend of James by the name of Cheek and known for his courage approached them. "James, you are going down the Missouri, and it is the general opinion that you will all be killed. . . . But I am afraid for myself as well as you," he said. "I know not the cause, but I have felt fear ever since I came to the Forks, and I never was afraid of anything before. You may come out safe, and I may be killed."[67]

Putting Cheek's premonition out of their minds, James, Dougherty, Brown, and Weir navigated their canoes toward the mountains, finding the river peaceful and even catching beaver that first day. Over the next two days, they were astounded by the spectacular beauty of the untouched wilderness, in James's words, "the peaks and pinnacles . . . resplendent in the sun," the "mountain sides . . . dark with Buffalo, Elk, Deer, Moose, wild Goats and wild Sheep," the pines and cedars waving "their tall, majestic heads along the base and on the sides of the mountains."[68]

Dougherty was so taken with the majesty of the scene that he "broke forth in one of Burns' noblest lyrics,"[69] likely singing "My Heart's in the Highlands" or some such:

> Chasing the wild-deer, and following the roe,
> My heart's in the Highlands, wherever I go.
> Farewell to the mountains, high-covered with snow
> Farewell to the straths and green vallies below;
> Farewell to the forests and wild-hanging woods,
> Farewell to the torrents and loud-pouring floods.[70]

It was everything one would have expected from the Garden of Eden, said James. Such ecstasy was short-lived, however. Just a few days later, when Dougherty turned nineteen on April 12, everything came crashing down, and the world of paradise transmuted to an inferno.

* * *

At the end of May 1810, six years and two weeks after the Lewis and Clark Expedition had departed Camp Dubois and started up the Missouri River, John Colter, William Bryant, and a third man, whose name is lost to history, reached St. Louis. The naturalist John Bradbury wrote that he saw Colter on his arrival and that "this man" had completed the journey from the headwaters of the Missouri to St. Louis in thirty days. Bradbury added: "I . . . received from him an account of his adventures after he had separated from Lewis and Clarke's party."[71]

By "adventures" Bradbury was referring specifically to Colter's 1808 escape from Blackfoot warriors who, after killing Potts, gave Colter a head start before chasing him, an eleven-day odyssey later called "Colter's run" that took him into present Wyoming and Yellowstone Park, and then back into Montana and finally to Fort Raymond. Bradbury's account of Colter's escape, first published in 1817, was widely reprinted and heavily relied on by Washington Irving, who popularized the story more than anyone else. The first account of Colter's run, however, had been written by Dr. William H. Thomas and published in the December 7, 1809, issue of the *Missouri Gazette*. Thomas had gone up the Missouri in the summer of 1809 as part of the armada—which included Thomas James and John Dougherty—that returned Sheheke and his family to their North Dakota home.[72]

Colter and Bryant and their companion carried with them three letters—and possibly four—all written on April 21—one from Pierre Menard to Pierre Chouteau; one from Menard to his wife, Angelique; and one from Reuben Lewis to his brother Meriwether. "A party of our hunters was defeated by the Blackfeet on the 12th inst. [current month]," Menard had written. "There were two men killed, all their beaver stolen, many traps lost." He identified the dead as James Cheaque and "one Ayres," with three other men missing. "The unfortunate affair has quite discouraged our hunters, who are unwilling to hunt any more here."[73]

Reuben Lewis had also gone up the Missouri with the 1809 armada in an arrangement between the United States, represented by Governor Lewis, and the St. Louis Missouri Fur Company, represented by William Clark, Edward Hempstead, Pierre Chouteau, Manuel Lisa, William Morrison, Benjamin Wilkinson, and Auguste Pierre Chouteau. The US government agreed to pay the company seven thousand dollars "to engage and raise One Hundred and Twenty five effective men . . . for the safe conveyance and delivery of the Mandan Chief, his Wife, and child, to the Mandan nation." The company would bear all the expenses, but it would also be issued a license to trade with any Indian nation on the upper Missouri except the Arikara. Not only that, but the government, via Lewis, stipulated that no trading licenses would be issued to any other person or company to go any farther than the mouth of the Platte River (just south of present Omaha, Nebraska) for the purpose of trading with the Indians. [74]

In what would be now be considered a blatant conflict of interest, Governor Lewis had given his friends—and his brother, since Reuben was an officer in the company—an exclusive opportunity to sign the contract to escort Sheheke and a monopoly on the upper Missouri Indian trade. The upshot was that approximately 350 men started up the river that summer—a military detachment of around 160, led by Pierre Chouteau (which left St. Louis in May), and a trading group, led by Lisa, of around 190 (which left in June). [75]

When Reuben Lewis thus bade Meriwether farewell in June of 1809 (and boarded the same keelboat as James and Dougherty), the latter was in good health and, with the two fleets on their way, in reasonably good spirits, although he was continually harried by territorial secretary Frederick Bates, who seemed determined to undermine him at every turn. Ten months later, on that April night in 1810, when Reuben sat down by the fire at the Three Forks stockade and composed a letter to Meriwether, he had no way of knowing that his brother was not alive and well—nor did anyone else in the group.

"Dr Brother[,]" wrote Reuben, "The return of your oald acquaintance Coalter, gives me an opportunity of addressing you a few lines. I have written General Clark on the subject of our situation, of our trade and prospects in the Country, (which at the present are very unpromising)." He went on to discuss the difficulty of having partners in the Missouri Fur Company of "such different interests & opinions" and said he was confident that the Blackfoot Indians in the area were being urged on by British traders. "It will be impossible to trap on this River Unless we could have 2 or 3-100 men in this Country, we have already lost 5 Men by that Nation and I fear for the lives of those, who are going to try the experiment again."[76]

Despite his discouragement, Reuben hoped that trapping on the western side of the Continental Divide, away from the Blackfoot nation, would soon be possible. He wrote that the upper branches of the Columbia were full of beaver and that according to Peter Weiser, the area of the upper Madison River was almost without mountains and that five or six days' travel would take one to a tributary of the Columbia almost as rich with beaver as Three Forks. Reuben also said he would consider selling out his interest in the Missouri Fur Company and investing in the "Newyork Company" should it "go into operation."[77]

Reuben added that he was in good health and was also sending a letter to his and Meriwether's mother. (If he did write that letter, it would have been the fourth epistle given to Colter and Bryant, but no trace of it has been found.) In light of the tragic events at Grinder's Stand six months earlier, Reuben's last words to his brother are poignant indeed: "with high esteem your affectionate brother Reuben Lewis."[78]

Despite being attacked by Blackfoot Indians "just beyond the mountains," Colter and Bryant and the other man escaped by hiding in a thicket and made their way back to Fort Raymond, Menard's and Reuben Lewis's letters safe in hand.[79] If Bradbury's claim that Colter reached St. Louis before the end of May is accurate, the threesome in the small canoe plied their oars with incredible intensity, averaging one hundred miles per day for an entire month.

Colter had been updated on Lewis and Clark's activities by Reuben Lewis and others and fully anticipated seeing and talking with both of them on his arrival in St. Louis. Instead, he learned that Lewis had died by his own hand the previous October and that Clark had not yet returned from a long trip east. So-called civilization must have seemed quite lonely to the man who had never minded solitude in the wilderness.

After a long and difficult trip, Clark and his family finally made it back to St. Louis on July 7. "Julia is much disheartened & Says She 'Shall never go to See you all again She fears,'" Clark wrote to Jonathan.[80] Regrettably, neither Clark nor Colter recorded details of their reunion, but it must have been a joyful one. Recruited by Clark in October of 1803, Colter had been tried (but not punished) by a court-martial in March of 1804 for a few minor offenses.[81] He mended his ways, however, and was never disciplined again. He and Clark had gotten along well, and in August of 1806, when Colter requested permission to leave Lewis and Clark's party to trap with Dickson and Hancock, Clark's response was quite complimentary: "We were disposed to be of Service to any one of our party who had performed their duty as well as Colter had done, we agreed to allow him the prvilage provided no one of the party would ask or expect a Similar permission."[82]

It had been almost four years since the two men had seen each other, and, whatever topics they discussed—which must have included Lewis's death—one subject likely took front and center: the grand map Clark was producing for the history that Lewis had never really started and that Biddle (soon to be joined by Shannon) was then working on. Throughout the expedition, Clark, already a skilled cartographer, had meticulously noted the locations of everything from mountains, bluffs, prairies, rivers, and creeks to islands, hot springs, rapids, mineral deposits, and Indian villages, estimating the distance both from one place to another and from the mouth of the Missouri to a given landmark. He had used a variety of methods to determine latitude and longitude, carefully recording the results. At the same time, he was continually working on four types of trail maps—"large-scale compass traverse maps, small page-size maps sketched in his journals, copies of maps prepared by traders and Indians, and composite maps of the west."[83]

In addition, after Drouillard returned from the upper Missouri in August of 1808—and before he went up the river again in the spring of 1809—he had helped Clark create a map that depicted in considerable detail two journeys made by Drouillard to encourage Absaroka customers to trade at Fort Raymond (with the first trip occurring during the winter of 1807–1808 and the second in the spring of 1808). In the process, Drouillard had explored parts of the Yellowstone, Bighorn, Little Bighorn, and Tongue Rivers and had seen a good deal of present southeastern Montana and a section of northern Wyoming. As M. O. Skarsten has written, Drouillard's information "proved helpful to Clark in correcting errors in some of his earlier maps."[84]

Now, in 1810, Clark was synthesizing that depth of experience to produce his cartographic master work—just as Lewis had planned on producing a literary master work of the expedition. Because Thomas Jefferson had instructed Lewis and Clark to determine "the most direct & practicable water communication across this continent for the purposes of commerce,"[85] it had been crucial for Clark to discover as much as possible about the sources of important rivers. He and Jefferson both understood that finding a passage between the eastward-flowing Missouri and the westward-flowing Columbia was the key to "water communication across this continent." So it was no surprise that Clark unfailingly asked specific and probing questions of Indians about the course of rivers. Nor was it a surprise that Lewis and Clark knew they were crossing the Continental Divide when they reached Lemhi Pass along the present Montana-Idaho border in August of 1805.

Although Clark had personally explored the Yellowstone River from the site of present Livingston, Montana (where the northbound Yellowstone turns east) all the way to its confluence with the Missouri (at the western edge of North Dakota), he had not been able to search for the origin of either the Yellowstone or its principal tributary—the Bighorn (which is called the Wind River near its headwaters), both of which were particularly significant in finding a possible water communication route across the continent, and, of course, in producing an accurate map. Upon reaching the mouth of the Bighorn in July of 1806, Clark had recorded in his journal: "I am informed by the *Menetarres* Indians and others that this River [the Bighorn] takes its rise in the Rocky mountains with the heads of the river plate [Platte] and at no great distance from the river Rochejhone [Yellowstone]."[86]

Clark certainly could have reviewed such details three weeks later when he granted Colter permission to leave with Dickson and Hancock, especially since the two trappers had told Clark they were "on a trapping expedition up the River Rochejhone."[87] Regardless, Colter was well aware of Clark's interest in the course of rivers, and when he and Clark finally reunited in July of 1810, the subject naturally came up as they examined Clark's draft of his master map. Probably after several consultations with Colter, Clark made a critical addition to his map—a dotted line labeled "Colters rout" that circles from Pryor's Creek (as noted earlier, now on the Crow Reservation) southwest, around both

"Eustis Lake" and "L[ake] Biddle" and back along the Bighorn to Pryor's Creek.[88]

This section of Clark's map, which includes an area never seen by Clark himself, clearly shows Eustis Lake—now known as Yellowstone Lake—to be the source of the Yellowstone River, and Lake Biddle— now known as Brooks Lake—to be the source of the Wind River/Bighorn River. Moreover, the dotted line depicting Colter's route leaves little doubt that he had undertaken this journey specifically to search for the headwaters of these two rivers (rather than stumbling upon Lake Eustis and Lake Biddle in the midst of a trading mission to the Absaroka Indians, as has long been assumed). Colter thus made a significant contribution to what Jay Buckley has described as "a work of superlative craftsmanship and analysis . . . [that] remained the best available until Frémont's maps of the 1840s."[89]

The impressive progress that Clark and Colter made in the world of maps, however, was contrasted by bad news from the world of settlers and Indians. On June 2, a few days after Colter's arrival, three Indians attacked the Cox family, who lived on Shoal Creek in Illinois, killing the family's young son and kidnapping his sister. About the time of Clark's arrival, a post rider traveling from Vincennes, Indiana, to St. Louis was killed by Indians and the mail lost. Not long after that, Clark wrote to the War Department, "four men who reside near the Missouri . . . who had been in pursuit of horses which had been stolen from them were killed in their camp . . . by the Indians." Like many others, Clark placed the ultimate blame for such violence not on the Indians themselves but on the British traders and officials he was convinced were urging the Indians on.[90]

For both Clark and Colter, another report—this one published in a St. Louis newspaper on July 26—struck much closer to home: "A few days ago, Mr. [Pierre] Menard, with some of the gentlemen attached to the Misssouri Fur Company, arrived here from their Fort at the head waters of the Missouri, by whom we learn that they had experienced considerable opposition from the Blackfoot Indians." After describing the attack on April 12 and the sad fate of Cheek and the others—all of which was known to Colter, of course—the article announced something that had happened after Colter's departure:

Early in May, George Druilard, accompanied by some Delawares, who were in the employ of the company, went out to hunt, contrary to the wishes of the rest of the party, who were confident the Indians were in motion around them, and that from a hostile disposition they had already shown, it would be attended with danger, their presages were too true, he had not proceeded more than two miles from the camp before he was attacked by a party in ambush, by whom himself and two of his men were literally cut to pieces. It appears from circumstances that Druilard made a most obstinate resistance as he made a kind of breastwork of his horse, whom he made to turn in order to receive the enemy's fire, his bulwark, of course soon failed and he became the next victim of their fury. It is lamentable that although this happened within a short distance of relief, the firing was not heard so as to afford it, in consequence of a high wind which prevailed at the time. [91]

Born within months of each other, Lewis and Drouillard had now died violent deaths months apart. "A man of much merit . . . particularly useful from his knowledge of gesticulation and his uncommon skill as a hunter and woodsman," Lewis had written of Drouillard. "It was his fate also to have encountered . . . all of the most dangerous and trying scenes of the voyage, in which he uniformly acquited himself with honor."[92] Drouillard had never learned of Lewis's death.

Clark likely heard the news about Drouillard first and informed Colter during one of their mapmaking sessions, but again, neither man left a record of what had to be a somber moment, especially since Colter and Drouillard had worked well together on their second time together in the West. Colter (often called the first American mountain man) and Drouillard (Lisa's lieutenant on the first major fur trading expedition launched after Lewis and Clark's return) had left their mark on the fur trade and the exploration of the West, but now, with Colter back in "the States" for good and Drouillard gone, the subsequent trailblazing would be left to men who had not been present with Lewis and Clark.

With his 1807 and 1809 ventures up the Missouri, Lisa had led the charge west, but Menard's latest report cast considerable doubt on the Missouri Fur Company's ability to take advantage of the "emence number of beaver" at Three Forks. Not only that, but the immediate concern of the company was not trapping or trading but getting supplies to

Henry's men as soon possible.[93] Never one to leave such a task to others, Lisa prepared to lead a relief party, but because ice on the Missouri made travel on the river impossible for several months each year, he wouldn't be able to leave until the spring of 1811.

As the Missouri Fur Company's hopes were dimming, "the Newyork Company" mentioned by Reuben Lewis was rapidly gathering steam. Reuben had no doubt heard of the company from Meriwether, who had heard of it from Thomas Jefferson. "A powerful company is at length forming for taking up the Indian commerce on a large scale," Jefferson had written to Lewis in July of 1808. "They will employ a capital the first year of 300,000 D. and raise it afterwards to a million. . . . It will be under the direction of a most excellent man, . . . a merchant of N. York, long engaged in the business & perfectly master of it."[94]

The name of the "most excellent man" was John Jacob Astor.

2

"THE MOST DIRECT & PRACTICABLE WATER COMMUNICATION ACROSS THIS CONTINENT"

Lewis and Clark and their men got an early start on Saturday, September 20, 1806. They had left St. Louis twenty-eight months earlier and were chomping at the bit to get back. They had made eighty-four miles the previous day and had camped near the mouth of the Osage River, just east of present Jefferson City, Missouri. They were "extreemly anxious to get down" and plied "their ores very well," wrote Clark. "We Saw Some cows on the bank which was a joyfull Sight to the party and Caused a Shout to be raised for joy." The horizon was tinged with sunset when they finally saw a French hamlet called La Charette (long since washed away by the Missouri River). With Clark's permission, the party "discharged 3 rounds with a harty Cheer, which was returned from five tradeing boats which lay opposit the village."[1]

Clark wrote that everyone they met, both French and American, was thrilled to see them and "much astonished" at their safe return because the captains and their party "were Supposed to have been lost long Since, and were entirely given out by every person &." In this spirit of celebration, Lewis and Clark purchased two gallons of whiskey—at the exorbitant price of eight dollars—for the men to share. Among the traders were two young Scotsmen who "very politely received" the explorers and offered pork for the men and "a very agreeable supper" of beef and flour for the captains. Not only that, but with rain looking likely, continued Clark, "we accepted of a bed in one of their tents."

One of the Scotsmen was a man by the name of Reed; the other was nineteen-year-old Ramsay Crooks.[2]

Clark's account of the meeting with Crooks and Reed represented a sort of matching bookend to the encounter he had described on August 11, when he and his men "found two men from the illinoies [Joseph Dickson and Forrest Hancock] . . . on a trapping expedition up the River Rochejhone [Yellowstone River]."[3] Colter joined them, of course, and the trio was thus leading the rush westward, but a host of others were nipping at their heels. Over the next five weeks, as the Corps of Discovery descended the Missouri, they met an incredible collection of individuals charging upstream:

- August 21: "Three French men Comeing up . . . on their way to the Mandans . . . two of them Reevea & Greinyea [Francois Rivet and Grenier] wintered with us at the mandans in 1804."[4]
- September 3: "Two boats & Several men . . . [commanded by] a Mr. James Airs [Aird] . . . [a] Gentleman . . . of the house of [Robert] Dickson & Co. . . . who has a Licence to trade for one year with the Sieoux."[5] Aird and Dickson were Crooks and Reed's employers.
- September 6: "A tradeing boat of Mr. Ag. Choteaux [prominent merchant René Auguste Chouteau] of St Louis bound to the River Jacque to trade with the Yanktons [Yankton Sioux Indians] . . . in Care of a Mr. Henry Delorn [possibly Delaunay or Delorme, both later overland Astorians]" and "12 frenchmen."[6]
- September 10: "Mr. Alexander La fass and three french men . . . in a Small pirogue [a hollowed-out boat generally larger than a canoe but smaller than a keelboat] on [their] way to the River Platt."[7]
- September 10: "A large pirogue and 7 Men from St. Louis bound to the Mahars [Omaha Indians] for the purpose of trade . . . in Charge of a Mr. La Craw [probably Joseph La Croix]."[8]
- September 12: "2 perogues from St. Louis one [containing] the property of Mr. Choteau bound to the panias [Pawnee Indians] on River Platt, the other going up trapping as high as the Mahars."[9]
- September 12: "Mr. McClellin [Robert McClellan, a friend of both Lewis and Clark] . . . with a large keel Boat which roed with 12 oars. . . [and] was well loaded down with Marchandizes and is

going up to the Marhars and yanktons to winter there [accompanied by] Mr. Jo. Gravelin [interpreter Joseph Gravelines] . . . and old Mr. Durion [well-known trader Pierre Dorion Sr., briefly employed by Lewis and Clark in 1804]."[10]

- September 14: "Three large boats bound to the Yanktons and Mahars the property of Mr. Lacroy, Mr. Aiten & Mr. Coutau [Charles Courtin]."[11]
- September 16: "Eight Frenchmen with a perogue loaded with marchandize and bound for the Panies Nation on River platte."[12]
- September 16: "A large boat of 6 oars and 2 canoes . . . loaded with marchandize . . . to trade with the Panias Mahars and ottoes [Oto Indians] . . . under the charge of Mr Reubados Son [probably Joseph Robidoux] [with] about 20 frenchmen in Company."[13]
- September 17: "A Captain McClellin [John McClallen] late a Capt. Of Artily of the U States Army assending in a large boat . . . bound for the Spanish Country by way of River platte to the panies Indians & purchase horses and cross the Mountains leaving their goods on this Side and git the Spaniards to come and bring their silver & gold and trade it for goods . . . this gentleman an acquaintance of . . . Capt. Lewis."[14]
- September 20: "A perogue with 5 french men bound to the Osarge [Osage Indians] Gd. village."[15]

Thus, although Manuel Lisa is properly credited with launching the first major fur trading expedition (in the spring of 1807) *after* the return of Lewis and Clark to St. Louis—and although Lisa's group would eventually include Lewis and Clark veterans Colter, Drouillard, Weiser, Potts, Cruzatte, and Windsor—a crowd of traders had preceded Lisa upriver by several months, and among them, they would dramatically impact both the fur trade and subsequent westward expansion.

Nor was the trading frenzy limited to upper Missouri: As James Ronda has pointed out, September of 1806 was "an illuminating moment when the American West was in motion—a motion whose direction and consequences were to shape the political and cultural destiny of half a continent."[16] To the north, the North West Company, a Montreal-based fur trading business, was the driving force. More than a decade before Lewis and Clark, the company had sponsored two historic explorations of present western Canada by the incomparable Alexander Mackenzie, who had descended a river (now called the Mackenzie) eleven hundred miles from Great Slave Lake to its mouth at the Arctic Ocean in 1789 and had made the first transcontinental crossing of North America north of present Mexico in 1793 by descending the Peace River and reaching an inlet of the Pacific Ocean north of Vancouver Island.[17] Now, as Lewis and Clark were returning to St. Louis, three other North West traders had taken key roles in the company's efforts to explore the Oregon Country—which included all of Idaho, Oregon, and Washington and parts of Montana and Wyoming in the present United States and much of British Columbia in present Canada—and control its fur trade: Alexander Henry the Younger, Simon Fraser, and David Thompson.

To the west, a group of Russian traders led by Nikolai Petrovich Rezanov also had the Oregon Country in their sights. After trying unsuccessfully to navigate the Columbia River, they had sailed to Spanish California, which they had only recently departed.[18]

Despite all this international activity, little progress had been made on Thomas Jefferson's goal of connecting eastward- and westward-flowing rivers (assumed to be the Missouri and Columbia Rivers, respectively) for the purposes of commerce. Lewis and Clark had done their best to find a northwest passage[19] but had found nothing but trouble. Their plan had been good—early in August of 1805 they made the right decision by ascending the Jefferson River (rather than the Madison or the Gallatin) toward what they correctly concluded was the Continental Divide. Cross the Divide they did, at Lemhi Pass, later in August, on the present Montana-Idaho border (southwest of Dillon, Montana, and southeast of Salmon, Idaho). From the trickle of water called Trail Creek, a tributary of the Missouri (via Horse Prairie Creek, the Beaverhead River, and the Jefferson), it was only five or six miles across Lemhi Pass to another trickle called Agency Creek, a tributary of the Columbia (via the Lemhi River, the Salmon, and the Snake). If the western waters had been as navigable as the Jefferson and the Missouri, Lewis and Clark could have reached the Pacific in a month.

Such a hope quickly proved fruitless. When Clark, Colter, and a few others reconnoitered what they called Lewis River (now called the Salmon), they had not gone far when they found "five very Considerable rapids the passage of either with Canoes is entirely impossible, as the water is Confined between [huge] Rocks & the Current beeting from one against another for Some distance below." The farther they went, the more unnavigable the river looked. On top of everything else, they saw little game and concluded that the trees in the canyon were not suitable for building canoes. Then, when Clark asked his Shoshone guide, dubbed "Old Toby" by the captains, and the other Indians he met what the river was like farther downstream, he was told "the water runs with great violence from one rock to the other on each Side foaming & roreing thro rocks in every direction, So as to render the passage of any thing impossible."[20]

Little wonder that the Salmon River would one day be known as "the River of No Return," and that even today it is not possible to cross the state of Idaho to the west by vehicle anywhere near this point.[21] Abandoning the notion of navigating the Salmon, Clark questioned his guide about an Indian road he had seen coming in from the north. After Old Toby drew two maps in the sand and responded to further questions, Clark concluded the road would lead his and Lewis's party north to a different river system and different tributary of the Columbia and to the Salish Indians—called Tushepaw by Clark but now commonly known as the Flathead nation.[22]

After obtaining horses from the Shoshone, the party headed north to the Bitterroot Range, making their way "over high rugged hills" as a September rainstorm turned to hail. Later they "descended a Mountain nearly as steep as the Roof of a house." Over the next few days they battled their way to the crest of the seven-thousand-foot Continental Divide, cutting a road through thickets and underbrush, with the mountainside so rocky and steep that the horses were in constant "danger of Slipping to Ther certain destruction." The rain and snow continued, as did the meager meals of a little pheasant meat and some parched corn.[23]

Getting much needed help from the Salish Indians, Lewis and Clark followed the Bitterroot River north, stopping at a camp they called Travelers' Rest, near the site of present Lolo, Montana (just south of Missoula). Now they went west, over Lolo Pass, back into present Idaho, and over what Patrick Gass called "the most terrible mountains I ever beheld," with snow and steep trails and meager rations once more the order of the day.[24]

The irony was, as the captains themselves learned, that the party was now close to where they had been eight weeks earlier. Old Toby informed them of an Indian road to the east that followed an extensive plain to the Missouri River. "The point of the Missouri where this Indian pass intersects it, is about 30 miles above the gates of the rocky mountains [about twenty miles north of present Helena, Montana]," wrote Lewis. "The guide informed us that a man might pass to the Missouri from hence by that rout in four days."[25] Lewis and Clark had thus lost seven weeks—and a good deal of fair weather—because their route to the southwest and back north again had taken fifty-three days.[26]

Neither Lewis nor Clark, however, made much of this revelation, apparently considering their detour the natural consequence of exploring an unknown land and relying on the sometimes vague secondhand accounts from Indians and traders. They "proceeded on," once again contending with treacherous mountains, bad weather, a lack of game, and hunger that verged on starvation until they were once again saved by Indians, this time the Nez Perce nation. On October 7, near present Orofino, Idaho, the expedition boarded the canoes they had built and paddled west on the Clearwater River, which would take them to the Snake, the Columbia, and the Pacific.

The upshot of all of this was that the expedition had stopped ascending the Missouri in mid-August and had followed a meandering path by foot and horse over countless mountain ranges until early October, when they began descending the Columbia. And while reaching the Pacific coast was in itself a monumental achievement, they had failed miserably in their attempts to discover a northwest passage. Transporting goods—such as beaver pelts—from one coast to another via a water communication route was appearing much more difficult than Jefferson had imagined.

Neither Lewis nor Clark had intentions of returning to the West as fur traders. The task of finding a northwest passage would have to be left to others. The North West traders Henry, Fraser, and Thompson were vitally interested in a water communication route to the Pacific, but they were approaching that objective from the north, via key northern rivers, particularly the Columbia and the Fraser. The Missouri River was out of their bailiwick because the Louisiana Purchase had brought it under US control.

As Lewis and Clark had found on their return in the late summer of 1806, however, a horde of traders from St. Louis and elsewhere had set their sights on the Missouri River fur trade, with three groups—led by Colter, Charles Courtin, and John McClallen (despite his claim of being bound for the Spanish country)—going as far as present Montana. They were followed in 1807 by Lisa, of course, who established his Fort Raymond post at the mouth of the Bighorn River. Still, none of these had designs on a transcontinental beaver trapping venture—the one man ambitious enough to do so was Astor. In a letter to Jefferson written just a few months after Lisa and his fifty or sixty men arrived in the heart of Absaroka Indian territory, Astor proclaimed his plans to "carry on the trade so extensively that it may in time embrace the greater part of the fur trade on this continent."[27] But even that was an understatement because Astor's grand scheme eventually included not only New York, the Missouri and Columbia Rivers, and the Pacific coast, but also Cape Horn; the Cape of Good Hope; the Sandwich Islands; Canton, China; and London.

Born in Germany in 1763, Astor had immigrated to the United States in 1784, where his first business venture was disposing "of a cargo of flutes. On the advice of a chance acquaintance he became interested in the fur business. After the British evacuated the Old Northwest in 1796, Astor moved into the area and also traded with the fur companies in Montreal."[28] One successful business deal followed another, Astor's wealth quickly growing. In 1808, he founded the American Fur Company. As John D. Haeger has written, "What had begun in the late 1780s as the simple purchase and sale of furs in a single market, by 1808 had become an international empire that mixed furs, teas, and silks and penetrated markets on three continents."[29]

When Astor first conceived the idea of building a trading post on the Pacific coast is not known, but whether or not he ever specifically learned of Lewis's 1806 statement to Jefferson that an immense quantity of furs from the Rocky Mountains could be collected at the mouth of the Columbia each year and shipped to Canton, China, faster than similar cargo was presently shipped from Montreal to London,[30] he no doubt would have had similar thoughts as soon as hearing that Lewis and Clark had successfully traveled from the mountains to the mouth of the Columbia and had built a fort there. His plans for such a post continued to develop, and in New York on June 23, 1810—at the same time that William Clark was on the last leg of his journey from the East to St. Louis and a few weeks after Colter had arrived in St. Louis—

those plans were solidified with the organization of the Pacific Fur Company. Astor, who had pledged to invest $400,000 in the company—and received fifty of the one hundred shares of stock—would manage the concern from New York while his partners took their chances in the field. Alexander McKay, Donald McKenzie, Duncan McDougall, and David Stuart, who received five shares each, were all veterans of the North West Company and used to life in the wild. (Indeed, McKay had crossed to the Pacific with Alexander Mackenzie in 1793.)

The lone American partner present at the formal organization of the company, Wilson Price Hunt, who also received five shares, was a St. Louis merchant with no exploring or trapping experience. He had, however, gained a detailed knowledge of the captains' travels through extensive discussions with both of them shortly after their return to St. Louis. In addition, as a lifelong US resident born in New Jersey, Hunt's unquestioned citizenship and loyalty to his country were just what Astor needed for his American company. By 1809, Astor had asked Hunt to lead the overland expedition to Oregon.

At the founding of the company in New York in June 1810, Hunt had signed for another partner receiving five shares, one of the multitude of boatmen met by Lewis and Clark in 1806 but one the captains would have considered a lesser light, not likely to have a huge impact on the Americana fur trade for decades: the teenage Scotsman who had served them supper and loaned them a tent—Ramsay Crooks.

Just as the details of Hunt's first meeting with Astor have been lost, so have the details of Hunt's initial attempt to recruit Crooks for Astor's enterprise. Hunt had arrived in St. Louis in 1803 and opened a store with partner John Hankinson, selling all kinds of goods needed by either average residents or average traders headed up the Missouri (with an inventory that included boats). Given Crooks's wintering on the Missouri River for Robert Dickson and Company in 1805–1806 and 1806–1807—and presumably buying supplies in St. Louis beforehand—it would be surprising if Crooks and Hunt had not met by the time Crooks met Lewis and Clark in September 1806.

Crooks's association with Dickson put him in a curious circumstance. Dickson, a fellow Scot, was twenty-two years older than Crooks and had made a name for himself as a savvy trader and Indian ally by 1797, when he married the daughter of an influential chief of the Santee Sioux. A few years after that, Dickson had become a prominent trader in the region that now includes Iowa, southern Minnesota, and parts of Wisconsin and South Dakota. In 1805, he and James Aird and others had formed Robert Dickson and Company at Mackinac Island, a key trading center near the convergence of Lake Huron and Lake Michigan. That same year, eighteen-year-old Crooks began working for them as a clerk. Dickson and Company "was composed primarily of Canadian fur traders who hoped to protect their interests in the face of growing restrictions placed on them by the American government as a result of Jay's Treaty (1794), the heavy customs duties imposed on their British goods, and the increased competition from American traders throughout the area south and west of [Mackinac]."[31]

For Dickson and Aird, who focused their attention on the Missouri River, Lisa was naturally the chief competitor. So it was not surprising that Lewis and Clark had met both Aird and Crooks going up the river in September of 1806. A year earlier, however, territorial governor James Wilkinson had decided that the trading privileges granted to British citizens under Jay's Treaty did not apply to lands obtained through the Louisiana Purchase. "Notice is hereby given," Wilkinson's proclamation of August 26, 1805, stated unequivocally, "that no person the Citizen or Subject of a foreign power will be permitted to enter the Missouri River for the purpose of the Indian Trade."[32]

Nevertheless, Dickson and Aird had found a loophole. According to Jay's Treaty, those living near forts surrendered to the US in 1796 were free to declare themselves British citizens, but if no such declarations were made within a year, they would be classified as US citizens. Although they were still British subjects in spirit, Dickson and Aird had let the deadline pass without comment, thus making themselves Americans—at least for purposes of trade. As for Wilkinson, he saw them as "Zealous British Partizans" intent on spreading "themselves over the North and West of America" from their Mackinac headquarters.[33]

Wilkinson was not alone in his negative opinion of Robert Dickson and Company. In August of 1808, an American official at Mackinac by the name of George Hoffman had voiced his concerns about Dickson. "I have seen & read a paper which you granted [Dickson] giving him permission to trade in Louisiana, & and have also been informed that Gov. [Meriwether] Lewis feels very thankful & grateful towards Dickson on account of services rendered by him to our Government," Hoffman wrote to territorial secretary Frederick Bates in St. Louis. "I fear that neither of you know the man—he has done what has perhaps advantaged the U. States—But believe me not from any love he bears our Country. . . . He is a Br. Subject in heart & sentiment . . . [and] possesses not the smallest wish for the happiness of the American people."[34]

The question naturally comes up: What of Crooks's loyalties? As a clerk to Dickson and Aird, he would not have required a personal trading license when he met Lewis and Clark in 1806. But his status soon changed because he and Robert McClellan, another trader—and friend of the captains—encountered by Lewis and Clark on their return, had formed a partnership during the winter. On May 1, 1807, a license was granted in McClellan's name to trade on the Missouri River for two years.[35] McClellan is known to have been on the Missouri at the time, and the license was almost certainly obtained by Crooks. The high-strung McClellan, seventeen years' Crooks's senior, had wisely chosen a reliable, levelheaded man to work with. Crooks enlisted men, made preparations, and purchased supplies and when McClellan came downriver in midsummer, he and Crooks and their eighty boatmen, trappers, and hunters rushed upriver.

In May of 1808, also in St. Louis, Crooks, "partner of Robert McClellan," was granted a license "to ascend the Missouri with provisions for their trading establishment." By August, the busy Crooks was at Mackinac to purchase goods for the coming winter and apply for another trading license. Hoffman, the same official who had warned Bates about Dickson, interviewed Crooks and asked him to take a loyalty oath. "[Crooks] refused taking it—alledging that he conceived himself an American Citizen, that he was concerned with one Mc.Cleland, an American born, in the Illinois, and that he was in no wise interested or concerned with the Macinac Company [Dickson and Company], I, therefore thereupon, granted him a *Common* Clearance."[36]

True to his word, Crooks was an American businessman working for American companies from that time on. During his two-year partnership with McClellan, however, things did not go well. Their plans were frequently thwarted by Lisa, whom McClellan threatened to kill at one point. The future eventually looked so bleak that in the spring of 1809, Crooks arrived in St. Louis with a notice—soon published in the April

12 issue of the *Missouri Gazette*—that he and McClellan were dissolving their partnership.

Discouraged and not sure what would happen next, the twenty-two-year-old Crooks was delighted at hearing, within days of his arrival, that President Jefferson had signed legislation repealing much of an embargo act ostensibly aimed at Britain but unintentionally harmful to American traders. Crooks knew that fur prices would rise and trade goods would be much more accessible. About this same time, twenty-six-year-old Hunt approached Crooks with "electrifying news of his own. How would Crooks and McClellan like to join an expedition being formed by John Jacob Astor to follow Lewis' and Clark's route to the Pacific?" Thomas James offered key evidence confirming Crooks's ties to Astor when he wrote that during his and Dougherty and the others' journey up the Missouri in the summer of 1809 (just a few months after the meeting between Hunt and Crooks), "below Council Bluffs we met Capt. Crooks, agent for John J. Astor, and who was trading with the Mohaws [Omaha Indians]."[37]

Regardless of Crooks's exact status in 1809, his standing with Astor a year later was not in doubt: Crooks was granted five shares in the new firm, putting him on equal terms with the seasoned Nor'Westers. Likely at Crooks's urging, Astor also reserved two and a half shares each for McClellan and Joseph Miller, a "well educated and well informed" former army officer who began working with Crooks and McClellan in 1809.[38]

With capital that made the Missouri Fur Company's assets look sparse, Astor launched a two-pronged mission: One party, headed by Hunt, McKenzie, and Crooks, would go by land (thus called "overland Astorians"), following the Lewis and Clark trail from St. Louis to the mouth of the Columbia; the other party, commanded by McDougall, McKay, and Robert Stuart, would go by sea from New York, around Cape Horn and to the Sandwich Islands for goods and more men and finally to the mouth of the Columbia to build a trading fort. Ideally, the overlanders would reach the upper Missouri in the fall of 1810, winter there, and reach the Pacific by late fall of 1811 (as Lewis and Clark had done in 1804–1805). The seagoing party would depart New York in the fall of 1810 and reach the Pacific in the spring of 1811, giving them time to construct a fort and be well settled by the time the overlanders arrived. The signing of the papers late in June of 1810 thus pressured both parties to act fast, especially the seagoers, who absolutely had to leave in time to round Cape Horn in December or January, when the area was enjoying good weather, favorable winds, and long days.

While the partners recruited men, Astor got busy shopping for a merchant vessel. On August 23, 1810, he paid $37,860 for the *Tonquin*, "a ship of 300 tons mounting twelve guns and mustering a crew of twenty-one men."[39] Astor paid another $54,000 and change for the cargo and $10,000 to ensure it. On September 6, the ship's crew, and Astor's employees—consisting of the four partners, eleven clerks, thirteen boatmen, and five mechanics—set sail. They were right on schedule but about to endure a nightmare.

A few weeks before Astor purchased the *Tonquin*, Crooks learned that he was now an official partner in the Pacific Fur Company when he met Hunt at Mackinac Island. Hunt and McKenzie had been attempting to recruit men for the overland expedition with limited success. They had enlisted more than thirty men, mostly boatmen, and Crooks urged further recruiting in St. Louis to have a good corps of hunters and to hire at least a couple dozen Americans—this was, after all, an American company. So Hunt, McKenzie, and Crooks sailed by way of Lake Michigan and the Fox, Wisconsin, and Mississippi Rivers to St. Louis, arriving on September 3. Given his and McClellan's past history with Lisa, Crooks was not surprised to find that enlisting men would be difficult because Lisa was already busy finding hands for his spring of 1811 trip up the Missouri to resupply Henry and his men. Hunt and McKenzie, who both been in New York to sign papers on June 23, had already experienced delays at Montreal and Mackinac, and it was now obvious they would never reach the upper Missouri this year. Still, they would get as far as possible. As the three partners recruited men, they also purchased the endless list of supplies needed to reach the Pacific— everything from a large keelboat, a Schenectady barge, oars, oilcloth, sails, and anchors to handsaws, padlocks, copper kettles, bearskins, hulled corn, knives and forks, tin cups, coffee, tea, pepper, bacon, a medicine chest, tobacco, combs, shoes, and thread.[40]

"Mr Hunt & McKinzey are at this place, prepareing to proceed up the Missouri and prosue my trail to the Columbia," William Clark wrote to Secretary of War William Eustis on September 12. "I am not fully in possession of the objects of this expedition but prosume you are, would be very glad to be informed."[41]

What Clark meant by "my trail to the Columbia" is not at all clear. Nor had Astor himself shed any light on that issue in a letter to Albert Gallatin he had written a few months earlier, noting that he had "made arrangements to send a party of good men up the Missurie for the purpose of exploring the country . . . to ascertain whether it afords furrs suficient to carry on an extensive trade," adding that the men intended "to cross the Rockey mountains to columbia's river where it is hoped they will meet" with those who had sailed on the *Tonquin*.[42]

Following Clark's trail up the Missouri and crossing the Rockies to the Columbia—in the strictest sense—would have meant doing what Lewis and Clark did: ascend the Jefferson River to its source; cross the divide at Lemhi Pass; follow, on foot or by horseback, the Lemhi, Salmon, and North Fork of the Salmon to Lost Trail Pass; cross to the Bitterroot River and descend it to Travelers' Rest; cross to the Lochsa River and descend it to the Clearwater; and build canoes and navigate the Clearwater to the Snake and Columbia. But Clark, of course, never would have recommended the trial-and-error route to Travelers' Rest to anyone making the transcontinental journey. As he and Lewis had eventually learned from Old Toby, a much better route would be to ascend the Missouri to the mouth of the Dearborn River, ascend the Dearborn to its source, cross the divide to the Big Blackfoot River, follow it to its mouth at the Clark Fork River, follow the Clark Fork a mile or two to its confluence with the Bitterroot, and ascend the Bitterroot a mile or two to Travelers' Rest.

Lewis and Clark had also known in 1805 from talking to Indians that the Clark Fork, which they called Clark's River, flowed north before eventually joining the Columbia, but they lacked two key pieces of information—how far north it went and whether it was navigable. In his postexpedition discussions with Hunt and others, therefore, Clark would not have recommended the northern route as a possible link between the Missouri and the Columbia. Furthermore, as the great Canadian explorer David Thompson would discover a few years later, the northern route was not navigable, especially because of Metaline Falls on the Pend Oreille River. This meant Lewis and Clark had made the right decision in crossing Lolo Pass and going west rather than descending the Clark Fork, but it also meant that Jefferson's fervently hoped-for Northwest Passage allowing reasonable water commerce between the Missouri and the Columbia was looking more and more elusive.[43]

As James P. Ronda notes, "The Platte, the Green, and the Snake were not like the Rivanna, the James, or the Potomac. . . . Waterways, so much a part of the Virginia tradition, were left behind as a westering nation turned to railways and highways."[44]

Hunt had certainly talked to Lewis and Clark after their return to St. Louis in 1806, gaining detailed knowledge about the expedition in general and their path to the Pacific in particular, but whether he and Clark met in 1810 to discuss probable overland routes for the Astorians is not known.[45] There are definite hints, however, that Hunt indeed consulted with Clark, because by March of 1811, when Hunt departed St. Louis to join the Astorians already waiting at the mouth of the Nodaway River, he had decided to "ascend the Missouri to the Roche Jaune [Yellowstone] river . . . and at that place . . . commence his journey by land."[46]

Hunt had thus decided to follow Lewis and Clark's route only as far as the mouth of the Yellowstone River, which lies in far western North Dakota near the Montana border (southwest of present Williston). Whereas Lewis and Clark had ascended the Missouri River west across present Montana, Hunt apparently hoped to obtain horses and follow the Yellowstone to the southwest. And, as noted in chapter 1, the course of the Yellowstone had been a crucial topic in the recent consultations between Clark and Colter as the former prepared his master map and identified "Eustis Lake"—now Yellowstone Lake—as the headwaters of the Yellowstone. Given Clark's friendly relationship with Hunt and his interest in talking with anyone heading west, he easily could have discussed the Yellowstone as an alternative with Hunt. Such a dialogue would have been especially timely because it had only been two months since Pierre Menard brought news of the Blackfoot attack at Three Forks. The Yellowstone was not only "a large and navigable river with but fiew obstructions"[47] in Clark's words, it would also take the Astorians away from the hostile Blackfoot nation to the friendly Absaroka.

Still, although Clark could have shown Hunt his map of the headwaters of both the Yellowstone and the Bighorn (at Lake Biddle, now Brooks Lake), neither he nor Colter (nor anyone else in St. Louis, for that matter) could have told Hunt how to cross from either Eustis Lake or Lake Biddle—both on the east side of the Continental Divide—to

the Columbia River system on the west side. However, at the same time
that Clark was putting the finishing touches on his map and Hunt was
buying supplies for his westward trek, Andrew Henry and his men had
already crossed from the Yellowstone to the Columbia.

For Clark, Hunt, and other St. Louis residents, the latest word on
Henry had come from Menard, who reached St. Louis by July 20, 1810.
Menard told of the April attack and how Drouillard and two Indian
hunters had been killed in subsequent hostilities in May. Menard also
informed Clark and the other partners in the Missouri Fur Company
that when he left in June, Henry's party was preparing to cross to the
Columbia River and trap there. "The Blackfeet manifested so determined a hatred and jealousy of our presence, that we could entertain no
hope of successfully prosecuting our business, even if we could save our
lives, in their country," wrote Thomas James. "Discouraged by the prospect before us, most of the Americans prepared to go back to the
settlements, while Col. Henry and the greater part of the company,
with a few Americans were getting ready to cross the mountains and go
onto the Columbia beyond the vicinity of our enemies."[48]

After the departure of Menard's group, which included James, Henry's band reportedly faced Blackfoot aggression once again. Writing to
Colonel Henry Atkinson in 1819 from Cantonment Missouri (about two
miles above Council Bluffs), Major Thomas Biddle—younger brother
of Nicholas Biddle—stated that the Missouri Fur Company had erected
a fort at Three Forks in 1810 and begun trapping. "They had every
prospect of being successful, until their operations were interrupted by
the hostility of the Blackfeet Indians," continued Biddle. "With these
people they had several very severe conflicts, in which upwards of thirty
of their men were killed; and the whole party were finally compelled to
leave that part of the country." Interestingly, Biddle's informant was
none other than John Dougherty.[49]

Dougherty family history also confirms that Henry and his men endured attacks after Menard's departure. In a letter written in 1907,
O'Fallon Dougherty, John Dougherty's son, stated that his father—not
known to be wounded before Menard left—was "shot several times by
the Indians" during his "ventures on the Mo River" and that he "carried
a half of ball in his right side during his life."[50]

Another report came from unnamed members of Henry's party who
said that shortly before abandoning the fort at Three Forks, "there had

been a battle between eighteen or nineteen of [Henry's] hunters, and upwards of two hundred Blackfeet, in which twenty two of the latter were killed, and the hunters enabled to make a safe retreat to the fort with the loss of only one man."[51] Despite likely exaggerating the number of Blackfoot warriors involved, this account is consistent with Biddle's.

Mark Kelly, Dougherty's biographer, has speculated that this battle may have prevented Henry and his men from ascending the Madison River to the south and then crossing the Continental Divide into Idaho by way of Raynolds Pass, the route Menard, and subsequently Clark, had expected them to take.[52] Such a scenario makes a good deal of sense, given the Blackfoot nation's decades-long determination to defend not only Three Forks itself but the Madison River in particular.[53]

As Kelly points out, however, Henry's route to Idaho's Teton Basin "has long been a matter of dispute among historians of the fur trade; indeed, more than one route may be supported by the record."[54] What is certain is that a group that included Dougherty (no others are identified) did not ascend the Madison but took quite another path. The decisive evidence is a thirteen-by-sixteen-inch handwritten document with a map on one side and a lengthy script on the other, now known as the Dougherty Map and Dougherty Narrative, respectively. Produced by an unidentified scribe who interviewed Dougherty sometime around 1818, the map is one of the three earliest (along with those from Drouillard and Clark) of the upper Missouri River, and the narrative describes Dougherty's experiences in the area, including the evacuation from Three Forks.[55]

The Dougherty Narrative offers the following details about the route taken from Three Forks to the Columbia side of the Continental Divide:

> Mr Dougherty left the fort [Three Forks post] crossed over to the Yellowstone descended until he met the Rest they then crossed over from the Yellowston to Stinking River assended to its [word omitted] with the intention of crossing over the mountains onto the Columbia at a place further South below the Blackfeet Indians in crossing over they fell on the waters of a River which they mistook for Clarks fork, but which after descending 3 or 4 days they concluded was the Rio del Norte they assended this River going further West fell on Clarks River which they descended & he wintered on it.[56]

Combining his meticulous analysis of the Dougherty Map and Narrative with the reports of James and Biddle—and adding his personal reconnaissance of the area itself—Kelly offered a route consistent with the various sources: from Three Forks, the group ascended the Gallatin River until reaching Buffalo Horn Pass, signified on the map by the notation "18 miles across"; they then, as noted in the narrative, "crossed over to the Yellowstone [and] descended [it] until [they] met the Rest," meaning the men Menard had sent to resupply Henry; again quoting the narrative, "they then crossed over from the Yellowstone to Stinking River," meaning they followed the same route that some of them, including Dougherty, had taken on their way to Three Forks—ascending Pryor Creek to Pryor Gap and continuing (into present Wyoming) to the Stinking (Shoshone) River, northeast of Cody; next they ascended the Shoshone, then the South Fork of the Shoshone to its source, crossing the mountains, as Biddle said, "near the source of the Yellow Stone river";[57] they then crossed Shoshone Pass, picked up Du Noir Creek, a key source of the Wind River, and followed it to the southeast, thinking they had crossed the Continental Divide and were now on Lewis's River (now called the Snake);[58] they descended the Wind River for three or four days until concluding it was the Rio del Norte (Green River), at which point they backtracked to the Brooks Lake area and crossed the Continental Divide at Togwotee Pass, which offered a spectacular view of the Teton Range to the west; they soon picked up the Buffalo Fork and followed it to its mouth at the Snake River near present Moran Junction in Grand Teton National Park and then ascended the Snake to the southwest, presumably entering present Idaho via Teton Pass, west of Jackson, Wyoming.[59]

By September of 1810, Henry and at least some of his men, now viewing the Tetons from the west, had established "Camp Henry" in a pleasant valley east of present Drummond, Idaho, along Conant Creek, a tributary of Fall River. They wintered at "Henry's Fort," along Henrys Fork, farther west, between present Rexburg and St. Anthony. And while the question of whether Henry and the others arrived in Idaho in two groups or one is still debated, there is no argument about the value of the Dougherty Map; it offers the only solid evidence of the second American westward crossing of the Continental Divide—after Lewis and Clark's crossing at Lemhi Pass five years earlier.[60]

* * *

"Whilst at breakfast in a beautiful part of the [Missouri] river," naturalist and writer John Bradbury wrote on May 26, 1811, "we observed two
canoes descending on the opposite side. In one, by the help of our
glasses [spyglass telescopes], we ascertained there were two white men,
and in the other only one." Traveling up the Missouri with Hunt,
Crooks, McKenzie, and five dozen trappers, hunters, and boatmen,
Bradbury left the only firsthand account of what happened next. "A gun
was discharged, when they discovered us, and crossed over. We found
them to be three men belonging to Kentucky, whose names were Robinson, Hauberk, and Reesoner." Dubbed the "doomed trio" by historian
Robert M. Utley, these three were John Hoback, Jacob Reznor, and
Edward Robinson, a triumvirate whose wanderings and adventures—
and deaths—would become the stuff of legend. They had not seen their
families or plantations in the Bluegrass State since enlisting with Lisa
early in the spring of 1807. "They had been several years hunting on
and beyond the Rocky Mountains, until they imagined they were tired
of the hunting life," continued Bradbury. "But on seeing us, families,
plantations, and all vanished; they agreed to join us, and turned their
canoes adrift."[61]

A flesh-and-blood specimen illustrating the violence of the era, Robinson was sixty-six years old, "one of the first settlers in Kentucky," who
had fought Indians in "the Bloody Ground" and "in one of those en-
gagements . . . had been scalped, and was obliged to wear a handkerchief on his head to protect the part."[62] Washington Irving added that
Hoback, Reznor, and Robinson "had been in the service of the Missouri
Company under Mr. Henry, and had crossed the Rocky Mountains with
him in the preceding year [1810], when driven from his post on the
Missouri by the hostilities of the Blackfeet."[63]

Thus came the first word that Henry's men had survived the winter
on a tributary of the Columbia and were now returning east. Reaching
the Missouri River upstream of the mouth of the Niobrara River (along
the present border of southeast South Dakota and northeast Nebraska)
by late May meant that the threesome had started quite early in the
spring, wasting no time as they walked and canoed eastward. Because
crossing the formidable Teton Range before the spring thaw would
have been arduous and snaillike—if possible at all—Kelly's speculation

that Hoback and his two companions may have gotten an early start by leaving in the fall and wintering on the Snake River east of the Tetons seems reasonable. [64]

The best evidence further indicates that Henry's men departed Henry's Fort in at least three groups: one consisting of Hoback, Reznor, and Robinson; another that went south to the Spanish settlements, "perhaps in an effort to join others of the St. Louis Missouri Fur Company reportedly trapping in the vicinity"; and a third of at least fifteen individuals (including both Henry and Dougherty) who left considerably later than the doomed trio, returning to Fort Mandan by way of the Bighorn, Little Bighorn, Yellowstone, and Missouri Rivers. [65]

While the vast majority of Hunt's party was unknown to Hoback, Reznor, and Robinson, there were two familiar faces in the crowd: Benjamin Jones and Alexander Carson. Jones and Carson had gone up the Missouri in 1809, in the armada that included Dougherty, Thomas James, and Reuben Lewis, and had endured the Blackfoot attacks at Three Forks during the spring of 1810. They had fled Three Forks with Menard, but rather than return with him to St. Louis, they had wintered at the Arikara Indian villages in present northern South Dakota. On May 22, as they descended the Missouri in their canoe, they encountered Hunt and his men and decided—like their three compatriots would four days later, and like John Colter had done when he met Lisa in 1807—to abandon thoughts of home, family, and friends and return to the mountains in hopes of making a fortune trapping beaver.

"As we had now in our party five men who had traversed the Rocky Mountains in various directions, the best possible route in which to cross them became a subject of anxious enquiry," wrote Bradbury. "They all agreed that the route followed by Lewis and Clark was very far from being the best, and that to the southward, where the head waters of the Platte and Roche Jaune [Yellowstone] rivers rise, they had discovered a route far less difficult. This information induced Mr. Hunt to change his plan . . . [and] abandon the Missouri at the Aricara Town." [66]

Jones, Carson, Hoback, Reznor, and Robinson all agreed to act as guides in leading Hunt westward. "On July 18, 1811," Hunt subsequently wrote, "Messrs. Hunt, Mackenzie, Crooks, Miller, McClellan and Reed, who were accompanied by fifty-six men, one woman and two children"—the Indian wife and sons of Hunt's chief scout and interpreter, Pierre Dorion Jr.—"and had gone by water from Saint Louis to the Aricaras' village on the Missouri, left there with eighty-two horses laden with merchandise, equipment, food and animal traps."[67]

The Astorians, who up to this point had followed Lewis and Clark's route on the Missouri River, thus charted their own course, going west near the site of present Mobridge, South Dakota, and ascending the Grand River. This shifted America's westward vision drastically to the south: while Lewis and Clark had seen much of North Dakota and the breadth of Montana but none of Wyoming, the Astorians would bypass North Dakota, catch just a glimpse of Montana, and make an extensive, though sometimes accidental, exploration of Wyoming. And although Hunt's corps departed the Missouri well supplied, nothing could change the fact that they were leaving much too late in the season and had little chance of reaching the Pacific coast before winter. Hunt knew it had taken Lewis and Clark seven months to go from Fort Mandan to the coast. He could move faster because he was not conducting studies and keeping detailed journals, as the captains had done for Jefferson, but he could hardly expect to make the journey twice as fast. Not only that but he faced a huge unknown—he was confident Hoback, Reznor, and Robinson could get him to the branch of the Snake River they had seen with Henry (though that would be much easier said than done), but neither they nor any others of Henry's men could say if the river was navigable. If so, they *might* reach the coast early enough to avoid wintering in the mountains. If not, they could be in serious trouble, but Hunt had no way of judging how dire the situation might be. Whether there were friendly Indians in the area, ample game to support sixty people, or passable terrain were all unknowns. Hunt did not even know how far it was from Henry's Fort to the mouth of the Columbia River.

Whatever trials Hunt imagined over the next several months no doubt paled in comparison to the real thing. Irving, who interviewed several of the participants, described the crisis faced by Hunt on Christmas Eve, 1811:

> On the 24th of December, all things being arranged, Mr. Hunt turned his back upon the disastrous banks of the Snake River, and struck his course westward for the mountains. His party . . . amounted now to thirty-two white men, three Indians, and the squaw and two children of Pierre Dorion. Five jaded, half-starved horses were laden with their luggage, and, in case of need, were to

furnish them with provisions. They travelled painfully about fourteen miles a day, over plains and among hills, rendered dreary by occasional falls of snow and rain. Their only sustenance was a scanty meal of horse flesh once in four and twenty hours.[68]

On September 15, his company of sixty still intact, Hunt had found a new passage over the Continental Divide, crossing on an Indian trail at Union Pass, twenty miles south-southwest of Togwotee Pass, used by those with Dougherty. At the summit, one of Henry's hunters—Hoback, Reznor, or Robinson—"showed us three immensely high and snow-covered peaks which, he said, were situated on the banks of a tributary of [the Columbia] river."[69] The peaks, of course, were the Tetons, and the "beautiful green valleys" on the other side of Union Pass were all part of the Green River Valley, linked in subsequent decades to names like Bridger, Carson, Campbell, Wyeth, Whitman, Smith, Sublette, Jackson, Bonneville, Ashley, De Smet, Fontenelle, and Fitzpatrick.[70]

Hunt reached Henry's Fort on October 8 and made the well-intended but ultimately catastrophic decision to build canoes and paddle down the Snake River, leaving seventy-two horses behind in the process. Their second—and third—day out they hit rapids, losing two canoes and crucial supplies and food. Less than a week later, near present Burley, Idaho, the swift-flowing river was suddenly "confined between 2 ledges of Rock . . . less than 40 feet apart & Here indeed its terrific appearance beggars all description."[71] A canoe carrying Crooks and four others smashed into a rock, splintering the canoe into fragments and throwing the men "amidst roaring breakers and a whirling current." One man drowned—the others barely survived, more food and supplies lost. "This disastrous event brought the whole squadron to a halt, and struck a chill into every bosom."[72] Another canoe loaded with food was soon lost as a few voyagers tried to thread it through rapids with a rope.

Less than two weeks after having six dozen horses available for trade or travel and stowing a substantial supply of food in the canoes, Hunt, now without horses, announced they had less than five days' worth of food remaining. Cold, wet weather was coming on quickly, and with the river full of rapids and falls for at least thirty-five miles ahead, they now abandoned their canoes. Adding trouble to trouble, the Shoshone Indians in the area—most of whom were terrified at the new sight of Europeans—lived on the edge of poverty and had little to trade. Hunt sent eleven men—in three groups led by McKenzie, McClellan, and Reed—off separately to search for Indians who could help or a better route. Crooks and a few others ascended the river to the east, hoping to reach Henry's Fort and return with the horses. "We spread a net," wrote Hunt. "Only one fish was found in it."[73]

Crooks soon appeared, convinced that travel by foot was so slow that he had no chance of reaching the fort and returning during the winter. Hunt and Crooks divided the forty-odd people into two groups and traveled on opposite sides of the river, hoping for some kind of good luck. Soon they were reduced to obtaining their only drinking water from small pockets of rain—the canyon walls were so steep that getting water from the river was impossible. Within two weeks, both groups were on the verge of starvation, surviving by catching a few beaver or fish here and there or by buying a horse or a few dogs from the Indians—and slaughtering the animals on the spot for food.

One crisis followed another; another man drowned. By the time Hunt headed northwest from the vicinity of present Ontario, Oregon, on Christmas Eve, he was the lone partner in the group. Miller and others, including Hoback, Reznor, and Robinson, had stayed near Henry's Fort to trap; McKenzie and McClellan and their men had followed the Snake into another mammoth gorge (now known as Hells Canyon), a route Hunt had found impossible to take. If Hunt saw them again, it would be at the fort the seagoing Astorians had (hopefully) built at the mouth of the Columbia River—the odds of such a reunion, however, seemed miniscule.

But of the five partners, Crooks's plight was the most desperate. "Mr. Crooks was quite ill in the night," Hunt wrote on December 9. "Seeing that [Crooks's feeble condition] would delay for two days my arriving among the Indians, I left three men with him; and departed . . . with two others." With their food supply consisting of three beaver skins, Hunt and his companions left two with Crooks and "supped on the third. The weather was extremely cold."[74]

He had not seen Crooks since.

3

"WE COULD ALWAYS RELY UPON THEIR WORD!"

On January 1, 1812, eight days after Wilson Price Hunt led his beleaguered band into the Oregon wilderness to continue battling the elements, Lewis and Clark veteran Nathaniel Pryor faced a different kind of foe: eight armed Winnebago Indians. Although Pryor had been trading peaceably with the Winnebagos only days earlier at his trading post and lead smelter near present Galena, Illinois, they stormed his post and took him hostage. "About sun-down of the same day," explained an 1826 account, "sixty arrived, shooting down the oxen in the yard and killing two of his men. They rushed on him, and was in the act of putting him to death, when by the politic dissimulation of a female in the house, there were averted for the moment from their intention. They then placed him in the house with a sentinel over him, intending to burn him in it."[1]

What the bewildered Pryor did not realize was that he was a victim of a conflict unknown to him that had occurred seven weeks earlier—the Battle of Tippecanoe. By pure coincidence, a group of Winnebagos returning from Canada had stopped the night before the battle in present Indiana near the confluence of the Tippecanoe and Wabash Rivers to lodge at an Indian town called Prophetstown. The town was inhabited by an Indian confederacy founded by the Shawnee chief Tecumseh and his brother Tenskwatawa, called the Prophet.

Born in present Ohio around 1768 (making him two years older than William Clark), Tecumseh was educated in his youth, taking a liking to both Shakespeare and the Bible. He distinguished himself as a warrior in the Ohio Indian wars, in which his father and two older brothers were killed. In August of 1794, under the command of Shawnee chief Blue Jacket, he fought in the Battle of Fallen Timbers, near present Toledo. British agents and the American traitor Simon Girty were also in the group, while the American enemies, including junior officers Clark and William Henry Harrison, were led by General "Mad Anthony" Wayne. The Americans won a decisive victory. By 1805, when Lewis and Clark were making their wearisome northwest passage, Tecumseh and the Prophet were promoting the idea of an Indian confederacy, with the former as war chief and the latter as spiritual leader.

"The white men despise and cheat the Indians; they abuse and insult them; they do not think the red men sufficiently good to live," Tecumseh had reportedly proclaimed before the Creek, Chickasaw, Choctaw, Osage, and Delaware nations, among others. "My people are brave and numerous, but the white people are too strong for them alone. I wish you take up the tomahawk with them. If we all unite, we will cause the rivers to stain the great waters with their blood." At the same time, evidence from Euro-Americans shows that Tecumseh objected to the torture of prisoners inflicted by both sides and that he was a man of his word.[2]

Although Tecumseh had met with Indiana territorial governor William Henry Harrison several times and expressed his displeasure with treaties negotiated by Harrison and signed by other Indian leaders,[3] Tecumseh made it clear that he did not intend to fight and requested that whites stay out of the disputed region until the next spring, when an appeal would be made directly to President James Madison. In July of 1811, he told Harrison he planned to visit other tribes and that peace would continue during his absence. Tecumseh also gave the Prophet strict instructions to avoid conflict with the Americans. Harrison, however, writes one historian, "felt that this would be a golden opportunity to crush the Indians while they were without effective leadership." Without express authority, Harrison marched a force of 1,200 men up the Wabash Valley to Prophetstown. "Though he was trespassing on unceded Indian land, on November 6 [1811], his forces had advanced to the outskirts of the village. Harrison fully expected, indeed hoped, that the Indians would attack . . . [but] failed to mount an adequate night guard."[4]

Just after four o'clock the next morning, with a cold rain falling, Harrison was talking with drummer Adam Walker when a shot rang out. "The attack . . . began on our left flank," Harrison wrote, but the sentinels "abandoned their officer and fled into camps. . . . Such of [the soldiers] as were awake or easily awakened, seized their arms [while others] had to contend with the enemy in the doors of their tents."[5]

In the early-morning chaos, one soldier reported firing his flintlock with the muzzle pressed against the chest of his assailant. Harrison suffered heavy casualties but managed to repulse the attack after two hours of intense fighting. He took possession of Prophetstown and declared a victory, although from the American view, the battle had been a draw, at best. "Critics faulted Harrison for provoking the Indian attack and for neglecting to secure his camp against an Indian surprise," writes Alan Taylor. "But President Madison and the Republican press endorsed Harrison's claims that Tippecanoe was a great and glorious victory over bloodthirsty brutes armed by the British." A Kentucky newspaper proclaimed, "The blood of our fellow-citizens murdered on the Wabash by British intrigue calls aloud for vengeance."[6]

The Winnebagos traveling from Canada had expected to rise after a peaceful night and proceed on their way; instead they found themselves in the thick of battle and naturally fought with their Indian brethren. When word spread that twenty-five of them had been killed at Tippecanoe, the Winnebagos living near Pryor took revenge on his American post. "While they were plundering his stores and ravaging his premises," continued the 1826 report, "with the greatest difficulty, he made his escape. After crossing the Mississippi on the cakes of ice, he was still the object of pursuit to the hostile Indians."[7]

A Sac Indian woman who cooked for Pryor and his men—"the female in the house"—had distracted the guard while Pryor grabbed his musket. Then, in a scene reminiscent of Colter's run, Pryor hid under a pile of driftwood near the shore, and, with the Winnebagos searching elsewhere, made his way across the ice to the Iowa side of the river. Somehow surviving the wet and cold, he traveled fifteen miles south to a French village where the fur trader Maurice Blondeau resided. Blondeau and his neighbors helped Pryor, hiding him in a cellar for the rest of the winter as Winnebagos continued searching for him.[8]

Knowing that Winnebagos might retaliate against American posts because of the losses at Tippecanoe, William Clark had sent Alexander

Willard, another expedition veteran, to warn Pryor. Willard was working as a government blacksmith for the Sauk and Fox Indians on the
west side of the Mississippi, opposite the site of present Nauvoo, Illinois, and when he got Clark's message he hurried north, navigating the
frozen Mississippi with a horse-drawn sleigh in an attempt to cover the
two hundred miles as fast as possible. When he reached Pryor's station,
however, he found nothing but the burned-out shells of the buildings
and concluded Pryor was dead. Willard continued north to warn others
and keep himself out of harm's way. When he rode south again a few
weeks later, however, he found new hazards. "The Winnebagoes are
Deturmined for War," Clark wrote to Secretary of War William Eustis
in February of 1812. "On the 8th [of this month] a party of that nation
(some of whom were known) fired on my Express [Willard] about 40
miles above the Settlements, who was on his return from Prarie de
Chien, the Mines & Fort Madison." Clark added that the next day,
Willard discovered the bodies of nine members of an O'Neal family,
most of them women and children, just minutes after they had been
murdered by Winnebago warriors. [9]

A few weeks later, the Boston *New England Palladium* reported
Pryor's death: "General William Clark . . . has written to his brother in
Louisville, informing that a party of Pouount [Winnebago] Indians, who
reside on the waters of the Illinois river, and who belonged to the
Prophet's party, has robbed the trading houses of Mr. G. Hunt and
Nathaniel Pryor, Esq. killed Pryor, and two of Hunt's men. Hunt es-
caped." [10]

But, as would be the case with Mark Twain in 1897 and Ernest
Hemingway in 1954, the reports of Pryor's death were greatly exaggerated. When the Mississippi was finally free of ice, Blondeau came down
the river with a boatload of beaver pelts, appearing to anyone onshore
that he was traveling alone. But stowed away in his cargo was Pryor,
who had now escaped an Indian attack for the second time. (The first,
as noted in chapter 1, had come in 1807, when Ensign Pryor's squad of
soldiers and hunters, including George Shannon, attempted to return
Mandan chief Sheheke to his North Dakota home and were attacked by
Arikara warriors.) Unfortunately, no record has been found of what
must have been a joyous reunion between Pryor and Clark.

Although acts of Indian violence were frequently reported, the killing of the O'Neal family had struck a chord of fear throughout the

territory. On March 19, Governor Benjamin Howard wrote to William Eustis:

> On the 10th of last month, nine persons were murder'd, in the most barbarous manner on the Mississippi, within the limits of our settlements; It is believed that this mischief was done by the Kickapoos, or Pawtawatimies of the Illinois. . . . Strong apprehensions are entertain'd there, that [Fort Madison] will soon be attack'd by a combination of Wenebagoes, Kickapoos, Pawtawatimies, and Shawanese; The commanding officer has called for reinforcements.—Since Christmas—12 persons have been killed certainly. More are now missing. . . . I encouraged the raising of a company of mounted riflemen, to act as rangers, to be commanded, by Capt. Boon, (Son of the celebrated Colo Daniel Boon).[11]

The Captain Boone mentioned by Howard was Nathan Boone, a friend and neighbor of John Colter. Whether Pryor's status as "missing and presumed dead" was a factor is not known, but when Boone mustered his mounted rangers on March 3, Colter was one of the original forty-one enlistees. Since his return from the West in 1810, Colter had married a woman named Sarah Loucy, also called Sally, and had a daughter, Evelina. (His son, Hiram, had apparently been born before the expedition, from a different mother.) Colter and his little family had settled on the Missouri River, about halfway between present Washington and New Haven, Missouri. Rather than returning to "civilization" with the fortune he had hoped to earn fur trapping, he had come back with little except his canoe and paddle, his rifle and ammunition, and the buckskin on his back. He had sued the estate of Meriwether Lewis to obtain his pay from the expedition, and although he had received $375.60 in May of 1811, most of those funds were now gone. Days before enlisting with Boone, Colter had visited Clark in St. Louis and borrowed forty-five dollars, likely to prepare for his ranger duty, because "the rangers were to equip themselves with good rifles or muskets and side arms as well as with clothing, horses, and provisions."[12]

As far as is known, this was the last time Clark and Colter saw each other.

Boone's rangers had barely begun their service when Kickapoo and Winnebago warriors massacred a group of settlers north of St. Louis. About that same time, the Potawatomi chief Main Poc threatened to wage war against the Osage nation and attack whites while doing so. An editorial in the *Louisiana Gazette* warned there would not be peace "as long as there is a British subject suffered to trade within the lines of our territories." However, the article continued, "The new company of rangers now doing duty in the district of St. Charles are perhaps as fine a body of hardy woodsman as ever took the field. They cover, by constant and rapid movements, the tract of country from Salt River on the Mississippi to the Missouri near Loutre."[13]

Who could have been better suited for such duty than Colter?

At an Independence Day celebration in St. Louis, on July 4, 1812, a group of grateful citizens offered their sincere thanks to Boone and his men: "Our Frontiers—watched and protected by a hardy band of Spartan Warriors—the Rangers deserve well of their country."[14]

But at least one man was not there to enjoy the festivities: Colter. Two months earlier, on May 7, at about thirty-eight years of age, he had died. His military record lists no cause of death; in fact, his old trapping companion Thomas James offered the only known information about his demise, saying, "I heard of Colter's death by jaundice."[15] But jaundice, a yellowish discoloration of the skin, is a symptom, not a disease. Colter could have died of anything from pancreatic cancer or malaria, to kidney or liver disease or hepatitis. Whatever his illness, it came on suddenly because a sick man could hardly have qualified for what Boone's biographer called "a tough-handed lot."[16]

The man praised by Clark for his expedition service thus did not survive two years in "the States" after repeatedly overcoming bitter cold, near starvation, grizzly bears, and hostile Indians during his six years in the wild. Although his adventures were chronicled by others, we have nothing from Colter himself—not a reminiscence, diary, or letter. Nor did anyone record his final moments, the way Clark had as twenty-two-year-old Sergeant Floyd was dying along the Missouri in August of 1804. Did Colter think of the West and how he had forgone a chance to be the first American to traverse the continent for a second time? That question will go unanswered, but in March of 1811, a year before he enlisted with Boone, Colter had been visited by Hunt, Bradbury, and others as they went up the Missouri in a keelboat. Bradbury, who had talked with Daniel Boone (on the other side of the river) the previous day, had been told where Colter lived by Clark, and asked one of his neighbors by the name of Sullens about him when the group stopped near the mouth of Boeuf Creek. Sullens sent his son to inform Colter he had visitors, and Colter arrived at the camp early the next morning.

Although Colter could not give Bradbury any further information about Clark's mention of a petrified skeleton of a forty-foot fish seen on the expedition, Colter was quite interested in talking to Hunt and Bradbury and rode with them for some time as the men pushed and pulled the keelboat upstream. Bradbury did not offer details of the conversation, but Irving's speculation that Colter "had many particulars to give them concerning the Blackfeet Indians, a restless and predatory tribe," is reasonable. Bradbury concluded his description of the meeting by noting that Colter "seemed to have a great inclination to accompany the expedition; but having been lately married, he reluctantly took leave of us."[17]

A few days after Colter's death, near the mouth of the Umatilla River in present northeastern Oregon, a group of Astorians—who would have been Colter's companions had he chosen to go west with Hunt—were headed downstream on the Columbia when they heard a commotion on the south shore. Among the men in the canoes were McClellan and Reed. Although the two of them, with the men accompanying them, as well as McKenzie and his companions, had left Hunt in separate groups the previous November, the three bands had eventually united, forming a group of eleven, as they followed the Snake River downstream along the present Idaho-Oregon border. Struggling through a "rugged defile" (Hells Canyon) considered impassable by Hunt and Crooks, they found the banks of the river "so high and precipitous, that there was rarely any place where the travelers could get down to drink of its waters." Nor did they see any game, staying alive on strips of beaver skin "doled out in scanty allowances." When a blizzard immobilized them under a mountain ledge, they prepared to face death with courage. When all seemed lost, McClellan spied a bighorn sheep above them, grabbed his rifle, scrambled up through the deep snow, took careful aim, and saved all eleven men by bringing down the ram with a single shot.[18]

McClellan and the others eventually reached members of the same Indian nation that had saved Lewis and Clark—the Nez Perce—and obtained food and canoes. Without losing a man, they reached Fort

Astoria (built by the seagoing Astorians as planned) on January 18, 1812. There was no word of Hunt or any other of the overlanders.[19]

Also present among those in canoes who noticed a disturbance on the south shore of the Columbia was twenty-six-year-old Robert Stuart, nephew of David Stuart, who received two shares from the latter and traveled with him aboard the *Tonquin*. Near the Falkland Islands, in early December of 1810, young Stuart had saved the lives of his uncle and eight other men when Jonathan Thorn, the incredibly obstinate captain of the ship, took offense at the nine men and sailed away, fully intending to leave them behind. Clutching a brace of pistols, Robert Stuart ordered the captain to turn back. If not, he said, "you are a dead man this instant."[20]

Given what McClellan and Stuart and their fellows had already experienced, it was hard to believe anything could shock them. When the group of Indians on the shore yelled several times for them to stop, they expected nothing out of the ordinary. "To shore the canoes instantly steered," wrote Astorian Alexander Ross, "when, to the surprise of all, who should be there, standing like two spectres, but Mr. Crooks and John Day, who, it will be remembered, had been left by Mr. Hunt among the Snake [Shoshone] Indians the preceding autumn; but so changed and emaciated were they, that our people for some time could scarcely recognize them to be white men."[21]

All eyes were on Crooks as he added another stunning saga to the Astorian chronicle. As recorded by Ross, this was his story:

> After being left by Mr. Hunt, we remained for some time with the Snakes, who were very kind to us. When they had anything to eat, we ate also; but they soon departed, and being themselves without provisions, of course they left us without any. We had to provide for ourselves the best way we could. As soon, therefore, as the Indians went off, we collected some brushwood and coarse hay, and made a sort of booth or wigwam to shelter us from the cold; we then collected some firewood; but before we got things in order, John Day grew so weak that when he sat down he could not rise again without help. Following the example of the Indians, I dug up roots for our sustenance; but not knowing how to cook them, we were nearly poisoned. In this plight, we unfortunately let the fire go out, and for a day and a night we both lay in a torpid state, unable to strike fire, or to collect dry fuel. We had now been a day without food, or even

water to drink, and death appeared inevitable. But Providence is ever kind. Two straggling Indians happened to come our way, relieved us. They made us a fire, got us some water, and gave us something to eat; but seeing some roots we had collected for food lying in a corner, they gave us to understand that they would poison us if we ate them. If we had had a fire, those roots would have been our first food, for we had nothing else to eat; and who can tell but the hand of a kind and superintending Providence was in all this? These poor fellows staid with us the greater part of two days, and gave us at their departure about two pounds of venison. We were really sorry to lose them.

On the same day . . . a very large wolf came prowling about our hut, when John Day, with great exertions and good luck, shot the ferocious animal dead; and to this fortunate hit I think we owed our lives. The flesh of the wolf we cut up and dried, and laid it by for some emergency, and in the mean time feasted upon the skin; nor did we throw away the bones, but pounded them between stones, and with some roots made a kind of broth, which, in our present circumstances, we found very good. . . . For two months we wandered about, barely sustaining life with our utmost exertions. All this time we kept traveling to and fro, until we happened by mere chance, to fall on the Umatallow [Umatilla] River; and then following it, we made the Columbia about a mile above this place, on the 15th day of April. . . . Our clothes being all torn and worn out, we suffered severely from cold; but on reaching this place the Indians were very kind to us. This man [pointing to an old grey-headed Indian, called Yeck-a-tap-am], in particular treated us like a father. After resting ourselves for two days with the good old man and his people, we set off, following the current, in the delusive hope of being able to reach our friends at the mouth of the Columbia, as the Indians gave us to understand that white men had gone down there in the winter, which we supposed must have been Mr. Hunt and his party.[22]

We had proceeded on our journey nine days, without interruption, and were not far from the falls [Celilo Falls, now obscured by the Dalles Dam] . . . when one morning, as we were sitting near the river, gazing on the beautiful stream before us, the Indians in considerable numbers collected around us, in the usual friendly manner: after some little time, however, one of them got up, and . . . took [my rifle] in his hands; another . . . took John Day's rifle from him. . . . All began to intimate to us by signs, in the most uproarious and wild manner, that some of their people had been killed by the whites and threatened to kill us in turn.[23] In this critical conjunction, John Day drew his knife, . . . but I pointed out to him the folly of such a step . . . and he desisted.

The Indians then closed in upon us, with guns pointed and bows drawn, on all sides, and by force stripped us of our clothes, ammunition, knives, and everything else, leaving us naked as the day we were born, and . . . it appeared evident that there was a disposition on their part to kill us; but after a long and angry debate, in which two or three old men seemed to befriend us, they made signs for us to be off; . . . we slowly turned around, and went up the river again, expecting every moment to receive a ball or an arrow. After travelling some little distance, we looked back and saw the savages quarrelling about the division of the booty. . . . All that day we travelled without tasting food, and at night concealed ourselves among the rocks—without fire, food, or clothing. Next day we . . . picked up some fishbones, . . . pounding them with stones, tried to eat a little, but could not manage to swallow any: that night also we hid ourselves among the rocks, but at last we resolved to keep by the river. . . .

Soon after we arrived at the river, we unexpectedly fell on a small Indian hut, with only two old people and a child in it. . . . The good people, however, gave us fish, broth, and roots to eat; and this was the first food we had tasted, and the first fire we had seen for four days and four nights. Our feet were severely cut and bleeding, for want of shoes; yet we lost no time, but set off, and arrived here three days ago, and our good old friend, Yeck-a-tap-am, received us again with open arms, and gave us these skins to cover our nakedness, as ye now see.

The good old man then killed a horse, which his people cut up and dried for us, and with that supply we had resolved to set out this very day and retrace our steps back again to St. Louis overland, and when you came in sight we were just in the act of tying up our little bundles.[24]

Crooks and Day reached Fort Astoria on May 11, 1812. They fully recovered within a few weeks, and on June 17 Crooks and another man walked the five miles to see Fort Clatsop, where Lewis and Clark had spent the winter of 1805–1806. That same day, eager to strengthen relations with Indian allies, Clark was headed up the Ohio River with an entourage of chiefs, warriors, and three women from the Great and Little Osage, Shawnee, and Delaware nations, taking them on a visit to the nation's capital. Also in the group were several interpreters, including Pryor's advocate Maurice Blondeau, and Clark's wife, Julia, and their two sons. With a long war looking certain, Clark wanted his family safe in Virginia.[25]

So Clark was not surprised when he discovered while still en route to Washington that James Madison had signed a declaration of war against Great Britain on June 18. Debates in Congress had fallen on partisan lines, with every Federalist voting against war and the great majority of Republicans, led by Henry Clay and the "War Hawks," voting in favor, even though the US was conspicuously unprepared for war.[26]

Nor was Great Britain ready for a second war with America. For two decades, Britain had fought France in a series of wars so costly to both countries in terms of men and resources—the French Revolutionary Wars, from 1792 to 1802, and the Napoleonic Wars, which had begun in 1803. Britain and such allies as Austria, Hungary, and Spain had been defeated by France, Italy, Switzerland, Holland, and others in the War of the Fifth Coalition in 1809, and on June 24, 1812, six days after the United States declared war against Britain, Napoleon invaded Russia, predictably leading to the War of the Sixth Coalition in 1813, with Britain once again taking the lead in battling France. Ironically, one of the War Hawks' main complaints against Britain was its illegal impressment of American sailors into naval service, deemed necessary because of the continual loss of sailors Britain had suffered in its long conflict with France.

Just as his elder brother George Rogers Clark had fought an Indian war in the Illinois Country during the late 1770s and early '80s that was contemporary to, but in many ways separate from, the American Revolutionary War, William Clark had now been drawn into a western conflict with Indians that was distinct from the war in the East. And although the War of 1812 was "a war of diverse causes, and its history was to be shrouded in sectional politics and issues," writes Thomas D. Clark, "there was clearly a high degree of expansionist influence in the West . . . manifested in the rapid white settlement in the Northwest and the South, an aggressive attitude of which the Indians were fully aware."[27]

As a soldier fighting in the Ohio Indian wars of the 1790s, particularly the Battle of Fallen Timbers, William Clark had helped facilitate this aggressive westward expansion. As Landon Jones has noted, at the Treaty of Greenville, which was signed on August 3, 1795, General

Wayne established the pattern for future dealings between Indians and the US government: first, Euro-Americans trespassed on Indian lands; second, Indian retaliation resulted in calls from white settlers for help from a federal army; third, the Indians would be defeated, with the Americans burning their towns and villages in the process; fourth, the Indians would achieve peace by ceding more of their territory.[28]

Clark had no particular hostility toward Indians, and his individual treatment of them was better than that of many white officials involved with Indians—he sincerely hoped to improve their situation. In terms of western expansion, however, Clark had no problem with the tactics of General Wayne or William Henry Harrison, nor did he have any sympathy for Tecumseh's attempt to lead the Indians in their own war of independence. It came as no surprise that Indians who met Clark over the coming years were treated with respect and also no surprise that Clark did not object to Andrew Jackson's 1830 Indian Removal Act.

Clark's present concern was getting his Indian allies safely to Washington, ensuring their good reception, and escorting them back to their homes without incident. When he arrived in Washington in August, however, he received one report of bad news after another. The first report was personal—a letter waiting for him from Nicholas Biddle. "It is now almost a whole year since . . . I wrote to you that [the history of the expedition] was ready [for] the press whenever Mr. Conrad chose," wrote Biddle. "Yet notwithstanding all my exertions the publication has been prevented from time to time till at last Mr. Conrad's difficulties have obliged him to surrender everything to his creditors & give up business."[29]

Just as Clark had been frustrated three years earlier with Lewis's failure to make any progress on the history of the expedition, he was now exasperated with Conrad. "[Conrad] has disapointed me in a way I had not the smallest suspicion of," he wrote to Biddle. "I think we might have expected from him some intimation of his situation which would have prevented a delay of the work."[30] Hoping to somehow salvage the project, Clark made preparations to visit Biddle in Philadelphia.

Meanwhile, news of the war hardly lightened Clark's somber mood. Fort Michilimackinac (later called Fort Mackinac), a strategic post because it controlled the Straits of Mackinac between Lake Michigan and Lake Huron, had fallen on July 17. The commander, Clark would later learn, had not even heard of the declaration of war and was so taken by surprise when British troops and their Indian allies attacked that he surrendered without a fight.

Clark knew, as St. Louis resident Christian Wilt had written, that the capture of Fort Michilimackinac would make the entire Mississippi River valley much less secure and "encourage the Indians to ravage the frontiers." That same correspondent had hoped that General William Hull, the governor of the Michigan Territory, would successfully invade Upper Canada and seize Fort Amherstburg, a British post about twenty miles south of Detroit. Hull had summed up the situation when he wrote, "The British cannot hold Upper Canada without the assistance of the Indians," but the "Indians cannot conduct a war without the assistance of a civilized nation."[31]

Hull and his force of approximately 1,800 men had indeed crossed the Detroit River into Canada, and on July 12 and 13 he issued a written proclamation informing the citizens they would "be emancipated from tyranny and oppression, and restored to the dignified station of freemen." At the same time, he warned that "no white man found fighting by the side of an Indian will be taken prisoner; instant destruction will be his lot."[32]

From his new headquarters at Sandwich (now part of Windsor), where he had found no resistance to his invasion, Hull sent riders to distribute copies of the proclamation throughout the area. It immediately had the kind of impact he had hoped—more than four hundred militiamen deserted from Fort Amherstburg. Many were farmers anxious to harvest their wheat crop, and at Sandwich, Hull granted them parole to do just that. Some of the deserters even joined the American side. "Genl. Hull began to think that his Proclamation would reduce Canada without fighting," wrote one American.[33]

At age fifty-nine, his senses dulled by a recent stroke and too much alcohol, Hull was not the soldier he had been during the Revolution. Despite commanding a force twice as large as that at Amherstburg, he hesitated, fearing an onslaught by what he called "hordes of savages." On July 22, Hull wrote to William Eustis that he was waiting for heavy cannons expected from Fort Detroit before attacking Amherstburg. That same day, British general Isaac Brock issued a proclamation of his own, which included an eloquent defense of the "savages":

The brave bands of Natives which inhabit this Colony, were, like his Majesty's Subjects, punished for their zeal and fidelity by the loss of their possessions in the late Colonies, and rewarded by his Majesty with lands of superior value in this Province: the Faith of the British Government has never yet been violated, they feel that the soil they inherit is to them and their posterity protected from the base Arts so frequently devised to overreach their simplicity. By what new principle are they to be prevented from defending their property? . . . they are men, and have equal rights with all other men to defend themselves and their property when invaded, more especially when they find in the enemies Camp a ferocious and mortal foe using the same Warfare which the American Commander affects to reprobate.[34]

Although not yet attacked by the Americans, Brock had other battles to fight—convincing his superiors to send reinforcements and persuading the Upper Canada legislature to suspend habeas corpus so he could draft available men and deal with deserters. As one day after another passed without an assault on the fort, the momentum shifted in Brock's favor, especially after Hull, contrary to promises made in his proclamation, allowed his men to loot Canadian homes and shops, stealing livestock, supplies, and food. Eventually, the men who had harvested their fields began returning to Amherstburg. Although the British had prepared to evacuate the fort, they resolved to make a stand, especially when Hull's chaotic command became evident. "The British officers and soldiers began to laugh at Hull," wrote an American prisoner at the fort, "seeing he sends his men out skirmishing to the bridge [over the River aux Canards] and does not take possession of it and keep it, or come to [the fort]."[35]

On July 26, when Hull got word that Mackinac had fallen, he feared that a mass "of Savages from the North" would soon attack, a fear that no doubt intensified a week and a half later when Indians under Tecumseh's command attacked a supply train, killed seventeen men, and mutilated the corpses, with the men's scalps visible on long poles staked next to their bodies. Over the objections of his colonels, two of whom—Lewis Cass and Duncan McArthur—were planning a mutiny, Hull retreated back across the river to Fort Detroit on the night of August 7.[36]

In a bold move, General Brock, who had fewer men than Hull, decided to attack the fort although it was well armed with artillery. Some of his colonels disagreed, but unlike those under Hull, they remained loyal. Brock's knowledge of dispatches written by Hull and his men (intercepted when British troops captured an American ship) and his relationship of mutual respect and trust with Tecumseh, the effective leader of more than six hundred Indians, were key factors in his decision. "I got possession of the letters my antagonist addressed to the Secretary at War, and also of the sentiments which hundreds of his army uttered to their friends," he wrote. "Confidence in the General was gone, and evident despondency prevailed throughout."[37]

On August 15, Brock fired cannons from Sandwich. The officers' mess at Fort Detroit was hit, killing three men and reducing Hull to heavy drinking. On August 16, Brock and Tecumseh crossed the Detroit River with a force of 1,330 men, equal parts British and Indian. Brock had already sent a dispatch to Hull: "It is far from my intention to join in a war of extermination, but you must be aware, that the numerous body of Indians who have attached themselves to my troops, will be beyond control the moment the contest commences"[38]—a bluff pure and simple because Indian conduct both at Mackinac and Detroit had been measured and restrained. Now Brock and Tecumseh ordered the Indian warriors—stripped, well armed, and wearing war paint—to strut within eyeshot of the fort in a formation that exaggerated their actual number.

Before Brock even ordered his men to fire, a white flag appeared fluttering above the fort.[39]

"TREASON, if the following is true," ran a headline in the September 12, 1812, issue of the *Missouri Gazette* in St. Louis. The report claimed that Fort Detroit, with all troops, both regular and militia, was to be immediately surrendered to the command of Major General Brock. "The above intelligence received by last mail, is truely disastrous," wrote the paper's editor, "we yet hope that it may be incorrect, we cannot believe that Gen. Hull, with a gallant collection of choice spirits would tamely surrender."

The next day, with news of Hull's defeat sinking in, Christian Wilt wrote, "We are here in a continued preparation for war, several volunteer company's will march in a day or two for the frontiers, some have already started. . . . We have news of Hull's having surrendered with the articles of capitulation—if true we may have some hard fighting yet."[40]

Wilt and his neighbors had good reason to be alarmed: In June, less than two weeks before Madison declared war, there had been only 241 soldiers of the regular army west of the Mississippi—63 at Fort Osage; 44 at Fort Madison; and 134 at Fort Bellefontaine.[41] Federalist congressmen arguing that the US was unprepared for war had grossly understated the case.

Clark, who had been ascending the Ohio River on his way to Washington when he learned of the declaration of war, was descending it on his return to St. Louis when he learned of the fall of Detroit. Nor was he surprised that his old fur trading competitor, and Crooks's former employer, Robert Dickson, the man treated so well by Lewis and Bates, had been instrumental in the British victory at Detroit. Just as George Hoffman had warned Bates about Dickson in 1808 (as discussed in chapter 2), Illinois Territory governor Ninian Edwards had cautioned William Eustis in 1811 that "Dickson hopes to engage all the Indians in opposition to the United States by making peace between the Chippewas and Sioux and having them declare war against us."[42]

Clark was keenly aware of Dickson's activities, writing to William Eustis early in 1812: "Mr. Dickson and those British traders who are also Agents, who have smuggled an emince quantity of goods through [Green Bay] could be caught on their return as they go out in the Spring—This description of people grasp at every means in their power to wave the affections of the Indians from any thing that is American."[43]

Clark had learned in Washington that Dickson played a key role in the fall of Michilimackinac when Dickson and John Askin Jr. led about four hundred Sioux, Menominee, and Winnebago Indians in Captain Charles Roberts's successful attack against the Americans, a victory that persuaded several northwestern Indian nations to join with the British. "I fear for the effects which this may produce on the Indians, who may be prepared for action," Clark wrote to Governor Edwards on August 16.[44]

Unknown to Clark for weeks, his prediction had already been fulfilled. On the previous day, August 15, as Captain Nathan Heald was evacuating ninety-three men, women, and children from Chicago's Fort Dearborn on orders from General Hull, they were attacked by a band of Potawatomi warriors that Heald estimated at between four and five hundred strong. "In about fifteen minutes," wrote Heald, "they got possession of all our horses, provisions, and baggage of every description, and finding the [Miami Indians supposedly guarding the evacuees] did not assist us, I drew off the few men I had left, and took possession of a small elevation in the open prairie." With twenty-six regulars, all twelve militiamen, twelve children, and two women already killed, Heald had lost more than half of his small party and had no choice but to surrender. "The next morning," he reported, "[the Indians] set fire to the fort and left the place."[45]

Although Dickson had not been present at the fall of Detroit, he had sent a chosen band of thirty Menominee warriors to Amherstburg, where they arrived about the same time the fort received word of the US declaration of war. Twenty-two of them defeated Hull's force at the River aux Canards, and all of them joined with Tecumseh's men in the parade of terror that convinced Hull to surrender.[46]

In a portent of things to come two decades later, Dickson had also made contact during the summer of 1812 with Sauk chief Black Hawk, then living in the Indian village of Saukenuk (at present Rock Island, Illinois) and persuaded him to join forces with the British. Like Tecumseh, Black Hawk felt exploited by the way William Henry Harrison and others had pressured Indians without authority to sign away huge tracts of Indian land. Black Hawk also said the Americans made many promises and broke them, whereas "the *British* made few—but we could always *rely upon their word*!" Responding to Dickson's request, Black Hawk and his warriors traveled to Forts Dearborn and Detroit but arrived after the British victories. In 1813, however, Black Hawk would fight in the Battle of Frenchtown and in the unsuccessful attacks on Forts Meigs and Stephenson in Ohio.[47]

William Clark no doubt considered Robert Dickson a hostile enemy, but the irony was that this foe was in many ways Clark's counterpart. A nineteenth-century historian described Dickson, born four or five years before Clark, as "a red-haired Scot, of strong intellect, ardently attached to the British crown, the head of the Indian trade of Minnesota, and possessing great influence among the Dakotas." Clark, also an ardent patriot with impressive intellect, also had considerable influence among the Indians, who called him "Red-head."[48]

That a leading fur trader like Dickson found himself enmeshed in the War of 1812 was hardly coincidence. The causes of the war were varied and complex, but as Mark Kelly observes, "To the American and British traders of upper Louisiana, the war was principally fought for control of the fur trade." That reality had hardly gone ignored by the politicians who urged Madison to declare war. In February of 1810, new senator Henry Clay (replacing Buckner Thurston, who had accepted a judicial appointment) had proclaimed in his first speech from the floor: "The conquest of Canada is in your power. . . . I verily believe, that the militia of Kentucky are alone competent to place Montreal and Upper Canada at your feet. . . . Is it nothing to acquire the entire fur trade connected with that country?"[49]

By successfully ascending the Missouri River to its source—and bringing back a report of plentiful beaver—and by returning with seasoned frontiersmen like Colter, Drouillard, and Weiser, Lewis and Clark had been instrumental in accelerating the American fur trade and the conflict with Canadian traders that inevitably followed.

Within two months of the declaration of war, of course, the Americans had suffered one loss after another and had forgotten any dreams of acquiring the entire Canadian fur trade—or any of it. Moreover, the fur trader Dickson had been one of the major torches lighting up savage warfare. And although Dickson's chief trading competitor, Lisa, had been on his way up the Missouri and out of touch when Madison made war official, Lisa would find out soon enough how closely the war and the fur trade were linked.

Dickson's efforts did not go unnoticed by British officials, who would laud "the eminent services which he had rendered to His Majesty's government by his loyalty, zeal and exertions in bringing forward the Indians to aid in the capture of Michilimackinac and Detroit." As autumn came on, Dickson was optimistic but realistic. In an October 2 letter written at Mackinac to Green Bay trader Jacob Franks, Dickson expressed hopes that "the Shackles that have so long fettered us"— apparently a reference to American restrictions on the British fur trade—would soon be thrown off. Still, he added, "We are as yet quite in the dark respecting Politics, nor can any one form an opinion respecting the duration of the War."[50]

❉ ❉ ❉

On October 1, 1812, the day before Dickson wrote his letter from Michilimackinac, his erstwhile clerk Ramsay Crooks—as he had been ten months earlier—was fighting cold and starvation and sickness in the Idaho wild. In 1811 he had found himself going west along the Snake River in the present southwestern part of the state; now he was going east near the Teton River in the southeastern part. "Mr. Crooks," wrote Robert Stuart, "has such a violent fever, and is withal so weak as to preclude all idea of continuing our journey until his recovery—notwithstanding the urgent solicitations of my men, to proceed without him."[51]

Given Crooks's virtual miracle of surviving the trip west, how was it that he had ventured away from the safety of Fort Astoria so soon? It had happened like this:

At Astoria on June 27, nine days after the US had declared war (an event not known in Astoria for another seven months), the Pacific Fur Company partners made a decision: "Resolved, that it being necessary to send an Express to New York, and all the papers and other things being prepared Mr. Robert Stuart is hereby instructed to have and to take charge of them, with which he is to go as directly to New York as circumstances will admit." It was further resolved that Stuart, who had sailed to Astoria—and had saved the lives of the men almost left behind at the Falkland Islands during the voyage—but was now returning overland, should be accompanied by four skilled guides and hunters: Kentuckians John Day and Ben Jones and French Canadians Francois Le Clerc and Andre Vallé, all of whom had reached the fort by land.[52]

This five-man team, which would supposedly avoid conflicts with Indians by traveling light and fast, was quickly joined by two partners, or former partners. "Mr. M'Lellan again expressed his determination to take this opportunity of returning to the Atlantic States," wrote Washington Irving. "In this he was joined by Mr. Crooks, who, notwithstanding all he had suffered in the dismal journey of the preceding winter, was ready to retrace his steps and brave every danger and hardship, rather than remain at Astoria."[53]

McClellan had been on his way east with Reed and others several weeks earlier when the Indian attack at the falls brought their return east to a halt. Now Crooks had decided to go as well. Since the two of them were defaulting on their obligations as partners, they had agreed to give up their shares and all other profits related to their partnerships and not to "engage or be concerned in the Indian trade or in any business whatever which may effect the interest of said Company."[54]

In the four and a half years since they formed their partnership, Crooks and McClellan had seen nothing but trouble. Now, by agreeing not to compete with the Pacific Fur Company, they had effectively given up the fur trade for good—unless they again signed on with Astor, a prospect that looked highly unlikely. The two were so discouraged that rather than waiting for a ship on its way to New York, they had no qualms about venturing right back into the country that had nearly killed them on their way west.

"In the afternoon of Monday, the 29th day of June 1812," wrote Stuart, "we sailed from Astoria under a Salute of Cannon from the Fort." Five weeks later, the group of seven was reduced to six when John Day showed signs of insanity that Stuart concluded "amounted to real madness" and hired local Indians to return him to the fort.[55]

Less than three weeks after leaving Day with Indians, on August 20, the group was now on horseback and wending their way along the south side of the Snake River in southwestern Idaho near present Grandview. Stuart recorded one of the incredible instances of Astorian serendipity when he wrote that "going down to drink [from the river] we found John [Hoback] fishing and in an instant Mr. Miller[,] Edward Robinson[,] & Jacob Reznor who had been similarly employed came out of the Willows & joined us."[56]

Since bidding farewell to Hunt's group at Henry's Fort the previous October, Hoback, Reznor, Robinson, and Miller had reportedly hiked close to one thousand miles, seeing Bear River, the Green River, the Great Divide basin, the Bighorn River, and the Snake River again, in the midst of episodes of trapping, being robbed by Indians, and losing their way and almost starving. Their survival itself was astonishing enough, but the odds of their meeting Stuart by chance and thus obtaining safe passage back to their Kentucky homes were astronomical. Miller readily accepted the invitation to join Stuart, but the doomed trio was determined to stay in the veritable desert, eking out their existence on another two-year trapping excursion, "as they preferred that, to returning in their present ragged condition to civilized society."[57]

Hoback, Reznor, and Robinson had gone up the Missouri with Lisa in 1807 and over the next five years had rejected at least four opportunities to return to the families. Now they had declined their last opportunity. In January of 1814, they and seven others, including Reed and Dorion, would perish in the southwestern section of present Idaho that proved so dangerous to the Astorians. Only Marie Dorion and her two sons would survive.[58]

Shortly before meeting Miller and the others, Stuart had been told by an Indian guide that there was "a shorter trace to the South than that by which Mr. Hunt had traversed the R Mountains." Although this guide soon disappeared—stealing a horse as he did so—Stuart looked for any opportunity to save time by taking a more southerly path. For a man who never seen the area before, he had an incredible gift for getting his bearings and understanding the geography. He and his six companions ascended the Snake River to the site of American Falls, following Hunt's route in reverse. Then Stuart led them southeast, along the Portneuf River, "this being the Water course which guided Mr. Miller to the Snake River."[59]

Over the next ten days, based partly on Miller's recollections of his travels with Hoback, Reznor, and Robinson and partly on Stuart's intuition, the band of traders turned explorers ascended the Portneuf past present Pocatello, McCammon, and Lava Hot Springs; then crossed to the Bear River and ascended it past present Soda Springs and Montpelier and into western Wyoming. Stuart's forte at discovering good trails is well evidenced by the fact that the Whitmans and Spaldings, who went west in 1836—and the tens of thousands of pioneers who followed them along the Oregon Trail—would take virtually the same path.

On September 16, however, the group "lost the intended track" they thought would take them across the Rocky Mountains. Not only that, but they feared going south—presumed to be the right direction— would result in a second encounter with a large band of Absaroka Indians whose behavior had been "insolent in the extreme and indicated an evident intention to steal if not to rob." So they turned north, descending a waterway (Greys River), which the savvy Stuart correctly assumed to be a branch of the Snake River that would take them to a "spur of mountains"—the Teton Range—seen by Hunt's party.[60]

Now, on October 1, Stuart and his men indeed found themselves in the Teton Valley but not in the situation they had hoped. Like William Clark and Andrew Henry, they had lost their mounts to the incomparable horsemen of the region—the Absaroka. Not wanting to assist the Indians further, they had burned all the provisions and supplies they could not carry. Next, after an adventurous few days that included navigating white water on rafts, they killed a lame elk only to find it had previously been wounded by an arrowhead they concluded to be of Blackfoot Indian origin. Then "Rain, Hail and at last, Snow fell in the course of the evening and night." Even though the men saw three antelope a few days later, they didn't fire their weapons because if any

Blackfoot in the area heard the shots, "inevitable destruction would follow."[61]

Crooks next came down with a dangerous fever, and as he looked increasingly feeble, McClellan, now refusing to carry the group's only beaver trap or even the equivalent in dried meat, announced he would take a shortcut by himself, saving his "sore feet" despite the prospect of meeting hostile Indians. He had last been seen on the plain—later known as Pierre's Hole—as the others struggled through deep snow on the mountainside.

When Crooks could not go on, Miller, Jones, Le Clerc, and Vallé urged Stuart to leave Crooks behind to a certain death. But rather than express his moral outrage, Stuart acknowledged their desperate plight: If they didn't cross the Tetons as soon as possible, another blizzard might kill them all; they were out of food but afraid to hunt because of the Blackfoot warriors possibly nearby; could they survive the winter even if they reached a tributary of the Missouri?

The empathetic Stuart understood exactly why the others believed they must move on or perish and shared many of their feelings. He also understood that theoretical contemplations of right and wrong were one thing, but confronting a dilemma when one's life swayed in the balance was something altogether different:

> The sensations excited on this occasion, and by the view of an un-
> known & untraveled wilderness, are not such as arise in the artificial
> solitude of parks and gardens, for there one is apt to indulge a flatter-
> ing notion of self-sufficiency, as well as a placid indulgence of volun-
> tary delusions; whereas the phantoms which haunt a desert, are
> want, misery, and danger, the evils of dereliction rush upon the
> mind; man is made unwillingly acquainted with his own weakness,
> and meditations shews him only how little he can sustain, and how
> little he can perform—[62]

Stuart still could not bear the thought of abandoning Crooks, but rather than trumpeting his righteous indignation, he tried to gently persuade the others that Crooks would recover soon. One by one, they reluctantly agreed.

Early the next morning, Jones went out looking for a spot to set the beaver trap. "As he was making his way among the thickets, with his trap on his shoulder and his rifle in his hand," wrote Irving, "he heard a crashing sound, and turning, beheld a huge grizzly bear advancing upon him, with terrific growl. The sturdy Kentuckian was not to be intimidated by man or monster. Leveling his rifle, he pulled the trigger. The bear was wounded, but not mortally . . . [and] retreated into the bushes." Jones had fired by reflex, not realizing until afterwards that he had done so "contrary to [the group's] determination" to stay silent for fear of Blackfoot aggression. But the mishap worked in the men's favor: no Indians were seen, and Stuart sent Jones out a second time, this time "in quest of Game."[63]

Benjamin Jones, the man who had endured Blackfoot attacks at Three Forks with Dougherty, James, and all the others—the man who would name one of his sons after Crooks and another after Hunt and would leave behind a library of fifty-four books when he died—did not disappoint, killing five elk within an hour and providing himself and the others with all the meat they could carry (except Crooks, who was unable to walk and likely being transported via travois).[64]

By October 6, Crooks was recovering and able to walk and carry his rifle and pistols. Now tracing Hunt's route in reverse, the wayfarers passed the site of present Victor, Idaho, scaled Teton Pass, forded the "very rapid current" of the south fork of the Snake River ("Mad River"), and trudged into the wide valley of present Jackson Hole, Wyoming. Next they ascended the Hoback River to present Bondurant, running out of food—again—on October 11. Rather than crossing Union Pass to the Wind River (Hunt's route), Stuart continued his push for a more southerly path. Seeing "a large smoke at some distance to the South west," Stuart sent Le Clerc "to see what occasioned it—We had great hopes of its being Indians and sat up late waiting his return in expectation of getting something to eat." But Le Clerc did not appear, and for the second night in a row, the men retired "supperless."[65]

Le Clerc returned the next morning—October 13—with the news that the smoke had come not from Indians but from McClellan, who "had been very much indisposed and lived on little or nothing since he parted with us [on October 1]." The group proceeded on and found McClellan "lying on a piece of straw worn to a perfect skeleton & hardly able to speak from extreme debility . . . he said it was as well for him to die there as any where else, there being no prospect of our getting any speedy relief." Predictably, Stuart had no more intention of leaving McClellan than he had Crooks. The starving men carried all of McClellan's things and somehow continued for seventeen miles "over a level barren of sand."[66]

After a vain attempt to "procure some meat," the men "after dark returned to camp with heavy hearts." Then "one of the Canadians"—either Le Clerc or Vallé—advanced toward Stuart with a rifle in his hand. They had no chance of finding game until they reached "the extreme of this plain," he said, and that would take another three of four days. That meant, Stuart understood perfectly well, that they would all starve to death. The Canadian was determined to go no farther and said they should cast lots "and one die to preserve the rest." As an incentive to Stuart—although it had the opposite effect—the dissenter proposed that Stuart would be exempted from the deadly game of chance. Stuart shuddered at the thought of cannibalism and calmly reasoned against the notion, suggesting they were likely to find game the next day.[67]

"Finding that every argument failed—and that he was on the point of converting some others to his purpose," wrote Stuart, "I snatched up the Rifle cocked and leveled it at him with the firm resolution to fire if he persisted"—a scene hauntingly reminiscent of Stuart's confrontation with Captain Thorne near the Falkland Islands. At that, Le Clerc or Vallé (and historians have disagreed on that point) "fell upon his knees and asked the whole party's pardon, swearing he should never again suggest such a thought." The famished men all crawled off to their meager bedrolls, but Stuart, for what he said was the first time in his life, could not sleep. "Let the man who rolls in affluence," he thought, "but visit these regions of want and misery; his riches will prove an eye sore, and he will be taught the pleasure and advantage of prayer."[68]

Stuart, who would reach St. Louis with all six of his companions alive and well, found his prayer answered the next day when the men were able to shoot a buffalo, eating part of it raw before they wisely made and sipped a broth before supping on barbecued meat. Their good luck continued as they traveled southeast from present Pinedale, killed more buffalo, and met friendly Shoshone Indians who sold them the only horse they had ("the Crows in their late excursion through this country, having deprived them of these animals, as well as of a number of their Women," wrote Stuart).[69]

On Monday, October 19, the Astorian nomads loaded their old but reliable horse—which would serve them faithfully for six months and more than eight hundred miles before being given, in good health, to a Nebraska trader—with six days' worth of meat and everything else except their bedrolls, which they now found easy to carry. That night "the wind blew cold from the North East with some snow," but Vallé and Le Clerc had killed a young bull that made for a delicious supper. The next morning they pursued their course to the southeast "for 18 miles through a beautifully undulating country" bordered on the left by a mountain and on the right by an elevated ridge. "The ridge of mountains [Wind River Range] which divides Wind river from the Columbia and Spanish waters ends here abruptly, and winding to the North of East becomes the separator of a Branch of Big Horn and Cheyenne Rivers from the other water courses which add their tributary waves to the Missouri below the Sioux Country."[70]

Although Stuart's record leaves some confusion as to his precise location—and although he reached certain inaccurate conclusions—he clearly understood that this area of present central Wyoming occupied a crucial spot in relationship to the path of rivers, especially the Pacific-flowing Columbia, the Atlantic-flowing Missouri, and the Gulf-of-California-flowing Spanish (Green) River. And while Lewis and Clark had crossed the Continental Divide at Lemhi Pass, at the Montana-Idaho border, subsequent crossings (by Dougherty at Togwotee Pass and by Hunt at Union Pass) had successively moved to the south and east. Now, specifically on October 22, 1812, the seven Astorians shifted the crossing of the Divide even farther south and east when they "passed thro a handsome low gap" and soon found "a little water oozing out of the earth . . . of a whiteish colour [that] possessed a great similarity of taste to the muddy waters of the Missouri." They had found the southern trace, "the one opening through which wagons could cross the mountains," as Bernard DeVoto wrote, "the door to Oregon and California, the true Northwest Passage—the historic portal, South Pass."[71]

Portrait of Thomas Jefferson (1743–1826), by Edward Percy Moran, 1916. As early as 1784, Jefferson proposed an exploration of the "western Country" to George Rogers Clark, William's elder brother. Courtesy of the Missouri Historical Society.

Portrait of Meriwether Lewis (1774–1809) by Charles Balthazar Julien Févret de Saint-Mémin. On June 19, 1803, Lewis wrote to his friend and former commanding officer, William Clark, and invited the latter to join him as cocommander of the expedition. Courtesy of the Missouri Historical Society.

Portrait of William Clark (1770–1838) attributed to John Wesley Jarvis. On July 18, 1803, Clark replied to Lewis's inquiry with an enthusiastic yes. Courtesy of the Missouri Historical Society.

Portrait of Manuel Lisa (1772?–1820). Lisa employed several Lewis and Clark veterans and established a post at the confluence of the Yellowstone and Bighorn Rivers in 1807. Courtesy of the Missouri Historical Society.

Astoria in 1813, the same year it was sold to the North West Company. Courtesy of the Oregon Historical Society, #ba008002.

Jedediah Strong Smith (1799–1831). A gentle, educated, religious man, Smith was arguably the greatest explorer in American history. He had several dealings with William Clark and in 1827 wrote a letter to Clark detailing his treacherous journey across the Great Basin to California. Courtesy of the Utah State Historical Society.

Photograph of James Clyman (1792–1881). Clyman served in the War of 1812, went up the river with William Ashley in 1823, and left a powerful account of the Arikara attack and subsequent events. Courtesy of the Utah State Historical Society.

Arikara Village, by George Catlin, 1866. William Ashley and his men were attacked near this site on June 2, 1823. Courtesy of the Missouri Historical Society.

South Pass, Wyoming, by William Henry Jackson. Discovered in 1812 by Robert Stuart, Ramsay Crooks, and others, South Pass was "rediscovered" early in 1824 by Jedediah Smith, Thomas Fitzpatrick, and others. Tens of thousands of pioneers would cross the pass on their way to Oregon, Utah, or California. Courtesy of the Utah State Historical Society.

Rocky Mountain Rendezvous, by William Henry Jackson. Between 1825 and 1840, fur trade rendezvous were held every year, most in western Wyoming but some in northeastern Utah and southeastern Idaho. Courtesy of the Utah State Historical Society.

Photograph of Thomas Hart Benton (1782–1858). Benton reconciled with Andrew Jackson, although the two had tried to kill each other in a gunfight, but never reconciled with James K. Polk or Stephen Watts Kearny after their support of John C. Frémont's court-martial. Courtesy of the Missouri Historical Society.

Portrait of Jessie Ann Benton Frémont (1824–1902). The daughter of Thomas Hart Benton and wife of John C. Frémont, Jessie was a well-educated woman who helped create Frémont's legend by cowriting the reports of his expeditions. Courtesy of the Utah State Historical Society.

Photograph of John C. Frémont (1813–1890). By the early 1840s, Frémont was arguably the most famous man in the United States, with his maps widely used by westering pioneers. Courtesy of the Utah State Historical Society.

Photograph of Christopher "Kit" Carson (1809–1868). Dime novels about Carson brought him mythical status, but controversy rages over his military actions against the Navajo nation in the early 1860s. Courtesy of the Utah State Historical Society.

Photograph of Philip St. George Cooke (1809–1895). An 1827 graduate of West Point, Cooke commanded the Mormon Battalion in 1846–1847 and served as a Union cavalry officer in the Civil War. Courtesy of the Utah State Historical Society.

Photograph of Henry William Bigler (1815–1900). Bigler's diaries offer an important record of his march with the Mormon Battalion as well as his experience at Sutter's Mill when James W. Marshall discovered gold. Courtesy of the Utah State Historical Society.

MORMON BATTALION ENCAMPMENT
1896

Photograph of members of the Mormon Battalion, 1896, individuals not identified. The original battalion included thirty-five women, and five of them completed the entire journey from Council Bluffs, Iowa, to Southern California. Courtesy of the Utah State Historical Society.

Portrait of General Stephen Watts Kearny (1794–1848). Nine months after
Kearny's charges against Frémont were upheld by a court-martial, Kearny died of
yellow fever, which he had contracted while serving as military governor of Vera-
cruz, Mexico. Courtesy of the Utah State Historical Society.

An 1857 portrait of Ramsay Crooks (1787–1859), by Jules-Emile Saintin. Crooks, one of only five Astorians to make the complete overland trek to the Pacific and back to St. Louis, became a respected fur trader, well known as a competitive but highly ethical businessman and a tireless worker, despite chronic health problems. Courtesy of Wisconsin Historical Society, WHS-2593.

4

"LET THE NORTH AS WELL AS THE SOUTH BE JACKSONIZED!!!"

On the morning of Saturday, September 4, 1813, forty-six-year-old Andrew Jackson, major general of the Tennessee volunteers, walked with one of his junior officers, Colonel John Coffee, from the Nashville Inn, where they were staying, across the public square to the nearby post office. Coffee glanced at Talbot's Hotel and Tavern, off to their left and also located in the square, and saw a fellow colonel by the name of Thomas Hart Benton standing in the doorway watching them. Benton was not smiling.

"Do you see that fellow?" Coffee asked.

"Oh, yes," replied Jackson, not turning his head. "I have my eyes on him."

Jackson had mentored Benton, fifteen years his junior, and Benton had recruited hundreds of volunteers for Jackson's army and had marched faithfully with Jackson and the men on a long, debilitating, five-hundred-mile trek up the Natchez Trace to Nashville. Benton, however, had been enraged when he learned that while he was in Washington in June seeking reimbursement for General Jackson's use of personal funds to supply his men, Jackson had acted as second in a duel between Benton's younger brother Jesse and Major William Carroll, another of Jackson's junior officers. Carroll came out of the duel unhurt, while Jesse Benton suffered a painful and humiliating but non-fatal wound in the buttocks.[1]

Only weeks before that, Thomas Benton himself had challenged Major William B. Lewis, Jackson's deputy quartermaster, to a duel—a conflict that ended in a war of words. As Benton's biographer points out, "Yet to see real combat, Jackson and his subordinates vented their aggression over petty slights and personal jealousies."[2] (Although Jackson and his volunteers had made extensive preparations to defend New Orleans against the British and their Indian allies and had been more than willing to fight—with Benton and his troops risking their lives on the ice-jammed Ohio River—the men had been released by the War Department without ever encountering the enemy.)

As for Benton's reaction when he learned of Jackson's support of Jesse's adversary, he hardly minced words. "It was a very poor business in a man of your age and standing," he wrote to Jackson on July 25, "to be conducting a duel about nothing between young men who had no harm against each . . . you would have done yourself more honor by advising them to reserve their courage for the public enemy." After alleging that Jackson had insisted that the duel be conducted "in a savage, unequal, unfair, and base manner . . . contrary to [Jackson's] own mode," Benton questioned Jackson's honor as a gentleman and vowed, "the terror of your pistols is not to seal up my lips."[3]

Jackson responded by saying it was beneath the dignity of a man of honor, particularly a soldier, to quarrel "like the fish woman." He also said he would horsewhip Benton the next time they met.[4]

Now, as Thomas Benton watched the two men stride toward the post office, it could not have escaped his view that Jackson was wearing a small sword and carrying his riding whip. Moments later, when Jackson and Coffee exited the post office, they walked straight toward Talbot's rather than cutting diagonally back to the Nashville Inn. Thomas had disappeared, but Jesse Benton was now standing on the pavement in front of Talbot's.

Jackson and Coffee walked past Jesse, who turned and stepped inside the tavern. Jackson entered the hotel through the main entrance and saw Thomas standing in the hall. "Now defend yourself, you damned rascal," he called, drawing a pistol from inside his coat and leveling it at Thomas, who hadn't had a chance to draw his own pistol and backpedaled toward the portico. Jackson rapidly advanced and was eight or ten feet away from Thomas when Jesse, now behind Jackson, fired his pistol and hit Jackson in the shoulder. Jackson fired an instant after he was hit but missed Benton. As Jackson began to crumble, Thomas drew two pistols, firing both at Jackson. Then Coffee charged into the hall and fired at Thomas but missed. He then swung his pistol to club Thomas, but that parry missed as well.

Amid the bedlam, a bystander named James Sitler rushed to help Jackson, while Jackson's friend and nephew Stokely Hays, "a man of a giant's size and giant's strength," bolted through the door, saw Jackson flat on his back and bleeding profusely, and realized it was Jesse and not his brother who had shot the general. He lunged at Jesse with his sword cane, but the slender weapon broke when it stuck a button. Undeterred, Hays threw Jesse to the floor, not realizing that Jesse, weak from his duel with Carroll, still had a loaded weapon. Jesse "clapped [the] pistol to the body of Mr. Hays to blow him through, but it missed fire." Hays drew a dagger and flailed at his opponent, inflicting several flesh wounds but not the fatal blow he desired, as Jesse fought for his life. At the same time, Coffee, now joined by Alexander Donelson, another of Jackson's officers and his brother-in-law, attacked Thomas with their own daggers. Like Jesse, Thomas was wounded but not seriously. Another friend of Jackson—Captain Eli Hammond, there seemed to be no end of them—jumped in the fray and beat Jesse about the head as continual stabs came from Hays. Badly outnumbered, the Benton brothers were finally assisted when "a generous hearted citizen of Nashville," Mr. Sumner, "caught [Hays's] uplifted hand and prevented the further shedding of blood." Then several other bystanders filled the hall, and the melee ended as suddenly as it had begun.[5]

The firing of at least five shots—with only one hitting its target—was a testament not only to the inaccuracy and flawed production of the smoothbore flintlock pistols but also to the limited skills of the combatants. Be that as it may, Jesse Benton's weapon was loaded with a large slug and two balls and did its share of damage. "The slug took effect in Jackson's left shoulder," wrote one of Jackson's early biographers, "shattering it horribly. One of the balls struck the thick part of his left arm, and buried itself near the bone. The other ball splintered the board partition at his side."[6]

Jackson's friends and some of the bystanders carried the bleeding general to a room in the Nashville Inn. A number of physicians—all of the doctors in Nashville, according to one account—gathered in the room and had difficulty slowing the loss of blood despite their combined efforts. Most recommended the amputation of the arm, but a young doctor argued against the procedure. Jackson, drifting in and out of consciousness, settled the matter. "I'll keep my arm," he said. Even attempting to extract the ball was out of the question. He would not leave his sickbed for three weeks.

"For my own part," wrote Benton, "I think it scandalous that such things should take place at any time, but particularly so at the present moment when the public service requires the aid of all its citizens. As for the name of *courage*, God forbid that I should ever attempt to gain it by becoming a bully."[7]

While Jackson and his men had resorted to dueling among themselves after trying unsuccessfully for several months to engage the enemy, the western front had seen frequent warfare throughout the first eight months of 1813. On the morning of January 19, British colonel Henry Procter, who had ably assisted General Brock at Amherstburg and Detroit, learned that an advance guard of Harrison's army had taken Frenchtown (now Monroe, Michigan) from a small band of British soldiers and Indian allies the previous day. "We marched to the enemy, and attacked him at the break of day, on the 22nd instant," wrote Procter, "and after experiencing, for our numbers, a considerable loss, about half of the enemy's force, posted in houses and enclosures, and which, in dread of falling into the hands of the Indians, they most obstinately defended, at last surrendered in discretion." Procter added that as the other force of Americans attempted to retreat, "all, or perhaps excepting a very few, [were] killed by the Indians." A Wyandot chief by the name of Roundhead had taken Brigadier General James Winchester, the American commander, prisoner. "[Winchester] was cut off from those who were posted, and whom he afterwards surrendered."[8]

A confederacy of Indians from the Wyandot, Potawatomi, Ottawa, Chippewa, Delaware, Winnebago, Creek, Sauk, Miami, and Fox nations had made up more than half of Procter's total company. "The zeal and courage of the Indian Department were never more conspicuous than on this occasion," continued Procter. "The Indian warriors displayed their usual courage."[9]

After his stunning defeat of Winchester's men, Procter retreated to the north and crossed the Detroit River to Sandwich, avoiding any reprisal by Harrison's larger force. He was commended by the House of

Assembly of Upper Canada, and, more importantly, promoted to brigadier general. [10]

One young British soldier less than impressed with Procter's command, however, was John Richardson, a sixteen-year-old volunteer in the light infantry Regiment of Foot. "On the 22nd, before daybreak," wrote Richardson, "[we] came within sight of the enemy" and were surprised to see the Americans "lying in their beds undressed and unarmed." Richardson and his fellows realized that "a prompt and forward movement of the line" would have enabled them to surround the slumbering Americans and hold them at bayonet point or cut off their access to a nearby wall—or both. But the British soldiers were dumbfounded when Procter instead "commenced firing his three-pounders . . . thus affording [the Americans] time and facility for arming and occupying the only position from which they could seriously check our advance." [11]

Twenty-six-year-old Kentucky rifleman William Atherton was one of the slumbering Americans: "I slept soundly until awakened by the startling cry of 'to arms! to arms!' and the thundering of cannon and roar of small arms, and the more terrific yelling of savages." [12]

The Americans briefly gained the advantage before the two sides settled into an intense, hour-long battle. Then British militia and Indians broke through the American line and flanked them. Next, wrote Richardson, around four hundred Americans "threw themselves into the strong block-houses they had already constructed" and defended themselves gallantly. "Meanwhile their right, and part of the centre, closely followed across the ice by the Indians, fell almost unresisting victims to the wrath of their pursuers: and for nearly two miles along the road by which they passed, the snow was covered with the blood and bodies of the slain." [13]

The American force of approximately 950 men had been annihilated at the Battle of Frenchtown, with more than 900 killed or wounded, far outnumbering British and Indian casualties. By mid-February, the bad news reached St. Louis. "DISASTROUS," read a headline in the *Missouri Gazette*. "In this weeks paper we have the disagreeable task to record another failure of our arms near Detroit . . . an affair which will tend to brace the nerve to action." [14]

The editorial introduction was followed by two letters written to Isaac Shelby, the governor of Kentucky, home of most of the men serving under General Winchester. "I send colonel Wells to you, to communicate the particulars (as far as we are acquainted with them) of an event that will overwhelm your mind with grief, and fill your whole state with mourning," wrote General William Henry Harrison. "The greater part of colonel Wells's regiment, United States' infantry, and the 1st and 5th regiments Kentucky infantry, and Allen's rifle regiment, under . . . general Winchester have been cut to pieces by the enemy, or taken prisoners." As soon as Harrison had heard of the attack, he set out to reinforce Winchester but had not gone far when "certain information was received of general Winchester's total defeat." Harrison had sent some of his best men to go forward and assist those who had escaped. "The whole number that reached our camp does not exceed 30."[15]

Major Martin D. Hardin—later a US senator from Kentucky—had written the second letter to Shelby. "The whole number of our officers and men there, on the morning of the 22nd, was about 900. At daylight a cannonade commenced on them—it was contested for some time— finally we sustained a total defeat," he wrote. "Our men were completely overpowered—every man thinks the enemy were double, others threefold our numbered. . . . The stroke has been so severe, that my feelings are perfectly deadened." The thoughtful Hardin next recorded the names of the sixty-four officers serving under Winchester, including the two—Major M'Clannahan and Captain Glaves—who had reached safety, and noted his estimates of the number of missing noncommissioned officers and privates. By his count, a total of 919 men were missing; that one-third of those had survived was as much as he could hope for.[16]

The *Gazette* urged those on the frontier to build or repair forts, keep their arms and ammunition in order, and plant fields in groups, with guards on duty. "I expect we shall have to dig trenches around it [St. Louis] we have a few pieces of cannon which are to be mounted & 3 or 4 Spanish Blockhouses which will be put in Repair," Christian Wilt wrote on the same day the report of Winchester's defeat was published. Like many others living on the frontier, he focused his hopes on William Henry Harrison: "If Harrison has been successful in taking Maldon, it will tend greatly to the safety of this country—but should he have met with the fate of Winchester, who out of 900 men lost all but 30 who returned to Harrison we have hard times here."[17]

The rumors flew: savages were gathering at Green Bay; they would soon attack from the upper Mississippi; they had amassed at Prairie du

Chien; they had swarmed together in Chicago; "they were waiting for ammunition; they were waiting for the ice to melt; they were delaying only until the dark of the moon; they were waiting for the English leaders." There was no end to the hearsay, and the man inevitably said to be leading these Indian conspiracies of terror was the redheaded Scot: Robert Dickson, with the likes of Frederick Bates, Alexander McNair, and Maurice Blondeau naming him.[18]

Such gossip no doubt rankled Clark, but he was much more concerned about the news of "another failure of our arms near Detroit," which hit close to home because he had lived in Kentucky from the time he was fourteen until he and Lewis departed on their tour of the West. He knew some of the officers listed as missing by Hardin but was a surrogate father to one young man serving under Winchester as a noncommissioned officer or a private—and therefore not included in the list—his sister Fanny's son John O'Fallon. In early adulthood, Fanny had suffered a multitude of problems, including a nervous breakdown and the murder of her second husband (after her first husband, John and Benjamin O'Fallon's father, had died young). Clark had taken a special interest in the boys and eventually assumed guardianship over them.[19]

A long, anxious vigil began for Fanny, Clark, and the rest of the family as they hoped for but dreaded any news of what had become of twenty-one-year-old John. Finally, sometime in the spring, word came that he was alive, then a letter from him. One hundred and eighty men in his company had been killed, he wrote his mother, but it was his description of what happened after the main battle—as well as those of a host of other prisoners of war—that would ignite a rallying cry for vengeance throughout the States. Writing that "a greater degree of inhumanities and savage barbarity never was before evinced by a civilized nation," John said, "the Indians were so unrestrained in acts of barbarity that they were let loose upon the wounded who had been placed in houses and after butchering them consumed their houses reducing to ashes them all."[20]

Clark would later learn that William Bratton, a veteran of the Corps of Discovery, had also been taken prisoner at Frenchtown. "The ample support which he gave me under every necessary occasion," Lewis had written of Bratton, "and the fortitude with which he boar the fatigues and painfull sufferings incident to that long Voyage, entitled him to my highest confidence and sincere thanks." At age thirty-four, Bratton had enlisted in August of 1812, serving as a private in the Kentucky volunteer militia in Captain Paschal Hickman's Company of Riflemen, under Lieutenant Colonel John Allen. The details of his imprisonment are not known, but he was apparently paroled by the British because he was honorably discharged from military service on March 27, 1813.[21]

The debacle at Frenchtown touched Henry Clay, by this time Speaker of the House of Representatives, in an even more personal way. His friend and brother-in-law, Nathaniel Gray Smith Hart (brother of Clay's wife, Lucretia), had been commissioned a captain of the Lexington Light Infantry Company after the declaration of war, and he had been serving under General Winchester since August of 1812. Captain Hart, one of the officers included in Hardin's list, survived the battle but was wounded and taken prisoner.[22]

On January 22, not long after the surrender, Indians began plundering the US camps, even though General Procter had promised the Americans their personal possessions would be protected and they would be given safe passage to Amherstburg, Procter also announced he would leave that day and take with him most of his men and the able-bodied prisoners—who were forced to march in bitter conditions without coats, pants, and shoes, which were stolen by Indians. A small group of militiamen was assigned stay behind to guard the eighty American prisoners too wounded to march. Fearing they would be killed by the Indians, the Kentucky soldiers were pleading with the British to protect them when a British officer by the name of William Elliott happened on the scene. Captain Hart recognized him immediately—the two of them had been roommates at Princeton, and Hart had nursed Elliott through a serious illness when the latter visited Hart's family in Lexington. Pleased to see his old friend, Hart introduced Elliott to his fellow American officers. "Having in former life received great favors from [the Hart family]," wrote Atherton, Elliott assured Hart "that the Indians would not molest those that were left— and that, upon the honor of a soldier, he would send his own sleigh for [Hart] on the next morning and have him conveyed to Malden."[23]

Another American prisoner by the name of Thomas Dudley, however, wrote that Elliott "seemed quite restless and a good deal agitated . . . [and] proposed borrowing a horse, saddle, and bridle for the purpose of going immediately to Malden, and hurrying on sleighs to remove the wounded." After assuring Hart and the others that they were in no danger, Elliott "borrowed" the horse of an American officer and left, "which was the last we saw of Captain Elliott," said Dudley.[24]

As the healthy prisoners prepared to leave, wrote Atherton, several of the men, both wounded and not, "apprehended great danger in being left [with the Indians], and insisted on all that could go to do so. The brave Captain Hickman [too injured to leave] saw the danger, and desired all that could walk not to remain." Although Atherton could walk, he decided to "risk it, and stay and assist those who were not able to help themselves." Captain Hart's men were reluctant to leave him behind and offered to carry him, but he trusted Elliott to keep his pledge. After a solemn parting, said Atherton, the "wounded and defenceless" men were "doomed to death by the infamous Proctor and Elliott."[25]

The next morning, January 23, with the Indians looking more and more hostile, Captain Hart, barefoot despite the snow and clad only in a shirt and drawers, approached an Indian who appeared to be a chief and told the Indian he was an acquaintance of Elliott, who had promised to send a sleigh for him. "Elliott has deceived you," replied the Indian. "He does not intend to fulfill his promise." Hart said he would give the Indian a horse or one hundred dollars if he would take Hart to Malden himself. The Indian said Hart was too badly wounded to travel. "Captain Hart then asked the Indian, what they intended to do with them? 'Boys,' said the Indian . . . '[you] *are all to be killed.*'" Though Atherton was involved in the same crisis, he wrote that he "could but notice the calmness and composure with which the brave captain received the sentence of death."[26]

A moment later, an Indian dragged Captain Hickman out of the house and threw him facedown on the snow. "He was tomahawked, but not yet dead," recalled Atherton. "He lay strangling in his own blood." Although neither Atherton or Dudley witnessed Captain Hart's death, both heard from Indians that the nineteen-year-old Hart had been shot after two Indians argued over who would take him to Malden and receive his promised reward. Atherton never forgot that Hart's only reply when told he was about to die "was in the language of prayer to Almighty God to sustain him in this hour of trial."[27]

Although Hickman and Hart and a few others, including Atherton and Dudley, had been allowed to leave the homes where they spent the night of January 22–23, most of the eighty-odd American prisoners had been held inside. At the same time Hart was trying to negotiate safe passage to Malden, a mob of some two hundred Indians—far outnumbering the few British guards who dared not deter them—plundered the prisoners' meager remaining possessions and then set the homes on fire. A British officer remembered the "fierce glare of the flames, the crashing of the roofs, the sacrificing of the dying wretches enveloped in fire, and the savage triumphant yelling" of the Indians, who tomahawked or shot any Americans who managed to escape the infernos.[28]

This atrocity, described by John O'Fallon in his letter to Fanny Clark Fitzhugh, became known as the "River Raisin Massacre." Word of the carnage spread rapidly, especially in Kentucky, and on February 9, Governor Shelby wrote to General Harrison that "in consequence of the intelligence contained in your dispatches," the Kentucky legislature had authorized "the organization of three thousand militia." This was good news for Harrison, now in present Ohio, but in mid-March he sent an express to Shelby, urging him to send the reinforcements as soon as possible because he feared they would not reach him before the troops with him reached the end of their enlistment period. While that letter was in transit, Shelby wrote Harrison of his hopes that the men of Kentucky would respond patriotically to the call to arms and "avenge the massacre of our fellow citizens," but the news of Frenchtown had the opposite effect: men were reluctant to enlist. Less than half the approved number of three thousand was raised, and even then a draft had been necessary. Not only that, but many of those drafted had hired proxies to serve for them, and by early April Shelby confided to Harrison that of a regiment he had seen, most were "under size and in other respects hardly Kentuckians."[29]

Green Clay, a prominent Kentucky businessman and politician and a cousin of Henry Clay, was named a brigadier general of the Kentucky militia and ordered to lead the troops to the post recently constructed under Harrison's command: Fort Meigs. Responding to Harrison's request to come with all haste, General Clay and his 1,200 Kentucky volunteers—with Lieutenant Colonels William Boswell and William Dudley each leading a contingent—left Lexington on March 31. There had been little time for training, but Green did his best to inspire the men. "Should we encounter the enemy," he wrote in general orders issued a week after their departure from Lexington, "remember the dreadful fate of our BUTCHERED BROTHERS at the River Raisin— that British treachery produced their slaughter." To honor their fallen comrades, he reminded the "volunteers," they "must with fortitude meet the hardships, and discharge the duties of soldiers. Discipline and subordination mark the real soldier—and are indeed the soul of the army."[30]

No amount of high-minded precepts, however, could substitute for real field drills, mock battles, target practice, and discipline, discipline, discipline. The advance of both regiments—which traveled separately for much of the journey—was characterized by widespread insubordination, a shocking neglect of military protocol, and a virtual absence of discipline among both officers and enlistees. When constant rain, a lack of packhorses and wagons, and an outbreak of measles were added to the equation, it was no surprise that the closer the men got to their destination, the less they looked like an army—an apt portent of things to come.[31]

On April 24, General Procter's force of 522 British regulars, 464 Canadian militia, and more than 1,200 Indians commanded by Tecumseh had boarded ships at Fort Amherstburg and sailed southwest on Lake Erie toward the mouth of the Maumee River, at present Toledo, Ohio. Procter's objective: taking Fort Meigs, situated on the south bank of the Maumee, at present Perrysburg. General Harrison was in command of more than a thousand men at the fort—a ten-acre compound sitting atop a forty-foot-high mound overlooking the river and surrounded by fifteen-foot pickets, seven two-story blockhouses, and five elevated artillery magazines. On April 26 several British soldiers and Indian allies were seen across the river preparing for battle and eventually setting up four of their batteries on the north side of the river, directly across from the fort, and one battery on the south side, three hundred yards east of the fort. The next day the Indians fired small arms at American soldiers who were fishing and started with the heavy artillery on April 28. That same day, wrote Major Eubank, Harrison's deputy quartermaster, "the whole army was at work . . . one third at a time throwing up a transverse [embankment] from one end of the camp to the other." On the morning of May 2, the British "commenced a heavy fire from all their Batteries with Cannon and Bombs and our Camp completely Surrounded with Indians and British keeping up a heavy fire of musketry and rifles . . . they continued to throw over their shells this evening."[32]

When Clay and Boswell, traveling behind Dudley, reached Fort Winchester (at present Defiance, Ohio) on May 3, Clay was immediately informed by Harrison's envoy Major William Oliver that Fort Meigs was under siege. Clay, now leading an armada of eighteen scows—large, flat-bottomed boats—ordered one group of men to unload any nonessential supplies from the scows while others installed shields on the sides of the vessels to protect against rifle fire. Clay then embarked downstream, reaching "the rapids" (near present Grand Rapids, Ohio) about eighteen miles from the fort that night. Oliver and sixteen others went ahead in a small boat, reached the fort about midnight, and informed a relieved Harrison of the arrival of the Kentucky militia.[33]

Harrison conceived a plan and sent Captain John Hamilton and a companion upriver to communicate it to Clay. Benson J. Lossing, a nineteenth-century historian who interviewed participants and had access to key primary documents, summarized Harrison's strategy:

> He knew that the British force at the batteries was inconsiderable, for the main body were still near old Fort Miami [downstream from Fort Meigs, on the north side of the river], and the bulk of the Indians with [Tecumseh] were on the [south] side of the river. [Harrison's] object was to strike simultaneous and effectual blows on both banks of the stream. While Dudley was demolishing the British batteries on the [north] bank, and Clay was fighting the Indians on the [south bank], [Harrison] intended to make a general sally from the fort, destroy the batteries in the rear, and disperse or capture the whole British force on [the south] side of the river.[34]

Clay and Boswell would lead four hundred Kentuckians on the south side while Dudley would lead the other eight hundred on the north side. Harrison's men would attack and capture the key objective of the offensive: the British battery east of the fort. The plan, however, "was overly complicated and dependent upon a level of coordination and training utterly lacking in the troops assigned to its execution," writes Fort Meigs scholar Larry L. Nelson. Moreover, although "Clay, Dudley, and Boswell clearly understood their orders . . . none of these men passed these instructions on to their subordinates. Not a single junior officer or enlisted man in Clay's brigade was aware of the objective. . . . The result of this lack of communication proved catastrophic."[35]

Dudley's men landed upstream from the fort, on the north side of the river, as planned. Clay's boats, however, were caught in the swift current and fishtailed helter-skelter downstream, with most of them ending up on the wrong side of the river. Managing to reach the fort, Clay gathered the troops still with him and made two effective thrusts to the west (upstream from the fort), driving the Indians in all directions.

Meanwhile, Colonel John Miller led 350 men from the fort toward the British battery three hundred yards to the east. In the brutal, hand-to-hand clash that ensued, thirty of Miller's men were killed and upwards of ninety wounded, but others disabled the artillery battery by hammering barbed steel spikes into the vents of the cannons. With the post reinforced and the British guns on the south side silenced, Harrison had already saved Fort Meigs; Dudley could now make the victory complete by spiking the batteries on the north side and leading his troops across the river to the fort.[36]

Initially, wrote Lossing, "Colonel Dudley executed his prescribed task most gallantly and successfully . . . marching in three parallel columns . . . [and moving] through the woods a mile and a half toward the British batteries, which were playing briskly upon Fort Meigs, when the columns were so disposed as to inclose the enemy in a crescent, with every prospect of capturing the whole force." In a shockingly swift and effective sortie, Dudley "charged upon the enemy with wild vehemence [and] captured the heavy guns . . . without losing a man." Harrison and many others were watching, and a wild cheer rose from the fort when Dudley's men pulled down the British flag. Harrison then signaled for Dudley to retreat to his scows and cross to the safety of the fort—as explained, at least in Harrison's mind, in the orders sent to Dudley.

That was when victory collapsed into chaos. Captain Peter Dudley, nephew of the colonel, had been given the spikes to disable the batteries on the north side, but he had somehow landed on the south side, with Clay. Because of that, Dudley's men could not sufficiently damage the sturdy cannons even though they had captured them. They attempted to spike the guns with muskets and "knocked out the lynch pins and threw them away," but these minor annoyances were easily resolved by British gunners when they retained control of the weapons.[37]

Dudley's flank, led by Captain Leslie Combs, was at that moment ambushed by Indians. Dudley ordered them to be reinforced and led the sortie himself. The Indians soon scattered. "That work accomplished," wrote Lossing, "discipline should have ruled. It did not. Impelled by the enthusiasm and confidence of victory, and forgetful of all the maxims of prudence, they pursued the flying savages almost to the British camp."[38]

Rather than a rushed flight, however, the Indian retreat was a carefully planned strategy: They were drawing Dudley's men farther into the thick underbrush—and farther away from Fort Meigs—with warriors on both sides waiting for the right instant to make their assault. When that assault came, the American force, now with little semblance of a military unit, offered a frantic but ineffective defense, with Dudley's junior officers having no idea what the colonel intended.[39]

"Driven from the batteries, the [Americans] in vain sought for safety in the woods," wrote the young Canadian volunteer, John Richardson. "The murderous fire of the Indians, which had already dispersed their main body, drove them back upon their pursuers, until in the end there was no possibility of escape, and their army was wholly destroyed." Richardson added that of Dudley's entire division, not more than 150 men made their escape.[40]

The tragic scene was eerily reminiscent of the Battle of Frenchtown, and even the aftermath looked like history repeating itself. As the throng of Kentucky prisoners were marched toward the river to be transported north, "a few cowardly and treacherous Indians," wrote Richardson, launched a massacre, overcoming the British guard and commencing "the work of blood." When "an old and excellent soldier of the name of Russell" attempted to wrest a prisoner from his assailant, he was shot through the heart. Soon, at least forty Americans had "fallen beneath the steel of the infuriated party." While the bloodlust had run its course at the river Raisin, however, it was cut short at the Maumee River. "Tecumseh, apprized of what was doing, rode up at full speed, and raising his tomahawk, threatened to destroy the first man who resisted his injunction to desist." The ultimatum had an "instantaneous effect," and the perpetrators "retired at once humiliated and confounded."[41]

One of Dudley's men wrote that Tecumseh "seemed to regard us with unmoved composure, and I thought the beam of mercy had tempered the spirit of vengeance which he felt against the Americans."[42]

Despite this victory in the field, Procter was unable to take Fort Meigs. The embankments dug by Harrison's men proved an effective defense against the British artillery. With the Indian allies growing impatient and Canadian militiamen anxious to return home and plant their crops, the siege of the fort rapidly lost steam. The general loaded his boats and sailed for Lake Erie on May 9. The Kentucky losses were mourned in the American press, but because Harrison had held his ground at Fort Meigs, the result was seen as being "equal to victory," interrupting if not ending the string of British conquests.[43]

One day before Procter's departure, the *Missouri Gazette* ran a short news item on page 3. "Arrived here a few days ago from the mouth of the Columbia river, Mr. Robert Stuart, one of the partners of the Pacific Fur Company, accompanied by messrs R. Crooks, Jos. Miller and Rob. McClellan, with three hunters," read the one-paragraph article. The hunters, of course, were Ben Jones, Francois Le Clerc, and Andre Vallé; after making a two-month winter camp in present southeastern Wyoming, the seven men had continued east, reaching St. Louis on April 30. "We learn that Mr. Stuart is bound to N-York with despatches. Next week we shall present our readers with an account of their journey from the Pacific Ocean to this place, a short narrative, which will evince to the world that a journey to the Western Sea will not be considered, (within a few years) of much greater importance than a trip to New York."[44]

By a quirk of circumstance, the article immediately following news of Stuart's safe arrival in St. Louis dealt with Crooks's former employer. "ROBERT DICKSON," ran the headline, with the first line concluding, "The designs of this celebrated man are at length put beyond all question." However, rather than relating any specific news about Dickson, the editorial summoned readers to take courage, apparently in the face of the multitude of rumors circulating about the trader turned Indian commander. Dickson, it seems, had visited several of the Indian nations then at war with the US to distribute military supplies among them. "We have heard of his threats and boastings a long time ago—and indeed for the last six months, it has been no unusual thing for our wives and children to start from their sleep under dreadful imagination that he was thundering at their doors."

Tacitly complimenting Dickson time and again, the editor acknowledged that Dickson, a distinguished man, was a real danger. "But who are we in God's name?" Dickson thinks he has decided the fate of this country in his talks with the Indians, but he takes it to himself to dispose of everything near and sacred to us without our concurrence. "He may have adopted a random opinion that you are little better than down right cowards, and that he and general Tecumseh will have nothing to do, on their arrival, but to receive your homage and to make an apportionment among their followers of your property." I have a different opinion, said the editor, turning to the likes of George Washington, Paul Revere, and John Paul Jones for inspiration. "If the blood of our fore-fathers has not been contaminated in passing through our veins, we will meet [Dickson and Tecumseh] on the frontier, and perhaps succeed in giving them lessons, of which the allies both white and red, if they have either wit or wisdom will not fail to profit."[45]

Talk of Dickson hardly subsided, but by the summer of 1813, another man had joined him as a villain of the north: Henry Procter, now a major general. But rather than repeating vague rumors about the general, US officials gathered twenty-two pages of signed, sworn affidavits from a variety of witnesses. On July 31, Congress published these findings in a report titled *Spirit and Manner in Which the War Is Waged by the Enemy*.[46]

"Massacre and burning of American prisoners surrendered to officers of Great Britain, by Indians in the British service," read the summary. "Abandonment of the remains of Americans killed in battle, or murdered after the surrender to the British. The pillage and shooting of American citizens, and the burning of their houses, after the surrender to the British under the guarantee of protection."[47]

The report offered brutal details about helpless, wounded prisoners being tomahawked or shot—or burned alive—with their bodies then denied civilized burials and left instead to be foraged by wild hogs. Captain Hart's courage was praised and William Elliott's duplicity revealed, but there was no doubt as to who would be held responsible: Colonel Procter, whose parting words to an American surgeon distressed about the safety of his patients were memorialized, after a fashion: "Be under no apprehensions, you will be perfectly safe."[48]

The report concluded that "the massacre of the 23rd January after the capitulation, was perpetrated without any exertion on their [British forces] part to prevent it: indeed, it is apparent from all circumstances, that, if the British officers did not connive at their destruction, they were criminally indifferent about the fate of the wounded prisoners."[49]

The US Congress could hardly call Henry Procter to account for his actions; still, the July report was a bad omen for the general, whose glory days were behind him.

* * *

By the third week of September, an ailing Andrew Jackson was still recovering from the wounds inflicted by Jesse Benton. His wife, Rachel, was nursing him back to health at his Tennessee plantation called the Hermitage, about fifteen miles east of Nashville. Except for a skirmish between US troops and Creek warriors in July in the Mississippi Territory, the war in the South had been relatively quiet. US and British warships were battling on the Great Lakes, and the British still had the advantage. The good news was that General Procter had failed both in his second attempt to take Fort Meigs and his only attempt to take Fort Stephenson (near present Fremont, Ohio). A man of incredible willpower, Jackson was convinced his leadership would be needed in the war, and he was anxious to get back in action. From all appearances, however, it seemed that he would have time for a complete convalescence before once again leading his men southward.

That all changed when word came that a US post in the Mississippi Territory called Fort Mims (about forty miles north of present Mobile, Alabama), had been besieged by Indians. First were unconfirmed rumors that one thousand Creeks had attacked, taken the fort, and killed most of the sixty people inside, but the confirmed reports that followed shortly thereafter told of something much worse. "The dreadful catastrophe, which we have been some time anticipating has at length taken place," wrote Harry Toulmin, a prominent judge in the territory. "The Indians have broken in upon us, in numbers and fury unexampled. Our settlement is overrun."[50]

Despite warnings from slaves sent out as sentinels and from friendly Choctaw Indians that hostile Creek Indians were in the area, commanding officer Major Daniel Beasley concluded there was no danger—even ordering the whipping of one of the slaves for giving a false report. The stockade was guarded by a blockhouse and enclosed military quarters and outbuildings as well the log houses of about twenty-five families of settlers. Security was so lax that on the morning of August 30, approaching Creek Indians found the gates to the fort open. Several hundred Indians "set up a most terrible war whoop and rushed into the gate with inconceivable rapidity." The clamor sent Major Beasley rushing toward the gate, and he was shot in the abdomen. He called for his men to take their ammunition and retreat to the houses as he disappeared into a building.[51]

"Notwithstanding the bravery of our fellow citizens, the Indians carried all before them, and murdered the armed and the helpless without discrimination," wrote Toulmin. "Not more than 25 or 30 escaped and . . . almost all of the women and children fell a sacrifice either to the arms of the Indians or to the flames." He next tallied up his estimates of the number killed at Fort Mims: seven commissioned officers; about one hundred noncommissioned officers; about twenty-four families, including six families of "half-breeds" and seven of Indians, amounting to about 160 people; and most of about one hundred slaves (called "negroes" by Toulmin), bringing the total to around 350.[52]

As Robert Remini points out, the Creek War was first and foremost a civil war between two factions of the Creek nation—the "Red Sticks," who had been convinced by Tecumseh to wage war against the whites, and those friendly to and willing to embrace parts of European culture. In this case, the Red Sticks had obtained arms and ammunition from the Spanish at Pensacola (in present northwestern Florida) through the recommendation of a British general, and they attacked Fort Mims to strike at the Creeks and so-called half-breeds at the post, as well as the white soldiers, adversaries all.[53]

Tennessee governor Willie Blount immediately ordered Jackson to march 2,500 volunteers and militia "to repel an approaching invasion . . . and to afford aid and relief to the suffering citizens of the Mississippi Territory."[54]

Still weak and unable to use his left arm, the indomitable Jackson rose from his sickbed and began organizing his officers and issuing orders for the militia to rendezvous at Fayetteville (about ninety miles south of Nashville). "The late attack of the Creek Indians," he wrote, " . . . call a loud for retaliatory vengeance. Those distressed citizens of that frontier . . . implored the brave Tennesseans for aid. They must not ask in vain." Then, since it was widely known that Jackson had been seriously wounded in his showdown with the Benton brothers, he assured the troops that "the health of your general" was restored and that he would lead them in person.[55]

By the time Jackson issued the orders to his men, a twenty-seven-year-old backwoodsman eking out a living just north of the present Tennessee-Alabama border had already decided to enlist. "When I heard of the mischief which was done at [Fort Mims]," he later wrote, "I instantly felt like going, and I had none of the dread of dying that I expected to feel." Although the wife of the excellent hunter but unsuccessful homesteader protested that his leaving would leave her and two young sons in a "lonesome and unhappy situation," he had made up his mind. "The truth is, my dander was up, and nothing but war could put it right again."[56]

The young husband's name was David Crockett, and he and his fellow volunteers rode south to the Huntsville area, where they joined with several other companies of militia and were soon part of the 1,300-strong cavalry division of Colonel John Coffee, the same man who had fought the Bentons with Jackson. As for the general, he arrived later, his face ashen and his arm still in a sling but his will immovable. He had a fort built at the southern tip of the Tennessee River, and when scouts informed him that upwards of two hundred Red Stick warriors had inhabited the nearby town of Tallushatchee, he ordered Coffee and his mounted riflemen to attack.[57]

"When we got near the town we divided," wrote Crockett of the encounter on November 3, "one of our pilots going with each division." Soon the two groups of five hundred men each had encircled Tallushatchee. A few rangers rode into view and baited the Indians, who came running and yelling. Then Coffee sprung his trap, and both divisions moved in. Realizing their plight, one Creek after another ran inside a house—Crockett counted forty-six of them. "We now shot them like dogs; and then set the house on fire, and burned it up with the forty-six warriors in it." Any who attempted to escape were felled, of course, just as the American prisoners trying to flee the burning structures at Frenchtown had been slaughtered. And the memory of the King of the Wild Frontier was seared with an image as indelible as anything recorded in the river Raisin affidavits: a boy "shot down," his arm and leg broken, "so near the burning house that the grease was stewing out of him" as he tried to crawl, "but not a murmur escaped him, though he was only about twelve years old."[58]

Coffee had lost five men, but the 186 dead in the town included every Red Stick warrior and some women and children, in what could only be described as a massacre. "We have retaliated for the destruction of Fort Mims," Jackson wrote to Governor Blount, not adding that the Indians had been repaid in kind.[59]

Jackson, close to death two months earlier, was well known in Tennessee by that time as a judge, politician, and militia officer, as a natural leader of men who hated the British with extreme passion and was intent on resolving the so-called Indian problem. Still, his chance for true glory had somehow bypassed him during his quarter of a century in Tennessee. The massacre at Fort Mims, however, brought him face-to-face with the great opportunity of his life, and nothing would hold him back—not a lacerated shoulder, a soaring fever, or a pleading wife. Over the next five months, his string of victories in the Creek Wars vaulted him onto a national platform, and especially after his monumental victory at the Battle of Horseshoe Bend (in present central Alabama) on March 27, 1814—with almost nine hundred Red Sticks massacred and Colonel Coffee and a twenty-one-year-old lieutenant named Sam Houston among the American heroes (and Jackson's brother-in-law Alexander Donelson among the dead)—his name was spoken with esteem and a dose of fear throughout the States. Commodore Oliver Hazard Perry may have won a decisive American victory at the Battle of Lake Erie in September of 1813 and General William Henry Harrison another less than a month later at the Battle of Thames—with Tecumseh falling in battle and General Procter court-martialed for poor leadership—but *Jackson* was the name uttered again and again.

In mid-May of 1814 in St. Louis, no one was surprised that when a white man's body—"tomahawked, stabbed, and scalped"—was found floating in the Missouri River, the *Gazette* roared, "The BLOOD of our citizens cry aloud for VENGEANCE. The general cry is let the north as well as the south be JACKSONIZED!!!"[60]

* * *

Clark, meanwhile, was still contending with the redheaded man in the north. Early in 1814, relying on reports from his paid Indian spies, he wrote to Secretary of War John Armstrong Jr.: "The noted Robert Dickson is with the Sacs, keeping alive that assendency which the British has gained over those Tribes."[61]

In March, a more specific and more alarming report about Dickson convinced Clark it was time to act. "Information received from different sources, and from the Indians themselves state," he wrote to Secretary Armstrong, "that Dickson the British agent has taken into the Green Bay and across the Mississippi five large Boats loaded with goods Amunition &c. as presents for the Indians; and is at the time raising a large Indian force." Clark said he therefore felt himself compelled "to take Notice of [the report about Dickson], And prepare to flusterate the hostile plans of the enemy . . . and rely on the Genl Government to support me in my plans."

Clark had earlier reminded Armstrong of the strategic importance of Prairie du Chien, a trading post located at the confluence of the Mississippi and Wisconsin Rivers. Although it was American territory, the post had fallen into British hands, and Dickson had set up his headquarters there. Now, with General Harrison's recent order sending General Howard's first regiment from St. Louis to the Canadian front, Clark argued, "If we are attacked by a large force, . . . the Mississippi will be left undefended from its sourse to this place." With Colonel Russell sick at Vincennes, Clark continued, the responsibility of defending the territory fell to him. He next announced his unauthorized plan: "I have therefore determined to have about 150 Men raised to Serve in the Public armed boats engaged for 2 Months . . . [and] as soon as a sufficient number of men can be precured I shall send up three of the Armed Boats, properly equipped with Cannon, and fixed for the service." One boat would pass up and down the Mississippi; "the other two (larger) will scour the river as high as Prairie du Chien and will be able to destroy any fleet of small Boats or Canoes which they may meet with."[62]

Clark was in the initial stages of recruiting and organizing his men when the *Missouri Gazette* beat the Dickson drum for the umpteenth time: "It is a fact well ascertained, that Robert Dickson is now collecting a large body of Indians . . . ; it is also known as a fact that he has in his interest the Sioux, Winabagoes, Folsavoine, . . . Ottowas, Chippewas and Kickapoos. Does it not become the guardians of the common weal to ward the impending blow?"[63]

Five days later, an act of violence seemed to confirm the *Gazette's* warning and Clark's preparations. "Of the many murders committed during the [War of 1812]," read an 1876 account, "none excited so much feeling or caused such a cry of vengeance in the hearts of the frontiersman as the tragic death of Captain Sarshell Cooper, who was the acknowledged leader of the settlers north of the Missouri River." On the evening of April 14, Captain Cooper and his family were in their cabin sitting around the fire, the captain holding the youngest child, with his wife sewing and the other children playing, when an Indian worked the muzzle of his gun through an opening in the logs and shot the "kind and generous" captain, "who fell from his chair to the floor, among his horror stricken family, a lifeless corpse."[64]

On May 1, 1814, an armada of three gunboats and approximately two hundred men departed St. Louis, with Clark joining a few days later. There was minor resistance from a band of Sauk Indians at the Rock Island rapids (south of present Rock Island, Illinois) but even less resistance at Prairie du Chien, virtually deserted because Dickson and three hundred of his Indian troops and the British commander and an unknown number of soldiers had learned of Clark's mission and fled. The British officer left in charge, Captain Francis Dease, promptly surrendered.

His mission apparently accomplished, Clark left Lieutenant Joseph Perkins and sixty-five men behind to build a small fort and another eighty to patrol the area in a massive gunboat, *Governor Clark*. After Clark arrived back in St. Louis on June 13, grateful St. Louis residents honored him with a ball at the Missouri Hotel and with the endless patriotic toasts so common at such an occasion. A feature article in the *Missouri Gazette* announcing and describing "the fortunate result of that hazardous enterprise" concluded thus: "Such has been the fortunate issue of this well conducted expedition; more important to these territories than any hitherto undertaken."[65]

Clark's victory lasted for six weeks. On July 17, a combined force of 650 Indians, British soldiers, and a militia of Canadian trappers appeared on the northern prairie. Perkins refused to surrender, and he and his men did their best to defend the post but were outnumbered ten to one. After a fifty-four hour siege—and after the *Governor Clark* was forced downstream and Perkins could see he would soon run out of both food and ammunition, he surrendered the fort and all its arms and supplies on July 20; in return, the British allowed the Americans safe passage downriver.

Two American attempts to retake the post failed, with neither armada making it farther north than the rapids south of present Rock Island, Illinois. Black Hawk and his Sauk warriors played crucial roles each time, something not forgotten by Clark. These defeats, writes Jay Buckley, "prevented other American attempts to proceed upriver in the fall, and effectively returned the area to Indian and British control for the duration of the war."[66] Nor would Clark's political enemies forget the failed "retaking" of Prairie du Chien when Clark ran unsuccessfully for governor of the new state of Missouri in 1820.

5

"ENTERPRISING YOUNG MEN"

The Boats *Rocky Mountains* and *Yellow Stone Packet*, under the command of Gen. Wm. H. Ashley, from St. Louis, *for the mouth of the Yellow Stone River*, arrived here on Wednesday last, on their way up, and departed the next day," announced the Franklin *Missouri Intelligencer* on Tuesday, April 1, 1823. About one hundred men were aboard the keelboats, the article continued, and they were to join a similar number at the mouth of the Yellowstone, where a fort had been constructed and other measures taken "for prosecuting the fur trade upon an extensive scale."

William Henry Ashley, a Virginia native now in his midforties, was hardly just another fur trader going up the Missouri—he was a successful businessman and militia general who had run successfully for lieutenant governor, taking office when the new state of Missouri (and the first state located entirely west of the Mississippi River) was admitted to the Union in 1821. The citizens of the seven-year-old town of Franklin were so anxious to show their respect for the "highly esteemed" Ashley that they invited him to a hastily organized ball, which was attended "by most of the respectable gentlemen of the place" and "the greatest portion of the female beauty."[1]

Ashley did not disappoint, greeting the guests cordially and engaging in conversations likely including everything from his investments in a gunpowder factory and a lead mine to national politics to his upcoming voyage to Blackfoot country. The fine evening was marked by "social enjoyment" and "cheerful, yet tempered hilarity."[2] As one who had invested a good deal of money and effort in bringing new life to the upper Missouri fur trade, Ashley would have been particularly interested in talking with the Franklin resident who had reinaugurated the Santa Fe trade after Mexico's overthrow of Spanish sovereignty: William Becknell. Becknell's journeys between Franklin and Santa Fe in 1821 and 1822 had "laid the foundation for what became the Santa Fe Trail, over which hundreds of caravans and hundreds of thousands of dollars' worth of goods would flow in the 1820s and 1830s."[3] There is no evidence, however, that Ashley and Becknell met that night or any time thereafter.

The prominent Missourian who was closely linked with Ashley was Andrew Henry. Roughly the same age, the two men had become friends as early as 1805 when Ashley served as a witness to Henry's marriage. The next year they were both certified as justices of the peace in the St. Genevieve, Missouri, district. They collaborated on business interests and were both militia officers during the War of 1812. Hearing of the Yellowstone River, the Bighorn, and Three Forks from Henry himself, Ashley had been captivated by the region, even though he also knew that several of Henry and Menard's men had been killed and that Henry had fled south to a tributary of the Columbia. Early in 1822, Brigadier General Henry Atkinson wrote to Secretary of War John C. Calhoun that Ashley and Henry "have organized a company consisting of about an hundred men, for the purpose of ascending the Missouri the ensuing spring, as high as the Yellow Stone to hunt and trap, and trade with the Indian Tribes inhabiting that part of the country."[4]

Ashley and Henry's plan to follow Lewis and Clark's route up the Missouri to hunt and trap and trade produced one of the most celebrated newspaper notices in the history of the West:

To
Enterprising Young Men
The subscriber wishes to engage ONE HUNDRED MEN, to ascend the river Missouri to its source, there to be employed for one, two, or three years—For particulars, enquire of Major Andrew Henry, near the Lead Mines, in the County of Washington, (who will ascend with, and command the party) or to the subscriber at St. Louis.
Wm. H. Ashley.[5]

The word spread, and the enterprising young men came. Most were in their twenties, although one, David E. Jackson, a Virginia native who had served in the War of 1812, was thirty-four. Also present were two twenty-seven-year-olds—Daniel T. Potts, of Pennsylvania, and Etienne Provost, a French Canadian from Quebec who had already traveled to the head of the Arkansas River with Auguste P. Chouteau and Jules de Mun and had been imprisoned by Spanish authorities at Santa Fe. Another had been born in Virginia and orphaned in Missouri at age thirteen. Now, at eighteen, he was one of the youngest in the group but would become one of the most renowned: Jim Bridger. In terms of carrying on Lewis and Clark's vision of exploring the West for the purposes of commerce, however, none of the 1822 enlistees would compare with a thoughtful, resolute young man who was twenty-three years old and hailed from upstate New York by way of Pennsylvania, and Ohio: Jedediah Strong Smith.

"In the spring [of 1822] I came down to St. Louis," Smith wrote in his journal, "and hearing of an expedition that was fiting out for the prosecution of the fur trade on the head of the Missouri by Genl. Wm H. Ashley and Major Henry I called on Genl. Ashley to make an engagement to go with him as a hunter. I found no difficulty in making a bargain on as good terms as I had reason to expect."[6]

Henry commanded the men while Ashley remained in St. Louis. The first keelboat, with Henry onboard, headed up the Missouri the first week of April. The second boat, called the *Enterprize*, was delayed while more guns were obtained. Smith and a number of others thus waited until May 13, when the *Enterprize* finally departed St. Louis. By this time the men were quite eager to reach the mountains, but they quickly discovered, as Smith wrote, that traveling upstream on the Missouri was "slow Laborious and dangerous." They were still in the state of Missouri, about twenty miles below Fort Osage, when one of the boats, attempting to negotiate both wind and a point in the river full of sawyers, clipped the limb of an overhanging tree with its mast. The craft wheeled with its "side to the powerful current" and "was swept under in a moment." With the boat went supplies and property valued at ten thousand dollars; some of the crew barely escaped drowning.[7]

Most of the men, including Smith, made camp and tried to wait patiently. The commander of the sunken boat and a few others hurried downstream, reaching St. Louis on June 3 and informing Ashley of the loss of the boat. "Not discouraged by this unfortunate occurrence," wrote Smith, "Genl. Ashley immediately commenced fitting out another boat and in Eighteen days was prepared to Leave with another boat and cargo and 46 men."[8]

Ashley took command when he arrived, and the group proceeded up the Missouri, with Smith out hunting virtually every day. They reached the Arikara towns near the mouth of the Grand River in present South Dakota the first week of September. After buying horses from the Arikara, Ashley sent the boat ahead, instructing the men to stop at the mouth of the Yellowstone River. Then he led a group of men on horseback toward the same destination. In a telling detail, Smith wrote that Ashley "moved with great care being somewhat apprehensive of danger from the Arickara indians."[9]

On the second day after leaving the Arikara nation, continued Smith, "it seemed to my unaccustomed eyes that all the buffalo in the world were running in those plains for far as the eyes could see the plains and hills appeared a moving body of life . . . resembling the idea I have formed of the heavy columns of a great army."[10] Near the mouth of North Dakota's Knife River, Ashley smoked the pipe of peace with Mandan chiefs, and the men then proceeded on without incident to the mouth of the Yellowstone, where Henry and his men—after being robbed of some of their horses by Assiniboine Indians—had built a fort, the third named after Henry. Although the original plan had called for the group to winter near Great Falls, the loss of a boat and of the horses had made that impossible, so the adventurers settled into the post that lay on the tongue of land between the Yellowstone and the Missouri, about a mile above the confluence, closer to the Missouri. This was not the spectacular Rocky Mountains the men had anticipated, but it was the best of the Great Plains, described by Meriwether Lewis as "the wide and fertile vallies formed by the Missouri and Yellowstone rivers, which occasionally unmasked by the wood on their borders disclose their meanderings for many miles in their passage through these delightful tracts of country." Smith's fellow trader Daniel T. Potts called the area "one of the most beautiful situations I ever saw."[11]

Ashley's overland company had reached the mouth of the Yellowstone on October 1. He and Henry "immediately commenced arrangements for business and after furnishing the mountain parties with their supplies of goods and receiving the furs of the last hunt Genl. Ashley started for St Louis with a large Perogue" loaded with packs of beaver pelts and six or seven men. [12]

Ashley was leaving late in the season and could have found himself trapped by ice at virtually any point along the Missouri River passage that William Clark had estimated at 1,880 miles long. According to one account, "he returned to St. Louis from the Yellow Stone, along with the floating ice." Upon his arrival—likely in December—he met with Clark and reported that "the Indians in that quarter are friendly, except the Assinniboin Tribe, some of their warriors having taken off from his establishment 16 of his horses." [13]

Within weeks of his arrival, Ashley posted a new advertisement in the newspaper, this time making no mention of enterprising young men but simply announcing, *"For the Rocky Mountains."* Again, one hundred hands were sought to ascend the Missouri to the Rocky Mountains and work as hunters. "As a compensation to each man, fit for such business, two hundred dollars per annum will be given for his services, as aforesaid." The expedition would set out from St. Louis on or before March 1. The subscribers were Ashley and Henry. [14]

Although the *St. Louis Enquirer* had estimated the previous fall "that a thousand men, chiefly from this place, are now employed in [the fur trade]," Ashley made two-thirds of his goal, enlisting about seventy men. At least two of them were in their forties, close in age to Ashley and Henry and not likely to be called "young men" by anyone. Edward Rose, often—and with good reason—called "the ubiquitous Rose," was about forty-three, the elder statesman of the expedition, but upon seeing his powerful frame and the battle scars on his forehead and nose and hearing of his "reckless bravery" and "strong and vigorous constitution," no greenhorn would have called him "old man" to his face. Born in Kentucky and said to be the son of a white trader and a woman of Cherokee and African American descent, Rose earned a reputation as a New Orleans boatman and brawler while still in his teens. He had been with Lisa with 1807; had lived the next year or two with the Crow, who called him "Five Scalps" because of his heroics in battle; had guided Hunt's westbound Astorians in 1811; and had trapped the Yellowstone country with John Dougherty in 1812. He had also lived among the Arikara and spoke their language fluently. Ashley could not have found a better interpreter. [15]

Hugh Glass was reportedly forty years old and was said to have been a pirate in his younger days, but, as an editor wrote in 1825, "whether old Ireland, or Scotch-Irish Pennsylvania, claims the honour of his nativity, I have not ascertained with precision."[16] Glass had lived with the Pawnee for years, had taken a Pawnee wife, and had fought alongside Indian friends, just as Rose had done.

James Clyman was born in Virginia's Blue Ridge Mountains on February 1, 1792, making him thirty-one when he signed on as a clerk with Ashley. He had battled Indians in Ohio during the War of 1812, laboring as a farmer and surveyor afterward. He read Shakespeare and wrote poetry himself and would also leave the best record of Ashley's second Missouri voyage. "Mr Ashley . . . said he wished . . . that I would assist him ingageing men for his Rockey mountain expedition," wrote Clyman, who said he found some "in grog Shops and other sinks of degredation."[17]

Whether they were recruited by Clyman or Ashley himself, in grog shops or elsewhere is not known, but two twenty-three-year-olds would leave immense imprints on the American fur trade: Kentucky's William Lewis Sublette and Ireland's Thomas Fitzpatrick. Bill was the oldest of five brothers, all of whom would be fur traders. The family had immigrated to Missouri, and in 1820, at age twenty, Bill had been appointed deputy constable of St. Charles Township. His service was well received—two years later he was named constable. About this same time, however, both of his parents died, and he found himself unattached and facing west. He stood a lanky six foot two and was "Jackson-faced," with sandy hair. "Although he lacked advanced education and had no military training," writes his biographer, "he knew how to work with people and how to lead men."[18]

Little is known about Tom Fitzpatrick's youth. He was born to a Catholic family and received the basics of a good education before sailing to America as a teenager. He was of medium height and slim but strong build. He was apparently involved as a clerk in the Indian trade somewhere on the Mississippi, but no details are known. As for his life after signing on with Ashley, however, LeRoy R. Hafen hardly exaggerates when he says that "the life story of Thomas Fitzpatrick is an epitome of the early history of the Far West. . . . No other man is so representative of this epoch."[19]

Ashley, Rose, Glass, Clyman, Sublette, Fitzpatrick, and all the others had left St. Louis on Monday, March 10, 1823, with most of the men aboard two keelboats. On March 26, Ashley had been honored by the impromptu festivities in Franklin and by the newspaper article praising him for pointing "the attention of the community to vast sources of national and sectional wealth."[20] Still, there had been portents of trouble ahead, incidents more disturbing than the loss of a keelboat and all its cargo a year earlier.

First, the day of the departure, amid all the bustle and excitement, a man fell overboard from one of the boats and drowned. The details of the accident and even the man's name have been lost to history.[21]

Second, for some reason, the gunpowder ordered by Ashley was not loaded onto the keelboats at St. Louis, so he assigned three men to deliver the powder in a two-horse cart from St. Louis to St. Charles, where it would be transferred to the boats. "The powder, amounting to about five hundred pounds, was put up in large kegs, or half-barrels, and, without being covered with canvas, was loaded into a cart, and the [men] started." After stopping at a tavern for "their morning dram, . . . they lighted their pipes, . . . took their seats on the half-barrels of powder, and started." They had barely gone a half mile down the road to St. Charles "when fire was communicated to the powder by means of a pipe. The explosion was tremendous and produced a concussion similar to that of a slight earthquake. The men were blown into the air to the height of several hundred feet, the cart shivered to pieces, and the horses much injured." One of the men survived for a few minutes; "the others were entirely lifeless and burnt in the most shocking manner."[22]

Again, the names of the victims were not recorded, even though one newspaper article, a contemporaneous letter, and two reminiscences described the catastrophe.[23] Nor did Ashley—or Clyman—make any mention of it. Regardless, the accident cast Ashley in a negative light— as the owner of a gunpowder factory, he was well versed in the precautions necessary to transport powder safely. It is particularly ironic that one of the key factors—along with economic conditions—prompting Ashley and his partner, Lionel Browne, to abandon the gunpowder business was an accident in 1818 that was eerily similar to the one in 1823. A group of employees were transporting a wagon full of powder from the St. Genevieve area to St. Louis when the load ignited and exploded, killing two men.[24] Given that deadly explosion—and others that had occurred at the factory—it is incredible that Ashley acted nonchalantly in ordering the powder sent to St. Charles. There is no sign, however, that he chose the right men for the job or gave them stern orders on handling such deadly cargo. On the contrary, these men acted with extreme carelessness—leaving the barrels uncovered and smoking pipes *in transit*. Six weeks later, another failure by Ashley to take care in perilous circumstances would also result in tragedy.

Throughout the rest of March and all of April, Ashley's men sailed, rowed, or pulled the boats up the Missouri, called "a monotinous crooked stream" by Clyman. "A discription of our crew I cannot give," he added, "but Fallstafs Battalion was genteel in comparison."[25] From time to time, a few men would desert and others would sign on, essentially confirming the speculation that there were at least a thousand men working in the Missouri fur trade. Early in May, about sixteen miles north of present Omaha, Nebraska, the men saw the Stars and Stripes fluttering from a garrison atop a high bluff overlooking the Missouri.

"From the *Bluff* on the 2d rise imediately above our Camp," William Clark had written in 1804, "the most butiful prospect of the River up & Down and the Countrey opsd. prosented it Self which I ever beheld." More than a decade later, Clark suggested that the bluff, which offered such a scenic view of the "River meandering the open and butiful Plains, interspersed with Groves of timber," would be the perfect site for a fort. In 1819, Cantonment Missouri had been constructed on lower ground, but when it was flooded by the river, the post was moved to Clark's choice bluff and renamed Fort Atkinson. It was the westernmost outpost of the United States and housed 350 men quite securely.[26]

Ashley, of course, received special treatment, but Clyman and his fellows were hardly neglected, with the one detail mentioned by Clyman revealing what they appreciated most: "The officers [at Fort Atkinson] being verry liberal furnished us with a Quantity of vegetables." One of the junior officers welcoming the traders was Lieutenant Reuben Holmes, who struck up a friendship with Rose and became his chief biographer five years later. In addition, a number of free trappers loitering at the fort joined Ashley's expedition, and two or three soldiers whose enlistment was about to end also signed on. After savoring the food—and drink—and good fellowship of the post, Ashley and his men, now numbering close to ninety, proceeded on. "Here we leave the last appearance of civilization and [enter] fully Indian country," wrote Clyman, "game becoming more plenty we furnished ourselves with meat daily."[27]

About this same time, Henry sent Jedediah Smith downriver with a dispatch for Ashley. The document has been lost, but Ashley reported it had been "sent for the purpose of desiring me to purchase all the horses I could on my way." One fact of life on the Missouri was that the farther one went up the river, the harder it was to purchase horses and the more expensive they got. Not only that, but the one Indian nation that seemed to have such an abundance of steeds—the Crow—were seldom disposed to part with any of them. So Smith checked his weapons, replenished his supply of flints, balls, and powder, stocked up on food, and boarded a canoe. Whether anyone accompanied him is unknown— we just know that he navigated his way down the Missouri, past its confluence with the Yellowstone, past the Mandan and Hidatsa villages, and past the Arikara villages, meeting Ashley's keelboats shortly thereafter, at the northern tip of present South Dakota.[28]

Ashley had little news for Smith, but Smith had something to report to him: In April, Henry had taken eleven men and traveled from the fort to trap near the Great Falls of the Missouri, Henry's planned destination in 1822. Four of their horses were stolen by Blackfoot Indians on the way. A week or two later, near the mouth of Smith River, nine miles below Great Falls, a band of Blackfoot warriors ambushed Henry's party and killed four men. In their hurried retreat back to Fort Henry, the eight survivors had to leave behind two hundred steel traps.[29]

The site of the ambush was 150 miles north of Three Forks, where the group that included Henry, Menard, Colter, Drouillard, and Dougherty had been attacked thirteen years earlier, but this was still Blackfoot territory, and their hostility to American traders had not changed. Now, for the second time, Henry had been chased out of the region so rich with beaver. For the next fourteen months he would operate out of the post near the mouth of the Yellowstone, beyond the eastern edge of Blackfoot lands (which covered central and western Montana, as well as large sections of Alberta and Saskatchewan, Canada). But he would never return to Blackfoot country and would never again cross the Continental Divide. In early August of 1824, his boats loaded with "a considerable quantity of valuable furs," he descended the Missouri River to St. Louis for the final time.[30]

Neither Smith nor Ashley described the latter's reaction to the report of Henry's troubles in the north. There was nothing to do but push on, with Smith reversing his course and going upstream on the stretch of river he had just descended. On May 30 they reached the villages of the Indians Ashley had been so suspicious of a year earlier—the Arikara, called "Rees" by the Americans. Following the pattern established by Wilson Price Hunt, twelve years earlier, Ashley hoped to obtain a good number of horses here and send part of his men overland (while Hunt's entire group had traveled on horseback, or by foot, from this point).

For Ashley, however, there were more bad omens. As the keelboats approached the two Arikara towns on the west side of the river, just above the mouth of the Grand River, Ashley's hunters, wrote Clyman, saw the sandy beach along the river lined with Indian women—"thinking to have to stand a siege"—filling containers with water. Next came word that the previous winter, a Sioux woman being held prisoner by the Arikara had escaped and fled downstream toward a small trading post manned by the Missouri Fur Company. When the woman came in sight of the post, "the men in the house ran out and fired on the Puesueing arrickarees killing [two of them] so that Rees considered war was fully declared between them and the whites." Ashley tried to convince the Arikara that he and his men were not responsible for the deaths, "but the Rees could not make the distinction." Although the Arikara chiefs agreed to be paid for losses suffered at the hands of the Missouri Company men, Ashley said he "would make them a present but would not pay . . . the damages."[31]

Ashley told a different story, and the discrepancies between his accounts and those of Clyman and others reveal how Ashley's failure to take rigorous precautions in such a hazardous situation led to calamity on the morning of June 2 (after negotiations on May 31 and June 1). For example, Ashley said nothing about "squaws packing up water" or the chiefs demanding a payment for damages, each of which was valid cause for alarm. Next, Ashley reported warning the Arikara about attempting to harm him or his men. In his words, "I made [the chiefs] a small present, which appeared to please them very much, I then told them that I had understood that a difference had taken place between a party of their men and some of the Missouri Fur Company, that in consequence of which they might feel disposed to do me an injury, and went on to state what I supposed would be the consequence should they attempt it."[32]

Not only did Ashley not say what retaliation he threatened, subsequent events offer no evidence that he had any plan at all for delivering swift retribution in the case of an Arikara offensive. When the attack finally materialized, Ashley gave every appearance of being disorganized and unprepared. Clyman described things perfectly: "We had no Military organization diciplin or Subordination."[33] As a general in the Missouri militia, Ashley had trained his volunteers how to respond to Indian aggression, but he had neglected even the basics with his traders. The "consequence" of the Arikara "doing an injury" to Ashley's men was virtually nil.

As to Clyman's claim that "the Rees could not make the distinction" between the actions of the Missouri Company men and those of the Henry-Ashley traders, Ashley confidently reported: "They [the chiefs] answered that the affray alluded to, had caused angry feelings among them, but that those feelings had vanished that they then considered the white people as their friends and would treat them as such."[34]

Ashley's taking such declarations at face value, however, flew in the face of continual signs of danger. First, one of the leading Arikara negotiators was Grey Eyes, the same unpredictable chief who had treated Lewis and Clark kindly in 1806 but who had helped initiate the unprovoked attack against Pryor and Chouteau a year later.[35] Whether Ashley knew this is not clear, but he certainly could have learned it from Clark. Second, as Ashley himself states, one of the two Arikara warriors killed by the Missouri Fur Company men was the son of Grey Eyes, making the situation that much more volatile. Third, according to Clyman, Ashley obtained the horses—nineteen according to Ashley, twenty according to Clyman—and 250 buffalo robes by giving the Indians "a fine supply of Powder and ball," a crucial detail omitted by Ashley, who said he sent "some goods" to make the purchase. Fourth, even though the location and topography of their towns—on a rise overlooking a narrow horseshoe bend of the river—gave the Arikara a strategic position for both attack and defense, Ashley observed that "the towns are *newly pickited* in with timber from about 6 to 8 inches thick 12 or 15 feet high dirt in the inside thrown up about 18 inches high." Not only that, but at the head of the large sandbar at the edge of the river—where Ashley's men keeping the horses would be virtually defenseless—the Arikara had constructed "a breast work made of dry wood." Regardless of whether the Indians had strengthened their fortress specifically to attack Ashley's men or simply for general defense, their overwhelming advantage left little doubt how any clash between the two sides would end.[36]

In discussing how precarious things looked for Ashley, Hiram Chittenden wrote:

> It should be stated, although Ashley makes no mention of it, that he was warned at this time to be on his guard. His interpreter, the noted Edward Rose, cautioned him that, from signs apparent to those versed in Indian wiles, trouble of some sort was brewing. Ashley seems to have been about as suspicious of Rose as Hunt had been twelve years before, and with just as little reason. He rejected Rose's advice to moor the boats for the night against a bar on the opposite side of the river, and not only remained near the shore next to the villages, but even left his land party camped on the beach.[37]

Such a scenario seems likely, but, to the frustration of modern historians, Chittenden failed to provide a source for this claim—in a chapter called "important [and] well-researched" by James Ronda.[38] Therefore the question of whether Rose, who knew the Arikara far better than Ashley or any other trader present, sounded the alarm days before the attack must remain a mystery.

No mystery, however, surrounds the warning blared by Rose hours before the volley of gunfire rained down from the Arikara. "In the night of the third day Several of our men without permission went and remained in the village amongst them our Interpreter Mr [Edward] Rose," wrote Clyman, who was on the sandbar with three dozen of Ashley's other hunters—and two and a half dozen horses. "About midnight he came running into camp & informed us that one of our men [Aaron Stephens] was killed in the village and war was declared." For the rest of the night, added Clyman, "we laid on our arms e[x]pecting an attact as their was a continual Hubbub in the village."[39]

An unidentified member of Ashley's expedition who was on one of the keelboats—anchored about thirty yards from the shore—offered a less detailed but similar report: "About midnight we were alarmed by the information that one of our men was killed in the village."[40]

These independent mentions of "about midnight"—one recorded forty-eight years after the Arikara assault by a man who had been on the beach, and the other at Fort Kiowa fifteen days afterward by a man who had been aboard a boat—offer solid evidence about the timing of Rose's warning, confirming that Ashley knew of Stephens's death roughly five hours before the Arikara opened fire at sunrise, giving Ashley plenty of time to do *something* to protect the men on the sandbar, who were conspicuously in imminent danger given Rose's news about Stephens. Analyses of the Clyman reminiscence and the Fort Kiowa letter reveal both to be generally reliable; their agreement on when Rose reported Stephens's demise thus outweighs Ashley's claim that he didn't hear Rose's warning until 3:30 a.m. (and even then Ashley's three descriptions are not entirely consistent).[41]

Moreover, events described by Clyman and others—but not by Ashley—indicate that a good deal of time elapsed between Rose's warning and the Arikara attack. "Several advised to cross over the river at once but thought best to wait until day light," wrote Clyman, "but Gnl. Ashely our imployer Thought best to wait till morning and go into the village and demand the body of our comrade and his Murderer Ashly being the most interested his advice prevailed."[42]

"A friendly Indian informed us he would bring us the body of the man that was killed, if we would let him have a horse, (this was about day break, and the wind had lulled)," stated the Fort Kiowa letter. "We were preparing to depart, having come to the conclusion it would be best for the men and horses to keep with the boats for a couple of days; the men refused to quit the beach until a horse was given the Indian. Ashley at last consented to let him have one." But later the Indian returned without the horse and announced that Stephens's body had been mutilated. At that point, the Indians "immediately commenced firing."[43]

Finally, the Fort Kiowa letter also describes a warning that came a few hours before Rose's: "One of the friendly Indians informed us of their intention to attack us before our departure; if they did not, we might calculate on their attacking us when we separated; he advised Ashley to swim the horses that night across the river, but having that day seen several Indians on the opposite side, we deemed it more prudent not to follow his advice."[44]

True, the various sources depicting the events of May 30–June 2, 1823, are not entirely consistent, and some details mentioned in one source are not mentioned in others. Still, a close look at all the documents leaves little doubt that Barton Barbour has it right: Eager to buy horses for an overland trip to the mouth of the Yellowstone River, "Ashley and his men"—but mainly Ashley because he was the one giving orders—"put themselves at grave risk." By the evening of June 1, when the thunder, wind, and rain that blew up earlier that day "had increased to a perfect gale, . . . the situation had already spun out of [Ashley's] control."[45]

"About sun rise the Indians commenced a heavy and well directed fire," wrote Ashley. "Seeing that some of the horses were killed and others wounded, as well as two or three men I attempted to have the horses crossed to a sand bar about the middle of the river, . . . but before any thing to effect that object could be done, the fire became very destructive, aimed principally at the men on shore."[46]

"They immediately commenced firing upon us," wrote the author of the Fort Kiowa letter. "The men on the beach were drawn up in front of the boats; their horses forming a breastwork. So severe was the fire, that in a few minutes all the horses were either killed or wounded, and many of the men. Ashley ordered the boats to weigh anchor and make for the beach . . . the boatsmen could not be made to touch an oar."[47]

It was left to Clyman, however, to tell firsthand of the carnage on the beach. "Finally one shot was fired into our camp the distance being however to great for certain aim Shortly firing became Quite general we seeing nothing to fire at." After describing the Arikara towns and their pickets, he continued: "You will easily perceive that we had little else to do than to Stand on a bear sand barr and be shot at, at long range." The irony of Ashley's bargaining hardly escaped him. "We having the day previously furnished them with abundance of Powder and Ball."[48]

The horses had overwhelmed everything—the thud of balls striking them; the animals crumbling amid their screaming, screeching, and bleating; the stench of burning horseflesh.

The men sought cover behind the fallen horses, but the endless hail of gunfire from the pickets gave them no pause to measure powder, handle ramrods, or prime pans. Each time they fired a shot, they had to complete the interminable process of reloading the best they could while also trying to stay low and not get wounded. Now came the thuds of balls striking human flesh, followed by moans and cries and cursings.

"Send the boats ashore!" someone called out. "Take us onboard!"[49] But neither of the boats moved. A chorus rose for the boats, but it was drowned out by the welter of gunfire and the whiz of arrows. Some of the men were dead, some wounded, but the others managed to keep on reloading and firing.

"When his party was in danger," a friend of Jedediah's wrote, "Mr. Smith was always among the foremost to meet it, and the last to fly; those who saw him on the shore, at the Riccaree fight, in 1823, can attest to the truth of this assertion."[50] Smith, who had been in the mountains for the last year and was thus the senior Ashley man, apparently took the lead among those now valiantly fighting a lost cause on the beach.

Rose, a veteran of countless fistfights and gunfights, had reportedly "taken his station behind a small bunch of willows, from which, detached and alone, he fired as often as an Indian showed himself at the narrow spaces between the pickets that surrounded the villages."[51]

When the first shots were fired, thirty-six men had been fighting alongside Smith, Rose, and Clyman, including some whose names would long be remembered—Tom Fitzpatrick, Bill Sublette, Hugh Glass, and Louis Vasquez—and many more whose names would not— with Hiram Scott, James Kirker, Hiram Allen, George C. Jackson, and Charles Cunningham among them.[52] All of them were armed with rifles, as Lewis and Clark's men and the overland Astorians had been before them, and they were well supplied with powder and balls. In open country they no doubt could have defended themselves more than competently, but, now they were under constant heavy fire and, as Clyman said, were shooting at long range—probably 150 yards or more—and their assailants were well protected—and virtually invisible—behind the sturdy pickets.[53]

Ashley, who had bypassed one opportunity after another to get the men on the beach out of harm's way, now tried desperately to help them, but it was too late. The untrained and undisciplined boatmen "were ordered to weigh their anchors and lay their boats to shore," but they were so "panic struck, that they would not expose themselves in the least."[54] The swivel cannons on the bow of each keelboat—with ample range to reach beyond the pickets and do *some* damage, distracting and interrupting the Arikara gunmen if nothing else—were silent and unmanned. Nor is there evidence that anyone was even trained to aim and fire the swivels.

What happened next is not at all clear.

"Several men being wounded a skiff was brought ashore," wrote Clyman. "All rushed for the Skiff and came near sinking it but it went the boat full of men and water the shot still coming thicker and the aim better we making a breast work of our horses (most) they nerly all being killed the skiffs having taken sevarl loads on Board the boats . . . one of the skiffs (was turned) was let go the men clambering on Board let the skiff float off in their great eagerness to conceal themselves from the rapid fire of the enemy."[55]

Ashley, by contrast, wrote that when the two skiffs, which between them held thirty men, reached the shore, most of the riflemen were determined "not to give way to the Indians as long as there appeared the least probability of keeping their ground," and five of them at most made use of the large skiff. Two men, one of them mortally wounded, took the other skiff to the opposite side of the river. When the large skiff reached his keelboat, Ashley started it back immediately, but "one of the men that worked it was shot down and by some means the skiff set a drift."[56]

The Fort Kiowa letter offered yet another perspective, saying that both skiffs were manned but "had not advanced a rod from the boat before those at the oars were shot down; finding all lost, those on the beach attempted to swim to the boats; some who could not, fell alive into the hands of the Indians; many who attempted to swim, were, by the violence of the current, driven below the boats and drowned."[57]

Things were happening so fast and so chaotically that it's little wonder the three witnesses remembered the scene so differently.

Seeing no hope of another skiff coming ashore, Clyman ran for the river, ramming the muzzle of his rifle in his belt, "the lock ove my head with all my clothes on," and plunged into the swift water. The strong current took him by surprise, and he was quickly carried past a keelboat. Thomas Eddie, onboard the boat, could not move freely because of "the shot coming thick" and could not reach Clyman though he reached out with a pole.[58]

Several men lay dead on the beach; the survivors were all in the water or in a skiff or a keelboat. It had been fifteen minutes since the first shot was fired. The Arikara now set their sights on the boats.

Clyman was about to drown. "My first aim was to rid myself of all my encumbrances and my Rifle was the greatest." He tried to pull it over his head, but the lock caught in his belt. "Comeing to the surface to breathe I found it hindred worse than it did at first." He tried again as he went under, turning the lock sideways, and the rifle slipped free. Still "much encumbered," he unbuckled his belt and let his pistols fall away, then his ball pouch, and finally one sleeve of his "Hunting shirt which was buckskin and held an immence weight of water." Rising to the surface, he heard "a voice of encoragemnt": "Hold on Clyman, I will soon relieve you."

It was Reed Gibson "who had swum in and caught the skiff the men had let go afloat"—he was fifteen or twenty feet away. "I was so much exhausted that he had to haul me into the skiff wh[ere] I lay for a moment to catcth breath." Half-recovered, Clyman stood and took the only remaining oar. "Oh, God, I am shot," Gibson moaned, falling forward in the skiff.

"I encouraged him," wrote Clyman, "and [said] 'Perhaps not fatally give a few pulls more and we will be out of reach.' He raised and gave sevreral more strokes with the oar using it as a paddle when [he] co[m]plained of feeling faint" and fell forward again. Clyman took Gibson's place in the stern, rowed to the east shore (opposite the Ree villages), and hauled the skiff up on the shore. When he got on the bank, Clyman saw several Indians swimming toward him. "I spoke to Gibson telling him of the circumstance he mearly said save yourself Clyman and pay no attention to me as I am a dead man and they can get nothing of me but my Scalp." A moment later, Gibson managed to stand. "Run Clyman, but if you escape, write to my friends in Virginia and tell them what has become of me." Then Clyman "ran for the open Prarie and Gibson for the brush to hide."

Three Indians with knives, tomahawks, and bows and arrows pursued the defenseless Clyman for several miles, but he managed to evade them, traveling downstream all the while and continuing in that direction long after the Indians disappeared. Concluding his prospects "ware still very slim," he saw a grove of trees near the river and "made for the water intending to [drink and] take a good rest in the timber."

He got a drink and sat down to rest when he "chanced to look [at] the [river] and here came the boats floating down the stream."

One of the boats picked him up, and he was informed that Gibson was also aboard. "I immediately wen[t] to the cabin where he lay but he did not recognize me being in the agonies of Death the shot have passed through his bowels I could not refrain from weeping over him who had lost his lifee but saved mine." Gibson died less than an hour later, and the men buried him—the only burial among the thirteen men killed.

Clyman added this postscript: "Before I had an oppertunity of writeing to his friends I forgot his post office and so never have written."[59]

* * *

"Ironically," writes Will Bagley, "the ambush at the Arikara villages set in motion events that led to the rediscovery of South Pass."[60]

In 1813, however (as noted earlier), upon the return of Stuart, Crooks, McClellan, Miller, Jones, Vallé, and Le Clerc, the *Missouri Gazette* had confidently prognosticated that "a journey to the Western Sea will not be considered, (within a few years) of much greater importance, than a trip to New York."[61] So, how was it that over the next decade, not only did an east-to-west crossing of the United States not become the norm, it didn't happen at all? Even more puzzling is the detail that Stuart's route across the Continental Divide—which had been described in a subsequent *Gazette* article that was widely reprinted—had to be rediscovered.[62]

Although the *Gazette* estimate of "within a few years" overstated the case considerably, there was good reason to believe that the Pacific coast might be a reasonable destination for common travelers within a decade because between 1805 and 1812 crossings of the Continental Divide had become surprisingly frequent. Lewis and Clark, the first to traverse the present continental US, had gone westbound in 1805 and eastbound the next year. In 1807, John McClallen and Charles Courtin had both led groups of trappers into present Montana (ahead of Lisa), with both parties eventually crossing to Columbia waters.[63] In 1810, Henry and Dougherty—whether in two groups or one—had crossed the Continental Divide to Henrys Fork, although not attempting to reach the coast. That had been accomplished by Hunt in 1811–1812, and, of course, Stuart had traveled east from Astoria, discovering South Pass in October of 1812.[64]

More than any other concern, Astor's Pacific Fur Company showed that the transcontinental commerce hoped for by Jefferson was a practical possibility. As Stuart and his six companions made their way east along tributaries of the Missouri, they had information that would allow other of Astor's employees to follow the same route west. Not only that, but Astorians in the West were already working on both sides of the Divide. From a post on the Columbia River, Russell Farnham "was fitted out for the Selish or Flathead tribe—crossed with them the Rocky Mountains—visited the headwaters of the Missouri—saw much of the country, and made a good trade."[65] Farnham likely made his trip in the summer of 1812, meaning that Stuart's had been the third Astorian crossing of the Divide.

The War of 1812 changed everything.

Although Astor had appointed Wilson Price Hunt the managing partner of the Pacific Fur Company, the latter spent very little time at Astoria after his arrival in February of 1812. He left that summer to negotiate trade with the Russian American Company and was thus absent in January of 1813 when Duncan McDougall and the other partners, Donald McKenzie, David Stuart, and John Clarke, learned that the US had declared war on Britain seven months earlier. The four partners, Canadians all, found themselves in the precarious position of managing an American post that could be attacked at any moment by British warships. After considerable debate, they agreed to abandon the enterprise, informing Hunt of this when he was briefly in Astoria in August of 1813 before departing on international business again. Hunt and McDougall agreed that the latter could transfer men and wages to the Montreal-based North West Company. The fort itself, however, as well as Astor's other property, was to be protected until Hunt's return. He was thus astonished when he arrived back at Astoria at the end of February 1814 to find that McDougall and the others had sold the post and all its contents to the North West Company in October of 1813. American cross-country trade thus came to an abrupt halt.

The war likewise cooled the capability and enthusiasm of the Missouri Fur Company to go anywhere near the Continental Divide. Although Lisa had established Fort Manuel (along the Missouri, just south of the present North Dakota-South Dakota border) in 1812, he was driven out the next year by hostile Indian nations encouraged by the British. When Lisa returned to St. Louis in 1813, the Missouri Company's business had reached a low point, its only posts one in central South Dakota for the Sioux trade and one in Nebraska for the Omaha trade. Although Lisa effectively secured vows of friendship from many Missouri River Indian nations during the war, the exploring efforts of the company, such as those of Colter, Drouillard, and Henry from 1807 to 1810, had stalled. That had not changed when Lisa died in August of 1820.[66]

Still, others had pushed west. The expedition of Auguste P. Chouteau and Jules de Mun, organized in 1815 to trap the headwaters of the Arkansas River (in present central Colorado), turned out to be a long-term, meandering excursion that eventually landed the coleaders and twenty-four of their men in "the dungeons of Santa Fe" for forty-eight days. In a letter to Governor William Clark, de Mun wrote of plans "to go in search of the Crow Indians, whom we knew to be somewhere about the head waters of the Columbia," but did not explain exactly what he and Chouteau had in mind. He simply said that "the coming of the Spaniards" caused a delay, "making it impossible to proceed to the head waters of the Columbia by the route we had first intended."[67] Nor did Chouteau and de Mun take any route across the Divide. William Becknell fared much better in Santa Fe after Mexican independence, but even his impressive trek from Franklin, Missouri, to Santa Fe did not span the Continental Divide, which lay farther west.

While the War of 1812 dampened the fur trade and western exploration in many ways, one aftermath of the war was a distrust of the British that motivated US officials to protect the country's border frontiers by establishing forts in the Northwest. William Clark, who was appointed governor of the Missouri Territory and served until 1820, recommended building a fort at the mouth of the Platte River, an idea that appealed to James Monroe, serving as both secretary of state and secretary of war under President James Madison.

Several months after Monroe became president in March of 1817, he named John C. Calhoun secretary of war. Calhoun, one of the leaders of the War Hawks, developed a strategy for defending the northern borders by erecting forts on the upper Mississippi and Missouri Rivers. In March of 1818, Calhoun wrote to a general at Fort Bellefontaine that "it has been determined to establish a permanent military post at the mouth of the Yellow Stone river."[68]

Enter Stephen H. Long, a young topographical engineer and brevet major in the US Army—and predecessor of sorts to another officer of similar skills by the name of John C. Frémont (then a toddler living in the South). Long had reconnoitered the upper Mississippi early in Monroe's tenure, recommending a fort at the Falls of St. Anthony (in the present Twin Cities area), and also putting forth the idea that the Missouri River could be best mapped by steamboat. "Long's proposal for mapping by steamboat was the genesis of a Missouri River scientific expedition that was to be distinct from the military expedition. . . . Calhoun agreed and showed his strong support by usually working directly with Long rather than through the military chain of command." Mindful of a previous government-sponsored study of the West, Calhoun advised Long to scrutinize Jefferson's instructions to Lewis in 1803.[69]

At the same time, Calhoun found it necessary to explain to General Andrew Jackson, commander of the army's Southern Division, why significant resources were being shifted to the Northwest. Employing logic bound to resonate with Jackson, Calhoun argued that a post on the upper Missouri would help "break British control over the Northern Indians." In the same letter, Calhoun revealed an apparent change of heart about the best site for a fort when he said, "I am inclined to think that the principal post ought to be at the Mandan Village."[70] Calhoun, however, kept such sentiments private, and Long's mission was widely publicized as the "Yellowstone Expedition." By December of 1818, Long had relocated to Pittsburgh to supervise the construction of a steamboat for the scientific mission. The craft, christened the *Western Engineer*, was seventy feet long and thirteen feet wide, designed to feature a cabin that appeared to be riding the back of a huge serpent, with the steam flowing from the creature's mouth. Such a grandiose façade, however, proved to be ironic; both the construction and the voyages of the *Western Engineer* were so plagued by problems that the boat looked to be anything but a swift, powerful monster of the sea.

Colonel Henry Atkinson, who had been assigned to command the military expedition, reached St. Louis with his men on June 1, 1819, fully expecting to find Long and the *Western Engineer* already there, but Long had stopped for necessary repairs in Cincinnati and Louisville and did not arrive for another week, much later in the season than he had hoped. Still, the four thousand inhabitants of St. Louis were enthusiastic about the forthcoming expeditions, and at a public dinner, complete with an "elegant band of music, and two pieces of artillery," a series of toasts praised Calhoun, "who has taken the Missouri frontier into the line of the national defense"; the scientists, "who ascend the Missouri to enlarge the boundaries of human knowledge"; and even the river itself, with the "year 1819 [marking] the era when its majestic current yielded to the power of steam."[71]

The hosts of the dinner were William Christy, a prominent businessman and judge, and a rising, thirty-seven-year-old attorney who had relocated from Tennessee to St. Louis four years earlier: Thomas Hart Benton. In the rough-and-tumble politics of St. Louis, Benton had aligned himself with Clark, Edward Hempstead, and John Scott, a group called "the little junto" by *Missouri Gazette* editor Joseph Charless, whose allies included William Russell, John B. C. Lucas and his son Charles, Frederick Bates, and David Barton. Insults inevitably followed, with a particular conflict brewing between Benton and twenty-five-year-old Charles Lucas. The two fought two duels in 1817, with Benton killing Lucas in the second. Benton's reputation was damaged, but he had fought his last duel, and his public standing was well on the mend by the time Long departed St. Louis on June 21. Two months later Benton would assume editorship of the *St. Louis Enquirer*, where he would push his expansionist views and launch a tacit campaign for public office.[72]

Benton's elaborate philosophy of westward expansion included hoped-for trade with India. "Benton's thought concerning the passage to India and the related theme of Anglo-American rivalry can be traced through almost four decades of public discussion," writes Henry Nash Smith, starting with his *Enquirer* articles in 1818–1819, then his 1825 Senate speech on the Oregon question and his "fostering of the exploring expeditions of his son-in-law, Lieutenant John Charles Frémont," and concluding with his support of the proposed railway to the Pacific in the 1850s.[73]

Not surprisingly, Benton was a faithful disciple of Thomas Jefferson. "He believed, according to his daughter Jessie Benton Frémont, that a visit he paid to the aged statesman at Monticello in 1824 was the occasion of a laying on of hands, a ceremony at which Benton received the mantle of the first prophet of American expansionism."[74]

The Missouri River hardly "yielded to steam"; the *Western Engineer* grounded twice not long after entering its waters. But this was hoped to be an anomaly, and spirits were again lifted at St. Charles when Benjamin O'Fallon, the newly appointed Indian agent for the upper Missouri, came aboard with a personal servant—presumably a slave—named Peter, and an experienced interpreter, John Dougherty. Three months later, when O'Fallon requested that Dougherty be named his subagent, he wrote: "I know of no person better than Mr. John Dougherty, he . . . has lived, between this [Council Bluffs] and the Yellow Stone, for the last 8 years and speaks several Indian languages tolerably well."[75]

The *Western Engineer*'s initial difficulties turned out to be no anomaly at all but a shadow of things to come. For those onboard, it was one thing after another after another: frequent groundings, boilers clogged with hardened mud, wood that didn't burn well, widespread sickness among the crew. Luckily for Dougherty, he spent much of his time the next several weeks leading scouting parties on foot, acting as both interpreter and hunter, and representing O'Fallon as an Indian diplomat. One of those joining him was Major Thomas Biddle. Thomas Biddle could not tolerate Long and had reportedly challenged him to a duel.[76]

"[We] with some difficulty extricated ourselves," wrote crewmember Titian Peale on July 7. "Just at the time we were surrounded with snags, sawyers, and floating logs, the main steam clock blew out." A week later, the crew idled their time at Franklin, waiting six days for repairs to be made. Less than a week after that, Peale recorded more aggravation: "In the afternoon came opposite the Miami Bottom. It lays on the south or left side ascending. Here is the most rapid water we have met in the Missouri with 90 lbs. pressure of steam to the square inch, and 10 men at the cordelle we could not move."[77]

One of the scientists, the well-respected Dr. William Baldwin, who had enjoyed Dougherty's explanations of Indian botanical cures, stayed behind in Franklin because of illness and died there on September 1 of a "pulmonary complaint."[78]

Meanwhile, writes William Lass, "the movement of Atkinson's 1,100-man expedition was a logistical nightmare." Planning to send his men upriver on three steamboats supplied by James Johnson, Atkinson experienced continual delays. When the three boats finally got started, several groundings and a strong current slowed them to a crawl. Hitting his limit, Atkinson abandoned steamboat travel and went overland. None of the three boats would reach its destination.[79]

On September 17, Long and his men guided the *Western Engineer* to shore at Council Bluffs, twelve hundred miles below the original destination of the mouth of the Yellowstone. Colonel Atkinson arrived twelve days later and began constructing "Camp Missouri" in a wooded bottom on the west side of the river, about a mile and a half from the bluff where Lewis and Clark had met in council with Otoe and Missouri chiefs. A comparison of the travel times of the captains' keelboat with Long's steamship pretty much told the whole story: Lewis and Clark had gone from St. Louis to the Council Bluffs in eleven weeks—it had taken Long twelve weeks and four days, at considerably more expense. So it was no surprise when Congress, already gun-shy from the Panic of 1819, cut off further funding and Calhoun subsequently halted the military expedition, giving Long revised orders to explore the Platte and Arkansas Rivers with a small group of scientists—and not by steamboat. When the group reached Fort Smith in September, Major Long met an officer ten years his junior who had also recently arrived: Captain Stephen Watts Kearny. The next month, Long and Kearny traveled together to St. Louis and both were struck with fever at St. Genevieve. Both survived, although Kearny's case was serious and lasted several weeks.[80]

Back at Camp Missouri, twenty-one-year-old Lieutenant James D. Graham, a West Point graduate who had become the chief operator of the *Western Engineer* during the brutal summer of 1819, was assigned to pilot the boat back to St. Louis. He did so without serious incident, arriving in June of 1820. Four months later, under the minor heading "STEAM BOAT NEWS," the following announcement appeared in the *Missouri Gazette*: "Sailed on the 4th October, the steam boat Western Engineer."[81]

* * *

As to how the Arikara ambush—and Ashley's negligence—led to the "rediscovery" of South Pass, as the summer of 1823 waned, such a breakthrough looked highly unlikely. Ashley had initially fled downstream after the attack, rescuing Clyman in the process, but he hoped to take his uninjured men right back up the Missouri past the scene of the killings, fighting off any further Arikara aggression from a keelboat. When he asked for volunteers, however, only thirty men stepped forward. As a result, Ashley sent his injured and his deserters in the *Yellow Stone Packet* (the larger of the two keelboats) south to Fort Atkinson, with a request for help from Colonel Henry Leavenworth, and dispatched Jedediah Smith and a companion (a French Canadian whose name has been forgotten) north to the fort at the mouth of the Yellowstone, with a similar request from Henry. Ashley and his remaining twenty-eight faithful then navigated the *Rocky Mountains* to the mouth of the Cheyenne River (in present central North Dakota) to await reinforcements.[82]

On June 22, Colonel Leavenworth led 250 soldiers north, some by boat and others overland. They were eventually joined by several hundred Sioux warriors—more than willing to fight their longtime foe, the Arikara—and by William Ashley's men and by Andrew Henry and those he had brought from the Yellowstone, as well as by sixty traders commanded by Joshua Pilcher of the Missouri Fur Company. Pilcher brought the sad news that on May 31, two days before the Arikara attacked Ashley, twenty-nine of his men, whom he called the "mountaineers," were "defeated" by a party of Blackfoot warriors, "consisting of between three and four hundred, [who] had concealed themselves in the side of some cliffs adjoining the Yellow Stone [River] . . . [and] rushed furiously upon [the traders] from every rock and brush." The first aim of the Indians was to kill the leaders, Michael Immell and Robert Jones. Immell had been with Dougherty at Three Forks and Henrys Fork and had been at Fort Manuel when Sacagawea died in 1812. Like Dougherty, he had been among the most loyal of Lisa's men. Immell brought down the first Indian who charged him; "his gun was hardly empty when he was literally cut to pieces." Although Jones was severely wounded, he "rallied and assembled his men, . . . but the Indians rushed upon them again with great fury [and] mangled the whites with lances, battle axes—scalping knives—and every weapon used by Indians." Besides Immell and Jones, five other men were killed, "four wounded, every thing lost, say at least $12,000."[83]

Armed with heavy artillery, this collection of soldiers, trappers, and Sioux warriors reached the Arikara villages on August 9. The next week, writes LeRoy Hafen, was one of "mismanagement, indecision, and delay. . . . Nothing of benefit had been accomplished, but only harm." A disgusted Pilcher wrote to Leavenworth, "You came . . . to 'open and make good this great road [the upper Missouri River]'; instead of which you have, by the imbecility of your conduct and operations, created and left impassable barriers."[84]

Agreeing that the river was indeed impassable, Ashley and Henry consulted and "together they made the momentous decision to break free of the upper Missouri River and its hostile tribes altogether and follow their tentative plans of mid-July to probe the western slopes of the Rocky Mountains unexplored by Americans since the War of 1812."[85]

Henry would lead half the men—and the few packhorses they had— back to Fort Henry at the mouth of the Yellowstone, close the post, and then take all the men to the mouth of the Bighorn (where the fourth "Fort Henry" would be built). Ashley would outfit a second overland party, captained by Smith, and send them west from Fort Kiowa (near present Chamberlain, South Dakota) to the Crow Country along the Bighorn. The two groups would winter together, then cross to the Columbia side of the Divide to trap. Ashley and Henry and many of the men had no doubt heard of the valley of a river that went by many names—including Rio del Norte, Seeds-ka-day, Siskadee, and Shetke-dee (or variations of the last three). It would eventually be known as Rio Verde—Green River. Trappers from the North West and Hudson's Bay Companies had reportedly found good success there. When Ashley and Henry determined their strategy, however, no specific mention of the Green River had been made, just of the Columbia.[86]

A crucial difference between the discovery of South Pass by Robert Stuart's group and the so-called rediscovery by Jedediah Smith's group thus becomes evident: Stuart, accompanied by six men who had previously crossed the Continental Divide (at Union Pass), was specifically searching for "a shorter trace to the South," while Smith and his men, none of whom had previously crossed the Divide, simply intended to reach "the waters of the River Columbia"—a destination that technically excluded the Green River because it flows into the Gulf of California (by way of the Colorado River) and is not a branch of the Columbia.[87]

After the War of 1812 had put such a damper on the American fur trade, simply getting men and boats back to the upper Missouri was a significant accomplishment for concerns like Ashley/Henry and the Missouri Fur Company. There was inevitably talk of crossing to the

Columbia as well, but no one was worried about how to get there. After all, *The History of the Expedition under the Commands of Captains Lewis and Clark*—the so-called Biddle edition, though it nowhere included his name—had finally been published early in 1814 and it included Clark's 1810 map, which, as William Foley notes, "altered long-held notions about American geography and launched a new generation of American maps."[88] Not only that, but Clark had kept up his passion for geographical complexities, talking to representatives of most of the expeditions that ventured to Columbia waters, and he was always eager and willing to spread maps on the floor and get down on his hands and knees—like he had with Jefferson—to explain all the details.

Even so, Clark was hardly the sole source of information about western geography. Whichever way he had reached the Divide in 1810—either by way of the Madison River or the Wind River—Henry had apparently become acquainted with Union Pass (west-southwest of present Dubois, Wyoming) and passed that information on to Smith, Fitzpatrick, and the others, who, as explained below, made their first attempt to reach the Columbia by way of that pass but were pushed back by heavy snows. When Hoback, Reznor, and Robinson—three of Henry's men—led Hunt and his overland Astorians toward the Pacific, they crossed the Divide at Union Pass, at least partially aware of its unique strategic importance—what other pass offered access within a ten-mile radius to the waters of the Missouri, Colorado, and Columbia Rivers?

Little wonder that the extant records from and about Ashley and Henry include no mention of South Pass before the 1824 rediscovery. That is not to say, however, that Stuart's discovery had been forgotten—quite the contrary because one of Stuart's companions—Ramsay Crooks—had shared the particulars of the 1812 journey with two of the most prominent advocates of western expansion in the country more than a year before Ashley issued his call for "one hundred men, to ascend the river Missouri to its source."

Crooks, it will be remembered, had barely survived the trek west, resigned his partnership days after reaching Astoria, and barely survived the return trip. It would have been no shock if his name were never heard again in connection to the fur trade. Astor, however, who received the year-old dispatches and a report from Stuart in June of 1813 (less than two months after Stuart and the others had arrived in St.

Louis), had other ideas. Something about the young Scot had impressed him, and on July 19 he wrote Crooks a letter. He was sorry to hear about Crooks's resignation, he said, but he expected the war to end shortly and when it did, he had every intention of continuing his Great Lakes fur trade. Would Crooks consider returning to his employ?

But Crooks wasn't in St. Louis to receive the invitation—he was already on his way to see Astor in New York, borrowing money from a friend in Pittsburgh in order to complete the one-way trip. Astor was glad to see him but was not thrilled with Crooks's idea of operating out of St. Louis. Instead, Astor assigned tasks in the East and the Great Lakes, even though the prolonged war often kept Crooks waiting for weeks on end. By this time, Robert Stuart, still an Astor agent and previously Crooks's superior, had willingly accepted a role subordinate to Crooks.

Besides Crooks's background in Canada, he had another intriguing connection to the British side—his sister had married William Procter, younger brother of the general, in 1807, but Crooks was content to sit out the war as an American. By the time the conflict ended with the Treaty of Ghent in December of 1814, and Jackson's victory at the Battle of New Orleans (fought without knowledge of the treaty) a month later, Crooks had gained high respect from Astor and was making a name for himself among many of Astor's influential friends.[89]

These friends never forgot that the eastbound Astorians had discovered South Pass. They had seen the reprints of the May 15, 1813, *Missouri Gazette* article—based on interviews with Stuart, Crooks, and McClellan—that appeared in the likes of the *Washington, DC, National Intelligencer*, the *Baltimore Weekly Register*, the *Boston Independent Chronicle*, and the *New York Herald*. In subsequent years, no doubt supplemented by reminders from Astor and Crooks, the Astorian adventure had been retold in *Annales des Voyages* (Annals of Travel), published in Paris in 1813; Henry M. Brackenridge's *Views of Louisiana*, in Pittsburgh in 1817; and John Bradbury's *Travels in the Interior of America*, in Liverpool in 1817.[90]

With a combination of corporate power and personal goodwill, Astor found rising stars everywhere. He likely learned of Thomas Hart Benton by reading his editorials in the *St. Louis Enquirer* and hearing about his skills as an attorney from St. Louis colleagues—and may have even remembered accounts of Benton's 1813 gunfight with Andrew Jackson.

Regardless, in the spring of 1818, Astor hired Benton to represent the American Fur Company in a fur trade lawsuit filed in St. Louis. Crooks and Russell Farnham, an Astorian who had become one of the first Americans to travel around the globe, both traveled to St. Louis to formally file charges and swear out affidavits. (While he was in St. Louis, Crooks hired another former Astorian partner, Wilson Price Hunt, to assist the American Fur Company with its business on the Illinois River.) Crooks and Farnham got along well with Benton, who taken up the cause of independent fur traders by arguing against the government system of trading "factories," which were essentially trading posts that provided goods to Indians.

In Benton's push for westward expansion, he found a kindred spirit in John Floyd, a congressman from Virginia (and later governor of Virginia) who happened to be an uncle of Benton's wife, Elizabeth McDowell, even though Benton was a year older than Floyd. (Floyd was also the cousin of Charles Floyd, Lewis and Clark's loyal sergeant who was the only expedition member to die during the journey.) In his memoirs, Benton wrote that the 1820–1821 session of Congress was "remarkable as being the first at which any proposition was made in Congress for the occupation and settlement of our territory on the Columbia River. . . . It was made by Dr. Floyd, . . . an ardent man, of great ability, . . . strongly imbued with western feelings."[91]

In December of 1820, four months before Benton took office as a Missouri senator, he and Floyd had met with Crooks and Farnham at Brown's Indian Queen Hotel (later the Metropolitan). "Their acquaintance was naturally made by Western men like us—in fact, I knew them before; and their conversation, rich in information upon a new and interesting country, was eagerly devoured by the ardent spirit of Floyd. He resolved to bring forward the question of occupation, and did so."[92]

In a January 25, 1821, report that ran for more than six pages in the dense *Congressional Record*, Floyd reviewed the history of the American fur trade from the time of Christopher Columbus to the present and included a healthy section on Astor's Pacific Fur Company. Getting to the heart of the matter—and clearly relying on Crooks and Farnham—Floyd wrote that a portage of only two hundred miles united the Missouri River with the Columbia. "The practicability of a speedy, safe, and easy communication with the Pacific, is no longer a matter of doubt or conjecture," added Floyd. "From information not to be doubted, the Rocky Mountains at this time, in several places, are so smooth and open, that the labor of ten men for twenty days would enable a wagon with its usual freight to pass with great facility from the navigable waters of the Missouri to that of the Columbia."[93]

Floyd's report was accompanied by a bill to authorize the occupation of the Columbia River and regulate the corresponding Indian trade. Although the presentation was treated with "parliamentary courtesy," Benton acknowledged that most of the members did not consider it a "serious proceeding." Nevertheless, "the first blow was struck: public attention was awakened, and the geographical, historical, and statistical facts set forth in the report, made a lodgment in the public mind which promised eventual favorable consideration."[94]

Some of Floyd's "facts" were questionable, but his prescience was the important thing. As Will Bagley has written, Floyd's "vision would eventually capture the imagination of a nation."[95] The first Rocky Mountain rendezvous—with beaver pelts from the Green River, the Great Basin, and branches of the Columbia all being sent to St. Louis—was less than five years away, and the first crossing of South Pass by husband-and-wife pioneers only fifteen.

Although Crooks had helped inspire Floyd's vision, his own perspective by the early 1820s and onward was that of a businessman. During the summer of 1822, for instance, when Henry and Ashley were taking their first group of recruits up the Missouri, Crooks made a visit to St. Louis, met several times with Thomas Hempstead, an acting partner of the Missouri Fur Company, and received letters from Joshua Pilcher, also an acting partner, and Indian agent Benjamin O'Fallon. O'Fallon encouraged Crooks to make some arrangement with Hempstead and Pilcher, but Crooks, for reasons unknown, declined to make a bid on providing the twenty to thirty thousand dollars' worth of goods the Missouri Company might want.[96]

Of course, Jedediah Smith, Tom Fitzpatrick, Bill Sublette, Jim Clyman, Ed Rose, Tom Eddie, and the seven or eight other Ashley men with them when they rode out of Fort Kiowa at the end of September 1823 may not have even heard of Ramsay Crooks and were not interested in such high-level discussions. They were focused on getting to good beaver country as soon as possible and salvaging what they could of the season that should have been already well under way.[97]

Clyman left the only firsthand account of the journey, and even it, as mentioned, was a late reminiscence, so it is not surprising that his memories of the route taken by the men is sometimes jumbled. As best as can be determined, Smith and the others ascended the White River—which flows into the Missouri just south of Fort Kiowa—to western South Dakota and then crossed to the south fork of the Cheyenne River and ascended it into present Wyoming. Continuing west, they hit the badlands west of the Cheyenne, and eventually, wrote Clyman, the route "became brushy mainly Scruby pine and Juniper," with ravines "steep and rugged an rockey." The streams were flowing west, so they assumed they "ware on the waters of Powder river." They followed one of the streams late one evening, "came into a Kenyon and pushed ourselves down so far that (our) horses had no room to turn." Now in darkness and trying to find a way out, "by unpacking and leading our animals down over Slipery rocks three of us got down to a n[i]ce open glade whare we killed a Buffalow and fared Sumpiously that night while the rest of the Company remained in the Kenyon without room to lie down."

Following any of the streams farther into the mountains was out of the question because they "ware shure to meet with rocky inaccessible places . . . this portion of the mountain furnished our horses with no food and they began to be verry poor and weak so we left 3 men and five horses behind . . . while the rest of us proceded on ther being some sighn of Beaver in the vicinity and hoping soon to find more where we Might all Stop for a time."[98]

Assuming Crow Indians were nearby, Rose, who had lived among the Crow almost fifteen years earlier, "was dispatched ahead to find the Crows and try to induce some of them to come to our assistance." Late that afternoon, "while passing through a Brushy bottom a large Grssley [Grizzly Bear] came down the vally [and] struck us about the center [of a file of men leading packhorses on foot] . . . Capt. Smith being in the advance he ran to the open ground and as he immerged from the thicket he and the bear met face to face." The bear lunged forward and slammed Smith to the ground, man and beast "pitc[h]ing sprawling on the earth," the grizzly going for Smith's head and "middle," with at least one blow being deflected by a ball pouch and butcher knife. Smith's comrades presumably saved him by shooting the bear, but Clyman was silent on that subject. What was clear was that the behemoth had broken several of the captain's ribs and cut him badly.

Clyman and his fellows knelt beside the groaning man, desperate to help him but "none of [them] having any surgical Knowledge what was to be done," bewildered at the same time. "I asked Capt what was best," wrote Clyman. "He said one or 2 [go] for water and if you have a needle and thread git it out and sew up my wounds around my head which was bleeding badly." Taking courage from Smith's remarkable composure, Clyman cut Smith's hair with a pair of scissors and began dressing the wounds. "Upon examination I [found] the bear had taken nearly all his head in his capcious mouth close to his left eye on one side and clos to his right ear on the other and laid the skull bare to near the crown of his head leaving a white streak whare his teeth passed," with one of Smith's ears "torn from his head out to the outer rim."

Clyman did his best, "stitching all the other wounds . . . according to the captains directions the ear being the last I told him I could do nothing for his Eare. O you must try to stich up some way or other said he then I put my needle stiching it through and through and over and over laying the lacerated parts togather as nice as I could with my hands." The men sent for water returned, saying they had found an ample stream about a mile away. Smith was somehow able to mount a horse, and the group set up a camp near the water, pitching the only tent they had for Smith and making him as comfortable as possible. "This gave us a lesson on the character of the grissly Baare which we did not forget," said Clyman.[99]

For the rest of his life, Smith wore his hair long, so that it would cover his scars, especially the one on his ear. And although he would become one of the best-known mountain men, the grizzly bear attack that entrenched itself into American memory was one inflicted not on Smith but on a lesser-known Ashley man: Hugh Glass. At the Arikara ambush in June, Glass had fought beside Smith, Fitzpatrick, and the others, and had written a memorable letter to the father of John Gardner, one of those killed on the sandbar, telling of Smith's powerful prayer at Gardner's burial. A few weeks before Smith's contingent ascended the White River from Fort Kiowa, Henry had led Glass and several others north to the Grand River, which they ascended to the west, just as Hunt's Astorians had done in 1811. Glass was out hunting for game late in September when, in the words of James Hall, who got his information secondhand, a grizzly bear "that had imbedded herself in the sand, arose within three yards of him, and before he could 'set his triggers,' to turn to retreat, he was seized by the throat, and raised from the ground. Casting him again upon the earth, his grim adversary tore out a mouthful of the cannibal food which had excited her appetite."[100]

Glass's companions killed the bear but could do little for Glass. In one of his less honorable moments, Henry decided to lead most of his men to the fort at the mouth of the Yellowstone while rewarding two—John S. Fitzgerald and young Jim Bridger—for staying with Glass until he passed. After five days, fearing an Indian attack and believing Glass was on the verge of dying, Fitzgerald and Bridger gave up, leaving Glass to die alone and taking his gun and ammunition. Somehow Glass survived, making it back to Fort Kiowa early in October, his exploit becoming the stuff of legend.[101]

Smith's "face to face" meeting with a grizzly had happened several weeks after Glass's and in Wyoming's Powder River basin, three or four hundred miles to the southwest. "After remaining here ten days or 2 weeks the capt. Began to ride out a few miles and as winter was rapidly approaching we began to make easy travel west ward and Struck the trail of Shian Indians the next day we came to their village traded and swaped a few horses with them and continued our march . . . to the waters of Powder River Running West and north." Not long after that, "Rose with 15 or 16 Crow Indians came to our camp as soon as we raised a fire in the evenin . . . they the Crows brought us several spare Horses which relieved our Broke down animals and gave us a chance to ride but they caused us to travel to fast for our poor horses and so Capt Smith gave them what they could pack sending Rose with them."[102]

Smith and his men followed at their "own gait stoping and Traping for beaver occasionly." The November nights were "frosty" but the days generally warm and pleasant. "On Tongue river we struck the trail of the . . . Crow Indians Passed over another ridge of mountains [Owl Creek Mountains] we came on to Wind River." They moved farther up the river; then, with "slight Snows and Strong north winds" prevailing and men and horses "completely exhausted," they "halted for the winter," likely near present Dubois, Wyoming, where John Colter had apparently wintered with a band of Crow Indians seventeen years earlier.[103]

"In February [1824]," continued Clyman, "we made an effort to cross the mountains north of the wind River [r]ange but found the snow too deep and had to return." This was Union Pass, which Hunt's westbound Astorians had crossed in September of 1811 (and which at least some of Henry's eastbound men had quite likely crossed in late 1810 or early 1811). Hearing of their interest in trapping beaver, a Crow chief gave them a tip. "While among the Crows the Major [Fitzpatrick] learned from a chief that a pass existed in the Wind river mountains, through which he could easily take his whole band upon the streams on the other side," wrote John S. Robb, who apparently interviewed Fitzpatrick. "He also represented beaver so abundant upon these rivers that traps were unnecessary to catch them—they could club as many as they desired."[104]

When Clyman spoke to Richard Tremaine Montgomery, a former newspaper editor who obtained Clyman's records for Hubert Howe Bancroft in 1871, he added this information: "I spread out a buffalo robe and covered it with sand, and made it in heaps to represent the different mountains, (we were then encamped at the lower point of the Wind River Mountains) and from our sand map with the help of the Crows, finally got the idea that we could go to Green River, called by them Seeds-ka-day."[105]

Ashley's men had started out with intentions of crossing to the waters of the Columbia. What they intended to do had they been able to scale Union Pass is not clear—because the Gros Ventre River (a tributary of the Columbia via the Snake) and the Green River were both accessible from that point. Now, however, like Stuart's men, they were clearly searching for South Pass and, also like Stuart, they had been told of the gap by Indians.

In attempting to find this "dividing ridge between the Atlantic and Pacific," wrote Clyman, they descended the Wind River to the mouth of the Popo Agie (near present Lander), then ascended the latter, and then "moved over a low ridge and Struck on [the] Sweet Water [River] . . . close to the East foot of the wind River mountain," where they encamped on a "cold and clear" evening. The next morning they moved to an aspen grove, where they "remained some two or three weeks Subsisting on Mountain sheep" because they were "overtaken by one of the heaviest falls of snow" they had ever seen.

Leaving the camp when the mountain sheep finally got scarce, they dug a cache to store "Powder Lead and several other articles supposed to be not needed in our Springs hunt." Next they "struck in a south westerly direction," but there was "no game to be found." Luckily, Clyman and his traveling partner, Sublette, managed to bring down a buffalo by shooting at different parts of the animal simultaneously. "Our company coming up we butchered our meat in short order many of the men eating large slices raw." Then they packed up their meat and went on in hopes of finding water but found only "large clumps of sage brush"—with melting snow as the sole hydration source for both horses and men. They camped, rose early the next morning, and proceeded on. Illustrating how little South Pass resembles the mountain defiles the men were used to, Clyman wrote: "Continuing on we found we had crossed the main ridge [South Pass] of the Rocky mountain [the previous day]."

South Pass had been rediscovered. As to whether credit should be given to Smith or Fitzpatrick, Clyman, who mentioned neither of them in his main narrative, settled the matter in his 1844 diary when he was in the area again and noted being "near to whare we encamped in January 1824 at which time we under J. Smith and T Fitzpatrick first traversed the now well known South pass." [106]

No one recorded the day—or the month—of this rediscovery; even Clyman wasn't sure because he said February at one point and January at another. Such scholars as Dale Morgan, LeRoy Hafen, and John Sunder agree the monumental passage took place in March. [107]

On June 7, 1824, as the postscript to a short news article reporting that three of Henry's men had been killed by Arikara Indians, the *St. Louis Enquirer* added that according to the same source, "Captain [Jedediah] Smith, with some of the party, had crossed the mountains." [108]

6

"THE MARCH OF OVER
TWO THOUSAND MILES"

On February 14, 1831, ten months after the church had been organized in New York, a Mormon missionary by the name of Oliver Cowdery, cofounder of the new American religion with Joseph Smith, wrote a letter from Missouri's Kaw Township to the superintendent of Indian affairs in St. Louis, William Clark. "As I have been appointed by a society of Christians in the State of New York to superintend the establishing Missions among the Indians," wrote Cowdery, "I doubt not but I shall have the approbation of your honour and a permit for myself and all who may be recommended to me by that Society to have free intercourse with the several tribes in establishing schools for the instruction of their children and also teaching them the Christian religion without intruding or interfering with any other Mission now established."[1]

Not long after their arrival in western Missouri in late January of 1831, Cowdery and two of his companions had crossed the Kansas River into unorganized US territory to preach to the Delaware Indians. The missionaries were well received and had a lengthy conversation with the Delaware chief William Anderson. During the previous two years, as a result of Andrew Jackson's Indian removal policies, the Delaware had been dislocated from southwestern Missouri to present Kansas—after their dislocation from Indiana to Missouri a decade earlier. Federal Indian agent Richard Cummins ordered Cowdery and the others to stop because they had no license. In a letter of his own to Clark, Cummins wrote:

A few days agoe three Men all Strangers to me, went among the
Indians Shawnees & Delawares, they say for the purpose of preaching to and Instructing them in Religious Matters, they say they are
sent by God and must proceed, . . . they say . . . that an Angel from
Heaven appeared to one of their Men and two others of their Sect,
and shewed them that the work was from God, and much more &c. I
have refused to let them stay or, go among the Indians unless they
first obtain permission from you or, some of the officers of the Genl.
Government who I am bound to obey. I am informed that they
intend to apply to you for permission to go among the Indians, if you
refuse, then they will go to the Rocky Mountains, but what they will
be with the Indians. The Men act very strange.[2]

There is no record of Clark responding to either Cowdery or Cummins. The missionaries stayed on the Missouri side of the border and
went about supporting themselves and preaching to the Missourians. In
May, Cowdery wrote another letter, this one to Joseph Smith and others in Ohio, saying he had been informed of a tribe of Indians "who
have abundance of flocks of the best kind of sheep & cattle and manu-
facture blankets of superior quality the tribe is very numerous they live
three hundred miles west of Santafee and are called navahoes."[3] It was
hardly a surprise that Cowdery's interest had been piqued by news of
the Navajo nation because he and his companions had journeyed west
for the express purpose of preaching to American Indians, whom they
believed to be descendants of a Book of Mormon people called Lamanites.

Cowdery offered no further details, but in recent days Kaw Township—formed only four years earlier—had likely been abuzz about the
arrival of a large company of traders from St. Louis. The party of eighty-
five men (well armed with knives, pistols, and rifles), scores of horses,
and twenty-three wagons overflowing with food, supplies, equipment,
and trade goods and drawn by six mules each, accompanied by the
predictable pack of barking dogs, must have made quite a commotion as
it lumbered across the Big Blue River into the helter-skelter town of a
few hundred settlers.[4]

The traders were making final preparations before embarking on the
Santa Fe Trail. It is quite likely that Cowdery heard about the Navajo
nation from one or more of these men. On May 4, three days before
Cowdery wrote his letter, the caravan had headed west, led by Jedediah

Smith, Bill Sublette, and David Jackson, now trying their luck in the Southwest after several years in the Rockies. As Dale Morgan writes, "Although none of them had traveled the Santa Fe Trail before, Jedediah and his companions were old hands on the plains and took in their stride the protracted drizzles, punctuated by occasional violent winds out of the northwest."[5]

In August of 1830, Smith, Sublette, and Jackson, who had bought out Ashley in 1826, sold their firm to Tom Fitzpatrick, Jim Bridger, Milton Sublette, Henry Fraeb, and Jean Baptiste Gervais. In March of 1831, Fitzpatrick had set out from the Yellowstone River to purchase supplies for the new company in St. Louis. This was the first time Fitzpatrick had returned to "the States" since his departure with Ashley in 1823. He happened to arrive in Lexington, Missouri, about the same time as Smith, Sublette, and Jackson—his potential suppliers. "The only thing that Fitzpatrick could do upon meeting them was to make arrangements for supplies on their terms," writes Hafen. "Thus it was agreed that Fitzpatrick would accompany the wagon caravan to Santa Fe and that there the traders would provide him with the desired goods. This would make a long, roundabout route, but what alternative was there?"[6]

Fitzpatrick was therefore among the band of traders when they pulled into Kaw Township. Also present was twenty-five-year-old Jonathan Trumball Warner, a year younger than Cowdery, and, like Cowdery, a native New Englander. He had suffered ill health in the spring and summer of 1830, and his physician recommended that he go west in search of a milder climate. "I was swept westerly by the strong and uninterrupted current of humanity flowing in that direction until I arrived in St. Louis in November [1830]," he later wrote.[7]

"Partly from the novelty of going to the mountains, and partly from the hope of further improvement in health, I sought for this purpose an interview with Mr. [Jedediah] Smith," continued Warner, who offered this description of Smith:

> Instead of finding a leather stocking I met a well-bred, intelligent and Christian gentleman, who repressed my youthful ardor and fancied pleasures for the life of a trapper and mountaineer by informing me that if I went into the Rocky Mountains the chances were much greater in favor of meeting death than of finding a restoration to health, and that if I escaped the former and secured the latter, the

probabilities were that I would be ruined for anything else in life than such things as would be agreeable to the passions of a semi-savage. He said that he had spent about eight years in the mountains and should not return to them.[8]

Circumstances caused Smith to change his mind, reported Warner, who readily accepted Smith's offer of employment. They had left St. Louis about the first of April.

Warner made no mention of meeting any Mormons in Kaw Township, but the presence of such prominent Mormons and such prominent frontiersmen at the head of the Santa Fe Trail was a powerful portent of things to come. Fifteen years later, an army commanded by William Clark's son-in-law would combine with four hundred Mormon volunteers and a handful of mountain men to make a historic odyssey along and beyond the Santa Fe Trail, with none other than Thomas Fitzpatrick playing a key role.

✿ ✿ ✿

In February of 1846, less than two years after Joseph Smith and his brother Hyrum had been martyred by a mob, the Latter-day Saints began fleeing their beloved city of Nauvoo, Illinois, and heading west across the frozen Mississippi. They were led by senior apostle Brigham Young (who would officially replace Smith as church president in 1847). After carefully studying John C. Frémont's maps, Young had decided to cross the plains and the Rocky Mountains and settle in the sparsely populated Great Basin. He had assumed that the Saints could reach the Missouri River from Nauvoo in five or six weeks, leaving plenty of time for an advance party to travel to the Great Basin that summer and for other pioneers to build way stations along the way. Unusually rainy weather, however, thwarted all these plans by turning southern Iowa into a muddy quagmire. The Mormons, many now sick, had labored for four months—in what seemed to be one endless wagon train fording flooded rivers and fighting virtual quicksand—to reach the Missouri at Council Bluffs, in present Iowa. Going farther west that year was clearly out of the question. As Richard E. Bennett has written, "Exhausted, ill-provisioned, unwelcomed, and scattered across a wilderness of three hundred miles, 12,000 to 15,000 Latter-day Saints camped in peril."[9]

Luckily—or providentially, from the Saints' perspective—an influential Pennsylvanian by the name of Thomas L. Kane began taking an interest in the Mormons at the same time they were trudging westward. On May 13, 1846, the same day that the United States declared war against Mexico, Kane attended a Mormon meeting in Philadelphia and met Jesse C. Little, an emissary of Young. Through Kane's efforts, Little was able to meet with President James K. Polk, who wrote in his diary: "I told Mr. Little that we were at war with Mexico, and asked him if 500 or more of the Mormons now on their way to California would be willing on their arrival in that country to volunteer and enter the U.S. army in that war, under the command of a U.S. Officer. He said he had no doubt they would willingly do so."[10]

Polk believed the Mormons would soon arrive in California and did not want them to enter the army before then. "Yet Polk's intentions were overruled by an ambiguous order that failed to convey clearly the decision so firmly agreed upon by both the president and the secretary of war."[11] The upshot was that the Mormons stranded at the Missouri were promptly recruited into military service.

The commander at Fort Leavenworth, in present northeast Kansas, was fifty-one-year-old Colonel Stephen Watts Kearny—who had married William Clark's stepdaughter, Mary Radford, in 1830. Clark and Kearny had known each other since at least 1826 and got along well. While there is no evidence they were particularly close, Kearny's style, both as a military officer and a family man, was quite reminiscent of Clark's.[12]

In mid-June of 1846, Kearny received orders from the secretary of war to conquer and take possession of New Mexico and upper California. The same letter authorized him to muster into service as many Mormon volunteers as possible—as long as the total did not exceed one-third of his entire force. Kearny welcomed the prospect of enlisting the Mormons and ordered Captain James Allen "to proceed to [the Mormon camps in Iowa] and endeavor to raise from amongst them 4 or 5 Companies of Volunteers to join me in my expedition to [California]. . . . They will under your command follow on my trail in the direction of Santa Fe, & where you will receive further orders from me."[13] Shortly after Allen went north, Kearny, now promoted to brigadier general, departed Fort Leavenworth for New Mexico. With him were "a total of 1,600 men, including infantry, cavalry, and artillery, with 1,556 wagons and nearly 20,000 oxen, mules and horses."[14]

Allen arrived at Council Bluffs late in June and made his first attempt to recruit Mormon men. The Mormons were quite skeptical at first but began enlisting in droves after Young and others, including Kane, who had recently arrived from the East, urged them to do so. The military pay would help send hundreds of families west in 1847, and the enlistment would also calm fears about Mormon loyalty to the US and secure permission for the remaining Saints to winter on Indian land near the Missouri.

Captain Allen spent three weeks recruiting men from the scattered Iowa camps; by mid-July more than 450 men had enlisted. Allen announced that they would be known as the Mormon Battalion, US Army of the West. "The battalion was mustered into service July 16, and Captain Allen took command as [Lieutenant] Colonel," wrote Henry Bigler, a single, thirty-year-old Mormon enlistee from present West Virginia. "The same day he marched us some six or eight miles to a trading post on the Missouri River kept by some Frenchmen. I think the proprietor's name was Sarpea. Here Colonel Allen issued to his men blankets, provision, camp kettles, knives, forks, plates, spoons, etc."[15]

The men, who also stocked up with coffee and sugar, had thus met the first of several mountain men they would encounter over the next several months—Peter Sarpy. Now forty-four, Sarpy had been a prominent trader along the Missouri, Kansas, and Platte Rivers for more than a decade. His station on the Missouri, made up of about twenty log homes whitewashed on the outside, has been called "one of the most strategically located posts" on that river, and he traded with trappers, pioneers, soldiers, and Indians alike. He was known as an expert in dealing with the Otto, Omaha, and Pawnee nations in the area. In a few years he would also do excellent business with California gold seekers. He offered "tin cups, traps, all manner of wearing apparel, blankets . . . and the inevitable whiskey supply," as well as robes and pelts.[16]

Like many a frontiersman, Sarpy had ridden with Fitzpatrick, but of the multitude of men who had trapped or explored with Fitzpatrick, Sarpy alone had explained why the Indians gave him the name "Broken Hand," also rendered as "Bad Hand" or "Three Fingers."

According to an 1847 Missouri newspaper article that named Sarpy as its source, in 1835 he and Fitzpatrick "were out together on an excursion thro' these desert regions, and had occasion to separate, with an understanding of where they were to meet." Not long after that, Fitzpatrick was chased by Blackfoot Indians and ran his horse off a cliff into the Yellowstone River in an effort to escape. Although Fitzpatrick then swam across the river, the Indians were still close behind. Fitzpatrick "had recourse to his rifle, but in his haste to pull off the cover, by some mismanagement received the contents of his piece in the left wrist, which was frightfully shattered with the discharge. Not daunted by the accident, he reloaded and fired, killing two of his pursuers before he left the spot. He then made for the woods, and dodged his enemies for some days, who . . . kept on his trail, until wearied with the fruitless result of their efforts to make a prisoner of the fugitive." Thirty days later, Fitzpatrick was reunited with Sarpy and related the details of his remarkable escape.[17]

"Broken Hand" Fitzpatrick had subsequently guided everyone from John Bidwell and Father Pierre-Jean De Smet to John C. Frémont across the Rockies. In addition, in 1845 he had led Kearny and five companies of the First Dragoons over the Oregon Trail to South Pass and Fort Laramie, returning to Fort Leavenworth by way of Bent's Fort (in present Colorado). The purpose of the ninety-nine-day expedition was to remind Indian nations of the military might of the US and discourage them from harming Oregon Trail pioneers. Next, when war with Mexico broke out, Kearny sent word to Fitzpatrick, then in St. Louis, to come to Fort Leavenworth straightaway.

Fitzpatrick complied, and shortly before Captain Allen left the fort for Council Bluffs, Captain Benjamin Moore, with two companies of Dragoons and Fitzpatrick as guide, rode south to stop a Santa Fe Trail caravan reportedly carrying weapons and ammunition to be sold to Mexican authorities. Moore advanced along the mountain route of the trail, ordering several wagon trains not to go beyond Bent's Fort but not catching the party in question. When Moore reached Bent's Fort, he sent Fitzpatrick back the way they had come with a message for Kearny. Fitzpatrick met Kearny that same day and traveled with him back to Bent's Fort, where hundreds of traders—who had arrived with more than four hundred wagons and with merchandise valued at more than a million dollars—were waiting for permission to proceed.

"The Fort is crowded to overflowing," wrote one observer. "Col. Kearny has arrived, and it seems the world is coming with him. . . . There is the greatest possible noise in the *patio*. The shoeing of horses, neighing, and braying of mules, the crying of children, the scolding and fighting of men, are all enough to turn my head."[18]

While at the fort, Fitzpatrick got notice that he had been appointed a federal Indian agent but would be allowed to continue with Kearny for the duration of the campaign. On July 31, 1846, Fitzpatrick wrote to his friend Andrew Sublette: "Late news which we received from Santa fee would indicate that we shall have no fighting, and indeed it has always been my opinion that there would not be a blow struck at Santa fee, whatever may be the case elsewhere. I know not, but from what I can learn the campaign will not end in New Mexico."[19]

On August 1, Fitzpatrick proceeded on to New Mexico with Kearny's Army of the West.

✿ ✿ ✿

General Kearny was now leading his troops into a West radically different from the one William Clark had known at his death in 1838. First, the Republic of Texas had joined the Union on December 29, 1845; second, the US and Britain had signed the Oregon Treaty on June 15, 1846, paving the way for the present states of Washington, Oregon, and Idaho, and sections of Montana and Wyoming to become a US territory (which happened in 1848); third, the war with Mexico would presumably allow Kearny to take control of present New Mexico, Arizona, California, Nevada, and Utah. Jefferson's vision of a sea-to-sea nation was on the verge of becoming reality. Anticipating and hoping for such events, in July of 1845, the prominent journalist and editor John L. O'Sullivan had urged the annexation of Texas as a response to foreign interference, which, he wrote, exists "for the avowed object of . . . checking the fulfillment of our manifest destiny to overspread the continent allotted by Providence for the free development of our yearly multiplying millions."[20]

The term *manifest destiny* "was not wholly new," writes Frederick Merk. "Phrases like it had been used before, but this precise combination of words was novel and right for a mood, and it became part of the language. It meant expansion, prearranged by Heaven, over an area not clearly defined."[21]

* * *

Colonel Allen and his battalion of Mormons arrived at Fort Leavenworth the same day Kearny left Bent's Fort. The two-hundred-mile journey had taken twelve days; it had not been easy.

Allen had requested able-bodied men, ages eighteen to forty-five. He got more than he bargained for. So many men volunteered that he relaxed the rules and filled five complete companies, one more than the total required for his two-rank promotion to lieutenant colonel. The oldest recruit of the 496 men was sixty-seven, the youngest fourteen. Virtually all of them marched, often in scorching heat the first several weeks. There were thirty-four women (twenty hired as laundresses) and forty-four children also present, some riding in wagons. Allen and six other members of the command staff rode on horseback, and teamsters drove the wagons, bringing the grand total to about six hundred people. Three days out, the battalion saw its first death when Samuel Boley died of an illness.[22]

The group spent almost two weeks at Fort Leavenworth and departed for Santa Fe on August 13. "The weather was still hot," wrote Bigler, "and the roads half-leg deep with dust and sand, water scarce, for the brooks and creeks were dry, and it seemed that some of our sick would die for want of water." A violent storm brought no relief but made things worse, capsizing tents and blowing some wagons "several rods into the brush." Hail fell so hard that the horses and mules "put for the timber, leaving their masters to face the storm themselves on an open prairie. This was severe on our sick."[23]

Colonel Allen, quite popular among the Mormons, had taken ill at the fort and remained there, hoping to catch up with the battalion later. The entire group prayed for his recovery, but "on the twenty-sixth," wrote Bigler, "our quartermaster (Mr. Gully) arrived from the garrison announcing the sorrowful fact of his death."[24] Three days later, the Mormons selected a shady grove near a creek and held a funeral service for Allen and also for teamster John Bosco and his wife, Jane, who had died two days apart from illness.

Now led by Lieutenant Andrew J. Smith, the group followed the Santa Fe Trail through present central Kansas. Enduring heat, cold, wind, wagon accidents, near drownings, a lightning strike that killed a cow, one desertion, conflicts with non-Mormon officers and among the Mormons themselves, and constant maladies that included blistered feet, and "ague and fever and billious and congestion," the battalion marched on.[25]

On September 8 the Arkansas River came into view. "This river is a curiosity in creation," wrote one of the Mormons. "It appears to be a river of sand with now and then a drizzling of water breaking out and then loosing itself again immediately."[26]

Smith knew they would soon reach an important fork in the Santa Fe Trail. The "Mountain Route" followed the Arkansas as it went west and slightly north, into present Colorado, to Bent's Fort. It then crossed the Arkansas and cut southwest into the northeastern corner of present New Mexico. This was the route taken by Kearny and Fitzpatrick several weeks earlier. The "Cimarron Route" crossed the Arkansas immediately and cut to the southwest, clipping the southeast corner of present Colorado and the northeast corner of present Oklahoma before entering New Mexico and rejoining the Mountain Route. Colonel Allen had planned on taking the Mountain Route, but circumstances had changed and Lieutenant Smith now planned to take the Cimarron Route because it was a good deal shorter.

This fork in the road took on added significance a few days later when the battalion met a party of eight men heading east. To the astonishment of the Mormons, most of the eight were fellow Latter-day Saints and some of them were well acquainted with the battalion members from the Nauvoo days. The leader was a convert from Mississippi by the name of John Brown. During the winter of 1845–1846, Brigham Young, still planning to cross to the Great Basin during the summer of 1846, instructed Brown to return to Mississippi, gather the Mormons there, and travel to the Platte River, where they would meet up with the main body of Saints trekking westward.

Brown reported that the Mississippi Saints had gone west as requested and on May 2, 1846, reached Independence, Missouri—near Cowdery's 1831 location at a spot now considered sacred—and joined there with some Mormons from Illinois and a few non-Mormon pioneers. The party, consisting of forty-three people and nineteen wagons, next followed the Oregon Trail into present Kansas and then to Grand Island on the Platte River (in present Nebraska), where they fully expected to meet a large company of Mormons heading west. They were puzzled when they saw no sign of the Nauvoo Mormons (then strung out across southern Iowa, of course).

This Mississippi company soon experienced a series of meetings with helpful mountain men, and one of those meetings, with an adventurer they called "Reshaw," turned out to be serendipitous for more than two hundred members of the battalion.

After waiting a week, Brown and the others reluctantly continued west along the Oregon Trail, more and more troubled about the absence of fellow believers. Around June 25, in western Nebraska, they met an experienced Spanish mountain man by the name of Jose. Although he was traveling east, he reversed his course and guided the Mormons west a few days. "He was of great service to me in camp life and helping to care for the animals," wrote Brown, "and also taught us how to approach the buffalo."[27]

On July 2, the Mormons met the storied mountaineer James Clyman, now in his midfifties, going east after having journeyed from California via present Nevada and Utah. "We arrived at the ash Hallow whare we found a company of Mormon Emigrants Encamped consisting of nineteen wagons," Clyman wrote in his diary. "These people are on their way to Oregon and informed us that the Pawnees had followed them and stole three horses last night."[28]

Clyman, who had traveled the Oregon Trail through most of Wyoming, told the Mississippi group that he had not seen any other Mormons on the trail. "There was considerable dissatisfaction in the camp," wrote Brown. "Some were in favor of turning back. However, we went on." On July 6 they passed Chimney Rock, stopping for the day at Horse Creek to repair wagons. The group now continued northwest, into present Wyoming and toward Fort Laramie (about twenty miles northwest of present Torrington, Wyoming). "A few miles below Laramie," wrote Brown, "we met with Mr. John Reshaw."[29]

This was thirty-six-year-old John Baptiste Richard, born of French descent in St. Charles, Missouri. He had gone west in the late 1830s and within a few years became a prominent trader along the North Platte River. He was a small but strong and athletic man who parted his shoulder-length black hair in the middle and was typically dressed in a buckskin frock, fringed leggings, and moccasins, all adorned with dyed porcupine quills. At Fort Platte, which was just a mile from Fort Laramie, Richard had made a name for himself because of his skill at smuggling liquor in from New Mexico.

Richard had heard that the Mormons were going up the South Platte River. If true, that meant they had abandoned the Oregon Trail, for the South Platte originated southwest of present Denver. "We held a council and concluded to go no further west but find a place for the company to winter on the east side of the [Rocky] mountains," remembered Brown. "Mr. Reshaw said that the head of the Arkansas River was the best place," wrote Brown, "as there was some corn growing there and it was near the Spanish country where the company could get supplies. He was going to Pueblo in a few days with two ox teams, there being no road and as he was acquainted with the route, we concluded to stop and go with him."[30]

There was one other advantage to going south to Fort Pueblo with Richard: They would travel along the South Platte River and be able to check for signs of the larger Mormon company—a slim possibility at best given their understanding that Brigham Young planned to lead the Saints along the Oregon Trail virtually all the way to the Great Basin. Regardless, the Mormons, who agreed to protect Richard's furs in return for his guiding them, moved over to Richard's camp, and on July 10 the combined party departed for Pueblo. "Mr. Reshaw proved faithful to us and rendered all the assistance he could on the plains and among the Indians," noted Brown.[31] Richard's friendship with the Cheyenne nation proved particularly valuable. On July 24, Richard, Brown, and several others were hunting buffalo with a friendly Indian when they became separated on the plain. Brown told what happened next:

> While thus scattered, we were discovered by a large party of Indians who had not seen us before. They immediately rushed upon us, apparently with great fury. We tried to get together before they could reach us, but in vain. . . . Our Indian was quite a distance away . . . but as soon as he saw what was going on, he came with all possible speed. He met his countrymen within one hundred yards of us. We yet did not know whether they were hostile or not. They soon reached out the hand for the usual "howdy do" which was a very pleasing sight to us. This kind of approach for friendship was new to

us. Mr. Reshaw was with us and I watched him all the time to see if he was alarmed, but he betrayed no fear. He was well acquainted with the chief whose name in English was Slim Face.[32]

Staying about fifteen or twenty miles west of the present Wyoming-Nebraska border, Richard led the Mormons south, entering Colorado just south of present Carpenter, Wyoming. They then followed Crow Creek to its mouth and ascended the South Platte past Fort St. Vrain, searching in vain for any sign of Brigham Young's party. Southwest of present Denver, they followed Plum Creek, then East Plum Creek, and then Fountain Monument Creek through the present Colorado Springs area and finally south to Fort Pueblo, arriving on August 7.

"We found some six or eight mountaineers in the fort with their families," wrote Brown. "They had Indian and Spanish women for wives. We were received very kindly and they seemed pleased to see us. . . . We counseled the brethren [who would be staying at Pueblo] to prepare for winter to build them some cabins in the form of a fort. The mountaineers said they would let them have their supplies, corn for their labor, etc."[33]

The Mormons built their new settlement below the fort on the south bank of the Arkansas River and called it Pueblo. "There the farmers planted pumpkins, melons, and turnips, and prepared fields in which to sow wheat and other crops in the early spring. In the meantime, they could purchase surplus corn at Fort Pueblo for three dollars a bushel or for an equivalent amount of labor, or journey to Taos for flour."[34]

News had reached Fort Pueblo that the main body of Mormons were camped for the winter along the Missouri River and that five hundred Mormons had joined Kearny's army and were on their way to New Mexico. (Such news could have come from Bent's Fort, about seventy miles to the southeast.) Learning this, Brown and several others who still had relatives in Mississippi decided to go east and accompany them the next year to the Saints' gathering place in the West. This group left Pueblo on September 1 and met the Mormon Battalion along the Arkansas River on September 12.

When Lieutenant Andrew Smith learned from John Brown that a group of Mormons were wintering near Fort Pueblo, he ordered Captain Nelson Higgins and ten enlisted men to escort nine or ten Mormon women and thirty-three children, many of them sick, to the new Mormon settlement. This was done over the protests of many battalion members, who wanted the Mormons to stay together, as instructed by Brigham Young.

Smith insisted, however—probably wisely, given the poor health of those in the detachment and the danger from Comanche Indians on the Cimarron Route—and the Higgins party headed west along the Arkansas on September 15, reaching Pueblo on October 5. As far as is known, no one in the group left a diary or other record of their trip, but the Mormons already at Pueblo no doubt gave them a warm welcome. It also quite likely that the friendly "Reshaw," waiting in Pueblo for permission to proceed to Taos, greeted them the way he had recently greeted another party of pilgrims, as described by Francis Parkman:

> Shaking us warmly by the hands, he led the way into the area. Here we saw his large Santa Fe wagons standing together. . . . Richard conducted us to the state apartment of the Pueblo, a small mud room, very neatly furnished, considering the material, and garnished with a crucifix, a looking-glass, a picture of the Virgin, and a rusty horse pistol . . . three or four Spanish girls brought out a poncho, which they spread upon the floor by way of a table-cloth. A supper, which seemed to us luxurious, was soon laid out upon it, and folded buffalo robes were placed around it to receive the guests.[35]

Still, the Mormon exodus to Pueblo had barely begun.

Not long after Higgins departed, the battalion crossed the Arkansas and began their journey along the Cimarron Route, where food and water were considerably less plentiful. On September 18, they had been without water for almost two days. "Finally," writes a leading scholar of the history of the battalion, "they came to a stagnant pond, but had to drive buffalo from it. The water was thick with buffalo urine, bugs, and rain water. The soldiers rushed to it, layed down, and sucked and strained the water through their teeth to keep from swallowing the bugs."[36]

Such miserable circumstances were compounded by a continual conflict between the Mormons, many of whom were sick, and the company surgeon, George W. Sanderson, who prescribed calomel for virtually any illness. Brigham Young had instructed the Mormons to rely on faith, the laying on of hands, and botanic cures and not to take medicine. The sick men found themselves with deeply divided loyalties, especially when their commanding officer, Lieutenant Smith, ordered them to comply with the doctor's treatment. When battalion member Alva Phelps died, Bigler wrote, "It was believed that Doctor Sanderson's medicine killed him; he give calomel, and the sick are almost physicked to death."[37]

"We marched nearly 15 miles," William Coray wrote on September 23. "Very sandy all the way . . . teams gave out. A storm this evening with every appearance of the equinox. Sickness raged high—10 in our co. and from 35 to 40 in the battalion—some of them very sick."[38]

On October 2, "some messengers . . . brought an express from Kearny stating that the Mormon Battalion if they were not there [Santa Fe] within 8 days could not be fitted out for California."[39] Smith quickly organized fifty men from each company to proceed with him—and with good teams and wagons—to reach Santa Fe by the tenth. Lieutenant George Oman, leading a group that included many sick men, women, and children riding in broken wagons—would follow at a much slower pace.

On October 9, the advance company, "a well drilled, shabby-looking set" according to one observer, fixed their bayonets, drew their swords, and marched into Santa Fe's public square.[40] The commander of Fort Marcy, situated on a hill overlooking the town, was Colonel Alexander Doniphan, who had been a friend of the Mormons in Missouri and had saved Joseph Smith from being executed by a military firing squad. Doniphan welcomed the Mormons with a one-hundred-gun salute. Several of the men soon met with their new commander, Lieutenant Colonel Philip St. George Cooke, "who received [them] with much courtesy & conversed freely."[41]

Thirty-two years later, Cooke wrote:

> Every thing conspired to discourage the extraordinary undertaking of marching this battalion eleven hundred miles, for the much greater part through an unknown wilderness without road or trail, and with a wagon train. It was enlisted too much by families; some were too old, some feeble, and some too young; it was embarrassed by many women; it was undisciplined; it was much worn by traveling on foot and marching from Nauvoo, Illinois; their clothing was very scant; there was no money to pay them or clothing to issue; their mules were utterly broken down; the quartermaster department was without funds and its credit bad; and mules were scarce.[42]

To deal with at least some of these realities, Cooke ordered Captain James Brown, a Mormon, to take the sick men and all twenty laundresses and their children to the Mormon settlement at Pueblo. The husbands of the laundresses objected to being separated from their wives and took the matter to Colonel Doniphan. He consulted with Cooke, who announced that the husbands, most or all of whom were in good health, could accompany their wives to Pueblo.

This meant that five women, all wives of battalion members, were still with Cooke's party. One of the women, Lydia Hunter, was pregnant, and another, Phebe Brown, had a young son with her. Cooke did not say why these women and their husbands were not sent to Pueblo.

On October 18, Brown and a lieutenant led sixty-six sick men, the twenty husbands of the laundresses, and the women themselves and their children southeast toward San Miguel. This party of well over a hundred souls would follow the Mountain Route to Bent's Fort and then go east to Pueblo. Two of the sick men died on the way. The group arrived at Pueblo on November 17 and pitched their tents near the eighteen log cabins already constructed. "The greetings which occurred between comrades and old friends, husbands and wives, parents and children, when the two detachments met, was quite touching," wrote one man. "A thrill of joy ran through the camp which none but those living martyrs can fully comprehend."[43]

❊ ❊ ❊

General Kearny and his three hundred Dragoons had set out from Santa Fe for California on September 25, with Fitzpatrick as guide and Antoine Robidoux as interpreter. They followed the Rio Grande south, and the first part of the journey went well. On October 6, at the New Mexico town of Socorro, Kearny was surprised to meet a party of sixteen mountaineers on their way to Santa Fe. "Came into camp late," wrote one of Kearny's men, "and found [Kit] Carson with an express from California, bearing intelligence that the country had surrendered without a blow, and that the American flag floated in every port."[44]

Fitzpatrick and his old friend Kit Carson no doubt shared a joyful reunion. Fifteen years earlier, in 1831, Fitzpatrick, fifteen years Carson's senior, had hired the twenty-one-year-old greenhorn in Taos, New Mexico, for a Rocky Mountain fur trade expedition, and they had crossed paths endless times since then. Carson now explained that he had been serving in California with John C. Frémont a few months earlier when US Navy captain Robert F. Stockton had assumed command—on his own authority—of all US forces in the area. Stockton promoted Frémont to major, and Frémont named Carson one of his lieutenants. Anxious to win the Mexican War in California, Stockton took San Diego without firing a shot. He next went to Los Angeles and employed sailors, marines, and Frémont's "Mounted Riflemen" to take that city. Convinced the war was won, Stockton announced that all of California was now US territory and Frémont was "Military Governor."

Stockton and Frémont then tasked Carson and fifteen rifleman to deliver letters to Senator Thomas Hart Benton—Frémont's father-in-law—and President James K. Polk announcing the victories. One of the men with Carson was Pauline Weaver, a half-Anglo, half-Cherokee Tennessean one year short of fifty. He had trapped and traded in the Rocky Mountains of both the US and Canada, had spent several years in New Mexico, and had trekked across Arizona and California as early as 1831. Carson and Weaver and the others had left Los Angeles on September 5 with orders to deliver the news as fast as possible. Carson later said they "had already worn out and killed thirty mules" by the time they met Kearny. [45]

Kearny did not consider Carson's report good news at all. Taking California had been *his* job, and Secretary of War William Marcy had assured him that US troops in California would be under his command. As Carson's biographer so aptly summed up, "Now, so far as the general knew, he was too late for the action. To make matters worse for him, the California business was commanded by an officer of the US Navy, acting on his own authority, in league with a junior officer of the army's Topographical Engineers." [46]

To Carson's dismay, Kearny announced that he wanted Carson and Fitzpatrick to trade places: Carson would guide Kearny to California while Fitzpatrick would deliver the dispatches. Carson protested. He had promised Stockton and Frémont that he would personally deliver the letters; not only that, but he was planning to stop and see his wife, Josefa, in Taos. Lastly, Fitzpatrick was fully capable of leading the way to California.

None of that moved Kearny, who ordered Carson to accompany him. Carson was so upset that he considered deserting, but he eventually agreed. Kearny, convinced he would see no action, sent two-thirds of his men back to Santa Fe with Fitzpatrick, a decision he profoundly regretted when he did face Mexican hostilities in California. Stockton and Frémont had been naively optimistic, and Kearny would lose some of his best officers in hard-fought battles. When the dust finally settled and Kearny "confronted Frémont, Frémont insisted that he was under Stockton's command, not Kearny's. He refused to take orders. As a result, the general would have him court-martialed for disobeying a superior officer."[47]

Tom Fitzpatrick reached Santa Fe on October 11, two days after Smith's advance party of the Mormon Battalion had arrived, and delivered a letter from Kearny to Cooke. According to one of the Mormons who talked with Cooke after he received the letter, Kearny had ordered Cooke to "fit [the battalion] out with 60 days provisions—not to encumber your selves with baggage as part of the route will be difficult for the passage of wagons & follow on my trail—Mr. Fitz Patrick the Pilot that I sent will conduct you to the Pacific, where you will await further orders. . . . I have sent Mr. Fitzpatrick (the bearer of this) who will conduct you through. He was with Capt Frémont as a pilot through his exploring expedition."[48]

Fitzpatrick had indeed been a scout for Frémont during the latter's second expedition, the same trip where Frémont, Carson, and a few others explored the Bear River valley and the Great Salt Lake late in the summer of 1843.[49] However, this secondhand report of Kearny's letter to Cooke raises two thorny questions. Was the letter (no longer extant) reported accurately? If so, why did Kearny claim—not only once but twice—that Fitzpatrick would "conduct" them west when Kearny had already ordered Fitzpatrick to deliver Stockton and Frémont's dispatches to Washington? Indeed, Fitzpatrick left on October 14 for St. Louis and Washington.

Thus, the well-respected Fitzpatrick, who had been among the eighty-five traders camped not far from Cowdery in 1831 and who would have been an excellent guide for the battalion, had but brief contact—if any—with them before going east.

"My guide," wrote Cooke on October 19, "is Mr. Weaver, sent to me by the general, who met him coming by the Rio Gila from California." That same day, Cooke received another note from Kearny. "I am informed that the wagons have been left rather as a matter of convenience," Cooke wrote in his journal. "I have brought road tools and am determined to take through my wagons. But the experiment is not a fair one, as the mules are nearly broken down at the outset. The only good ones (above twenty, which I bought near Albuquerque) were taken by Mr. Fitzpatrick, who brought an order for the twenty-one best in Santa Fe."[50]

Cooke's journal entry of October 23 showed he had not underestimated the difficulties: "All my servants, too, are sick, and many of the men. Notwithstanding every exertion on my part, eight mules were missing this morning. . . . The road is excessively bad, and it has taken one company seven hours to come eleven miles. . . . I have not one minute of time unoccupied and an unwell. An influenza is prevailing. For several days before today, the heat and dust has been great, whilst I have been kept awake at night (sleeping under three blankets) by cold."[51]

The Mormons had been issued one blanket each.

The next morning, at a ranch near Albuquerque, Cooke was pleased to exchange three worn-out mules for two fresh ones and buy two others. That same day, he met a guide assigned to his party by General Kearny. The new pilot was a forty-one-year-old mountain man with a unique history—though there is no record that he ever disclosed that history to anyone on the battalion. Meriwether Lewis had witnessed his birth, and he, with his French Canadian father and Shoshone Indian mother, had journeyed with Lewis and Clark all the way from the Mandan Indian villages in present North Dakota to the Pacific coast and back. He had been sent to St. Louis as a young boy, and William Clark paid for his room and board and clothing and education. He then went west, to the mouth of the Kansas River (not far from where Oliver Cowdery would preach to the Indians eight years later) to live the kind of life his trader/interpreter father had lived. This life was interrupted, however, when he was befriended by a German duke who took him to Europe. When the young man returned to the States four years later, he was said to have "acquired a classic education and could converse fluently in German, Spanish, French and English, as well as several Indian languages."[52] For the next two decades, he popped up everywhere and with everyone—at the Platte River with Joe Meek, at the Green River with Jim Bridger, on a buffalo hunt with Kit Carson. A traveler who saw him working out of Bent's Fort in 1844 called him "the best man on foot on the plains or in the Rocky Mountains."[53] His name was Baptiste Charbonneau.

William Clark's influence was everywhere.

Charbonneau had spent the last month scouting for Kearny and knew that the general's plan was to follow the Rio Grande south to the area near Elephant Butte and then go west, pick up the Gila River, and follow it into present Arizona. (Whether Kearny and Charbonneau realized they both had close connection to William Clark is unknown.) However, wrote Cooke, "Charbonneau . . . reports that he had examined a route different in part and farther than that taken by the general, viz., to descend the [Rio Grande] river farther and fall into a road from El Paso to the Copper Mines. The report is favorable; but [Charbonneau and the other guides] did not make a thorough examination by any means; and the practicability of the route from the Copper Mines to the Gila is still a problem."[54]

On November 1, Cooke noted that Weaver was dangerously sick. Luckily, another guide arrived the next day. "Of the guides sent me by the general," wrote Cooke, "only Leroux joined me this afternoon; the others have come up tonight more or less drunk."[55]

Born in St. Louis about 1801, Joaquin Antoine Jacques Leroux was a well-educated French Canadian who had been a boyhood friend of Antoine Robidoux, Kearny's interpreter. Leroux was an old Ashley-Henry man who had gone up the Missouri in 1822. Not long after that, he made his way to New Mexico, settled in Taos, married a Mexican woman, and became a Mexican citizen. In the late 1820s he trapped in southern Colorado with the Robidoux brothers. In the 1830s he trapped the Gila and Colorado Rivers and their tributaries. By the time the Mexican War began, Leroux had seen much of the Southwest.

Leroux said Cooke was "not half so well fitted out to carry wagons as the general was." Further, Leroux "asserts that it is twelve hundred miles and at least ninety days' travel from here. Very discouraging . . . I send [Leroux] forward in the morning with all the guides but Charbonneau and Weaver (sick), to explore the plains beyond the point we leave the river (perhaps not more than fifty miles) and return to meet me there."[56]

"A man of Company A has died this evening," Cooke wrote on November 3. The man's name was George Hampton. "His death was very sudden. . . . The last two nights have been very cold, with severe frost.

Today the sun was disagreeably hot. I have reduced the ration to nine ounces of flour and ten ounces of pork."[57] Cooke did not say if such reflections caused him to consider the prospect of sending others to Pueblo, but he would do just that less than a week later.

Also on November 3, Cooke made his first mention of the last of his four main guides, calling him "Doctor Foster, the interpreter."[58] At twenty-six, Stephen Clark Foster was much younger than the others but had a noteworthy background. A native New Englander, he had graduated from Yale College, studied medicine in Louisiana, and practiced medicine in several states. Unusually versatile, he served as interpreter, surgeon, and scout for Cooke.

Among them, Leroux, Charbonneau, Foster, and Weaver had very impressive credentials. Cooke had done about as well as he could have. True, he did not have Fitzpatrick or Carson, but neither of them had the kind of experience in the Southwest that Leroux, Charbonneau, and Weaver did. But even their previous travels did not make these scouts—or anyone else—experts at what Cooke was attempting: crossing a desert several hundred miles long in wagons. Going strictly by horse and mule—as Kearny was now doing—was a completely different matter. In his journal, Cooke would complain more than once about his pilots, but he was in uncharted territory that likely would have befuddled any mountain man.

Leroux returned from a scouting trip on November 9 and reported finding water holes about fifty miles away. "It has now become evident to all," wrote a discouraged Cooke, "that we cannot go on so, with any prospect of a successful or safe termination to the expedition." One by one, he listed the obstacles—mules in miserable condition, twenty-two men on the sick report, many people needing to be transported in wagons, many men weak or old or debilitated, insufficient rations. "I have then ordered that fifty-five of the sick and least sufficient men shall return to Santa Fe, taking with them twenty-six days of rations of four at ten ounces, and port at half a pound. I shall thus get rid of 1,800 pounds' weight of rations, and by means of what they leave, particularly the live stock [such as sheep and cattle], increase my rations for the remainder."[59]

Despite his discouragement and his acknowledgment that "making the road as we go, ten miles is sometimes a very hard day's march— equal to at least twenty-five miles on a good road," Cooke mustered

hope, determined to have "patience and perseverance and energy" as
he set out on his current mission of blazing a route of more than three
hundred miles to the San Pedro River, "of which the guides know little
or nothing—know not if there be water sufficient."[60]

Led by Lieutenant William Willis, the third detachment of fifty-
seven men and one woman (and no children) started back to Santa Fe
on November 10. "Such a sight I never saw," wrote Levi Hancock.
"They was stowed away in the wagon like so many dead hogs. No better
way could be done so it was said. I went to the Lieu and asked him if he
would see that they was well taken care of when he had it in his power
to do it and gave him my hand. He gripped it and I could say no more,
neither could he. Many gave me their hand and wept."[61]

John Green died the night of November 12, when the party was
camped near the spot where George Hampton had died nine days
earlier. Green was buried next to his friend.[62]

The Willis group went north to Santa Fe and then, rather than
taking the Mountain Route, they went farther north to Taos, then continued north into Colorado and crossed the Sangre de Cristo Mountains
to Pueblo, arriving on December 20. They had traveled farther than the
other two groups and had had harsher weather and fewer provisions.
Several more men died, and the group was without food the last few
days of their journey. They were thrilled when they saw the "street of
log shanties . . . built of rough logs of cottonwood, laid one above the
other, the interstices filled with mud, and rendered impervious to wind
or wet. At one end of the row of shanties was built . . . a long building of
huge logs, in which prayer-meetings and holdings-forth took place."[63]

"Reshaw" had made it all possible.

With four women and one child still in the group, Cooke proceeded
on. On November 13, he found a note on a pole from Leroux telling
him to go right and leave the Rio Grande, which at that point flowed
southeast toward El Paso. Two days later, with a bitter gale blowing all
day, "raining, snowing, and shining alternately," Leroux, Charbonneau,
Foster, and four others were sent out and urged to make "an active and
more distant examination of the country."[64]

Charbonneau returned the next day and said the wagons could pass
the gap in the mountains and that there was water six miles ahead.
Cooke found the spot and continued on. He climbed to the top of a
three-hundred-foot peak, gazed out in all directions, and asked himself,

"But alas, where shall the water be found?" He repeated that thought the next day: "Where is water or our most advisable course? Heaven knows! We are exploring an unknown region with wagons."[65]

On November 20, at the Mimbres River (north of present Deming, New Mexico), Cooke climbed a hill with all four guides and "had a long and anxious consultation with [them]." It had become increasingly clear that the maps they had were "worthless" and could be "depended on for nothing." Kearny had wanted them to follow the Gila River into present Arizona (which would mean going northwest to a mountain range at this point), but the pilots agreed to that they "would not attempt it." Instead, they proposed going "some three hundred miles and then [striking] the San Pedro," a tributary of the Gila. (The San Pedro rises in Mexico, just south of the Arizona border, and flows north, past Benson, and converges with the Gila at Winkelman, Arizona.) "What difference if this distance is doubled, it if is a better route?" asked Cooke. "I shall strike the Gila all the same by either."[66] So the decision was made: They would continue southwest toward San Bernardino Spring, a well-known oasis on the present Arizona-Mexico border.

The day of November 22 found Leroux, Charbonneau, and the others doing what they always did—searching for water, sometimes days at a time. "Suddenly, at four o'clock, exactly before us, at perhaps fifteen miles," wrote Cooke, "we saw a white smoke spring up. I knew then that it was Leroux, who had spoken of making a little smoke at the little water hole."[67]

That night, well after dark, Charbonneau straggled into camp on foot. He was carrying his saddle, but his mule was nowhere to be seen. He reported that when he had come to a grassy area, he had stopped to let the tired mule eat and rest. A half hour later, when Charbonneau tried to bridle his mule, the stubborn animal kicked him and ran off. He followed it for several miles but could not catch it. Finally, to keep his saddle and pistols from falling into the hands of Apache Indians—and partly, conjectured Cooke, from anger—Charbonneau shot it.[68]

"A severe trial has been undergone," Cooke wrote the next morning, "forty miles without water!" Fortunately, they reached the water hole later that day, but unfortunately, "there was not enough of water for the men to drink, as it leaked slowly into the little crevices of rock and stones. They eagerly watched, and dipped it up by spoons!"[69]

"It was exceedingly cold last night," Cooke wrote on November 25. "It is believed the thermometer would have indicated between ten and fifteen degrees. About seven miles brought us to the defile of the mountain; it is very long and quite rocky. It took the wagons about two hours and a half, and was probably three miles over." Cooke then described yet another memorable scene involving the son of Sacagawea:

> Charbonneau, who had killed an antelope before the column reached the mountain, I found near the summit (whilst the baggage was slowly crawling up) in pursuit of grizzly bears. I saw three of them far up among the rocks, standing conspicuously and looking quite white in the sun, whilst the bold hunter was gradually approaching them. Soon after, he fired and in ten seconds again; then there was a confused action, and we could see one fall and the others rushing about with loud and fierce cries that made the mountain ring. The firing having ceased whilst the young bears were close by, I was much alarmed for the guide's safety; and then we heard him crying out in Spanish, but it was for more balls; and so the cubs escaped. The bear was rolled down and butchered before the wagons had passed.[70]

More than the other guides, Charbonneau's multifaceted personality seems to have been frequently revealed on the journey. On April 26, 1847, in San Diego, Lydia Hunter died six days after giving birth to a baby boy. Charbonneau, whose own mother had died when he was seven years old, was said to be "very kind and helpful to Captain Hunter during this sad time."[71]

Charbonneau was a colorful guide, and a valuable one as well, but Cooke relied on Leroux the most, no surprise given his vast experience over the past twenty-five years and his knowledge of the Southwest. At the end of November, as the battalion made its way over Guadalupe Pass, in the southwest corner of New Mexico, Leroux told Cooke that they were probably less than one hundred miles from the San Pedro River. He was right. They reached San Bernardino Spring on December 2, stayed over to rest, wash clothes, and trade with the Indians, and on December 7, wrote William Coray, "the pilots . . . returned and said the San Pedro River was within 30 miles. The pilot, Weaver, professed to be acquainted all the way."[72]

"Beyond, toward the mountain towering before us white with snow, from which a northwester cut us to the bone, we had seen only a smooth slope of prairie," Cooke wrote on December 9. "My anxiety became very great and I pushed on at a faint gait to the guides, and after ascending a hill saw a valley indeed, but no other appearance of a stream than a few ash trees in the midst; but they, with the numerous cattle paths, gave every promise of water. On we pushed, and finally, when twenty paces off, saw a fine bold stream! There was the San Pedro we had so long and anxiously pursued."[73]

Leroux proved his value again on December 12 when he returned to the camp and offered an important report on the garrisoned town of Tucson. He and the other guides had concluded that rather than following the San Pedro River north, "over a trackless wilderness of mountains and river hills," it would be much better to cross west to Tucson and then follow the Santa Cruz River to the Gila. Leroux said there were two hundred Mexican soldiers in Tucson, and he also gave "an excellent account of the road beyond Tucson."[74]

Cooke made it clear, both to his own troops and to the soldiers and citizens in Tucson, that he "came not to make war against Sonora, and less still to destroy an unimportant outpost of defense against the Indians. . . . The property of individuals [will be held] sacred. The people of Sonora are not our enemies."[75] Cooke indeed passed through the area without bloodshed, even negotiating Foster's release after the latter had been held prisoner for three days.

The battalion reached the Gila River, just west of present Florence, Arizona, on December 21. "In the afternoon [we] encamped on the banks of the Gila River," wrote Bigler, "where the Pimas came out by the hundreds to see us. . . . They brought into the camp large quantities of corn and corn meal, wheat, and flour, also beans and squashes to trade for old shirts, old shoes, pants, vests, beads, and buttons. They would not have money."[76]

As the battalion descended the Gila River west, Cooke knew they would soon reach the mouth of that river and would have to cross the Colorado River (into present California) to continue west. On January 7, 1847, he sent Foster and Weaver ahead to check the difficulty of the road and to see if any troops had come from Sonora or if anyone was approaching from the west. All was clear. "I passed that river on the 10th and 11th of January. On the first day and night, the loading of the wagons, and many men, were boated over," Cooke wrote in a dispatch sent to Kearny. "On the morning of the 11th, the mules were driven two miles, from grass; then drew the wagons through the long ford of a mile, nearly swimming. The wagons were then loaded in the willow thicket, and I marched 15 miles over the sandy road, to the first well, the same day; a great effort and labor."[77] During the course of that march, Cooke had found a note stuck on a pole: "No water, 2nd January. Charbonneau."[78]

On January 13, men and mules fought their way through sand, covering thirteen miles in seven hours. Water from a well was "very bad and warm, and the supply scanty and slow." Cooke consulted with Weaver on Indians apparently in the area and on what route to take near the "Salt Lake" (Salton Sea). Two days later, Cooke marched before sunrise. "The road was the same flat, clay plain, and much to our surprise seven or eight miles brought us to the Pozo Hondo ["deep well"]. As I approached it, Major Cloud met me with letters."

However, wrote Cooke,

> The pleasure of this great relief was sadly changed to the most sorrowful feelings on hearing of our great loss in action of Captains Moore and Johnston and twenty-one dragoons. Then was genuine grief shown by all that knew them. Our difficult and straightened circumstances were lost sight of for the time. What a loss to my regiment! . . . Peace to their ashes! Rest their souls! . . . A weight was taken off my mind and that of others on hearing of the general's safety, though twice wounded.[79]

Based on Carson's report that "an American flag floated in every port," Kearny had sent most of his men back to Santa Fe, convinced he would simply be handling administrative matters in a conquered California. Stockton, however, apparently in an effort to impress President Polk and Senator Benton, had announced victory prematurely. When Kearny reached American settlements in present Southern California early in December, he learned that Mexico controlled much of the area and further discovered, as he approached San Diego, that about one hundred Mexican troops were nearby. Kearny and his junior officers did not hesitate about engaging the enemy.

A military historian summarized the battle thus:

Well before dawn on December 6 [1846], Kearny's augmented force of about 150 troops attacked an equal number of mounted Californio lancers near the village of San Pasqual. Kearny led the wild and poorly executed attack that quickly degenerated into a desperate mounted skirmish. Heavy rain the night before had dampened the dragoons' gun powder and made their superior firearms ineffective. Kearny had divided his force into several elements in column formation; but as the two foes met on the flats near San Pasqual, the dragoon officers lost control and the fight turned into a brawl, rather than a conventional battle. The Californios bested the dragoons initially in small clusters through the use of their lances; but eventually, the Americans gained the upper hand through individual discipline. The Californios retreated, taking their dead and wounded along. The Battle of San Pasqual, though not decisive, was nevertheless an American victory.[80]

William Emory touched on the human side of the conflict in his December 8 journal entry. "Robidoux, a thin man of fifty-five years, slept next to me," he wrote. "The loss of blood from his wounds, added to the coldness of the night, 28° Fahrenheit, made me think he would never see daylight, but I was mistaken." Robidoux, Emory said, "woke me to ask if I did not smell coffee, and expressed a belief that a cup of that beverage would save his life, and that nothing else would." Emory believed there was no coffee in camp and thought the veteran trader imagining things but to his surprise found the cook heating coffee over a small fire of wild sage. "One of the most agreeable little offices performed in my life," wrote Emory, "and I believe in the cook's, to whom the coffee belonged, was, to pour this precious draught into the waning body of our friend Robidoux"—who did survive.

"Last night the brave Sergeant Cox died of his wounds, and was buried to-day deep in the ground, and covered with heavy stones, to prevent the wolves from tearing him up," continued Emory. "This was a gallant fellow, who had, just before leaving Fort Leavenworth, married a pretty wife."[81]

Within two days, the force of lancers had grown to more than two hundred. Kearny and his surviving officers agreed that their only option was to fight to the death. Luckily, Stockton sent reinforcements, and on the night of December 10, approximately two hundred marines and sailors arrived—a number that must have both thrilled and pained the general. The lancers disappeared in the desert.

Kearny joined with Stockton, and the combined American force won crucial battles in Los Angeles and San Pedro on January 8 and 9. Kearny ceded command to Stockton in these battles because Stockton was commanding considerably more men and knew the territory. However, "these victories were successful, not due to Stockton's command, but because of Kearny's tactical control and generalship."[82]

Frémont and his California Battalion were not involved in these hostilities. In fact, though they had been active in various war maneuvers since the previous summer, they had never seen combat. By January 11, Frémont, who had been farther north, was camped with his troops at the mission in present San Fernando, north of Los Angeles. When Frémont heard that some of the Californios defeated by Stockton and Kearny had fled to the area, he sent an emissary with a peace overture. The upshot was that, without any authority to do so, Frémont held a peace conference and negotiated a treaty on January 13, offering better terms than the unconditional surrender demanded by Stockton.[83]

Meanwhile, Cooke and the Mormon Battalion, aware of the final victory, were heading northwest, past present Palm Springs. "Marched ten miles," wrote Bigler on January 21, "when we arrived at Mr. Warner's, the first settlement, and encamped."[84]

The link between the Mormons and the mountain men had now come full circle, for this was Jonathan Trumball Warner, the same man who signed on with Jedediah Smith and arrived in Kaw Township in May of 1831. He had followed the Santa Fe Trail to Santa Fe and had then, like the Mormons who were now his guests, made the difficult crossing to California, reaching Los Angeles on December 5, 1831. He decided to settle in the area and became a Mexican citizen and a successful merchant. Since his name was difficult for Spanish speakers to pronounce, he changed it to Juan Jose Warner. He married Anita Gale in 1837. In 1844 he applied for a land grant on behalf of his children, stating that he needed "a place in which to put a considerable number of cattle and sheep belonging to the children of my marriage with my aforesaid wife." His application was approved, and he established "Warner's Ranch," which quickly became a favorite station of emigrants taking the southern route to California.[85]

"The Colonel got some fresh beef cattle of this gentleman," continued Bigler, "and issued four and one half pounds of beef to the soldier per day. This did very well, although rather flat eating without salt or bread. The Colonel laid over at this place all the next day. I understand that Mr. Warner owned a ranch some fifteen leagues square with three thousand head of cattle on it. While lying here, some of our boys found a hot spring about a half a mile from camp, but after the water had run a few rods from the head, it became cool enough to bathe in, and most of the Battalion had a good time washing off."[86]

The war in California was over, but a personal war was about to begin.

Frémont arrived in Los Angeles on June 14, and he and Carson were quickly reunited. "As soon as Frémont joined," wrote Carson, "I left Kearny and joined him."[87] While Frémont was glad to see Carson, he was livid that Kearny had not allowed Carson to carry the dispatches to Washington. This was only one of several points of conflict between the two officers, but Frémont took this one quite personally, and his preoccupation with it got the wheel rolling toward his court-martial, which occurred early in 1848.[88]

Therefore, when Kearny summoned Frémont to his headquarters on June 17, he was dealing with a junior officer who—along with any other baggage he was carrying—had a huge chip on his shoulder. Things started out badly and went downhill from there.

As background to the June 17 confrontation, it is important to note that two days earlier, Kearny had learned that Stockton was organizing a civil government, with Frémont as governor—this despite the fact that Kearny had already shown Stockton his authorization from the War Department to act in such matters. (As for who had the highest rank, it was clearly Kearny, a brigadier general, not Stockton, a brevet commodore whose permanent rank was captain.) In a letter (the two were corresponding by letter even though their offices were within easy walking distance), Kearny asked by what authority Stockton was doing these things. Stockton responded with a letter of his own, saying he was not responsible to Kearny and then making the outlandish statement that Kearny should consider himself suspended from command of US forces in California.[89]

On January 16, the exasperated Kearny had one of his officers send a message to Frémont ordering him to stop making military appointments without Kearny's permission. When no reply came, Kearny sent word to Frémont that he wished to see him "on business."

So, on January 17, Frémont showed up at Kearny's office. Yes, he said, he had received the order and had written a letter in response. He further explained that a clerk was making an official copy of the letter. Moments later, Carson walked in with the letter. After reading it, Frémont signed it and handed it to Kearny. One passage stood out: "I feel therefore, with great deference to your professional and personal character constrained to say that, until you and Commodore Stockton adjust between yourselves the question of rank, where I respectfully think the difficulty belongs, I shall have to report and receive orders, as heretofore, from the Commodore."

Frémont even had the audacity to sign the letter, "Lieutenant Colonel, United States Army and Military Commandant of the territory of California."[90]

Kearny must have been speechless. A junior officer in the United States Army was telling a general with full authorization from the secretary of war that he would be answering to a brevet commodore in the navy. Had it been anyone else, Kearny would have arrested him on the spot. But this junior officer was arguably the most famous man in America and the son-in-law of a powerful senator and a friend of Kearny's. As Captain Henry Smith Turner wrote in a letter to his wife, "Genl. K. is evidently timid with respect to Frémont. He fears to do his duty lest some offense should be given to Col. Benton."[91]

Rather than losing his temper, Kearny told Frémont that if he took the letter back and destroyed it, all would be forgotten. Frémont declined and said Stockton would support him. Kearny warned Frémont that if he persisted, "he would unquestionably ruin himself." At that, Frémont stood and marched out of the office, with Carson hard on his heels.[92]

That same day, January 17, 1847, Kearny wrote two letters, one to the War Department: "I am not recognized in my official capacity, either by Com Stockton or Lieut. Co Frémont. Both of [them] refuse to obey my orders or the instructions of President, and as I have no Troops in the country under my authority, excepting a few Dragoons, I have no power of enforcing them."

And one to Stockton: "And as I am prepared to carry out the President's instructions to me, which you oppose, I must, for the purpose of preventing collision between us & possibly a civil war in consequence of it, remain silent for the present, leaving with you the great responsibility of doing that for which you have no authority & preventing me from complying with the President's orders."[93]

Making good on his pledge to avoid violence, Kearny and fifty dragoons set out for San Diego the next day. Like the privates, Kearny marched the entire way on foot, allowing a sick solider with severely blistered feet to ride his horse. The next day, January 19, in the midst of all his troubles, Kearny got the best possible news: Lieutenant Colonel Cooke and his Mormon Battalion had reached Warner's Ranch. In a few days, it would no longer be true that Kearny had no troops "excepting a few dragoons."

Kearny sent a letter to Cooke, an officer he knew well and trusted, ordering him to march the battalion to San Diego. On January 29, Cooke wrote: "This evening I rode down by moonlight and reported to the general in San Diego."[94]

A few days later, Kearny ordered the Mormon Battalion to San Luis Rey, where they would begin official combat training, something they had not had a chance to do when they enlisted six months earlier. (The activities of the battalion, of course, would naturally become known by Stockton and Frémont.) Kearny wanted the battalion to be ready in case hostilities broke out. At the same time, hoping to use diplomacy and leverage rather than force, Kearny and a few staff officers boarded a US warship on January 31 to sail to Monterey. This would give Kearny the chance to meet with US consul Thomas Larkin and gain his support, which happened. Army reinforcements from New York were also expected to land at Monterey soon.

Kearny arrived at Monterey on February 8 to more good news. Commodore W. Branford Shubrick had arrived two weeks earlier aboard the USS *Lexington* to replace Stockton. Shubrick had orders from the secretary of the navy, George Bancroft, authorizing him to form a civil government, but when Shubrick saw Kearny's orders, he promptly accepted him as the military and civil commander in the area. A week later, 113 army soldiers arrived. Among them were Colonel Richard Mason, who had replaced Kearny as commander of the First US Dragoons, and a junior officer by the name of William Tecumseh Sherman. On March 5, five hundred members of the First New York Volunteer Regiment reached Monterey. Kearny now had more than a thousand men at his command, and Stockton was no longer on the scene—nor was Carson, who once again had been sent to Washington with dispatches.

Frémont, however, didn't budge.

"Of all the forces available to him, Kearny chose the Mormon Battalion to perform the most dangerous mission: to confront Frémont's volunteers. . . . On March 19, Cooke led his four companies of the Mormon Battalion north to Los Angeles."[95]

Obtaining the arms and ammunition from Frémont's men now became Cooke's responsibility—Frémont had thus far refused to obey the order to do so. Frémont was still in Monterey, so Cooke met with the captain second in command to Frémont—none other than Kit Carson's old friend, the mountain man Dick Owens.

Owens refused.

"The general's orders are not obeyed?" the incredulous Cooke asked rhetorically in his report. "To be refused them [ordnance and artillery] by this Lieut. Colonel Frémont and in defiance of the orders of the general? I denounce this treason or this mutiny."[96]

Nevertheless, Cooke kept his patience. Over the next few weeks, he continued to drill his men, who knew about the conflict with Frémont. "Last night we were called up and ordered to fix bayonets, as the Col. [Cooke] had sent word that an attack might be expected from Col. Frémont's men before day."[97]

Fortunately, there was no attack. By the end of April, Frémont had finally given in. He handed over the arms and ammunition and offered to resign. Kearny refused to accept the resignation. On June 16, escorted by fifteen members of the Mormon Battalion, Kearny, Cooke, and several others left for Fort Leavenworth. Frémont and his loyal mountain men followed a few hundred yards behind in a separate group. When they all reached the fort in August, Kearny arrested Frémont.

The trial began on November 2, 1847, in Washington, DC. "The charges were mutiny, with eleven specifications; disobedience of the lawful command of his superior officer, with seven specifications; and conduct to the prejudice of good order and military discipline, with five specifications." On January 31, 1848, the court found Frémont guilty of all three charges and all of the specifications. Frémont was sentenced to be dismissed from the US Army. President Polk "concluded that the facts proved did not constitute the military crime of mutiny. But he believed that the charges of disobedience to the lawful commands of a superior officer and conduct to the prejudice of good order and military discipline had been sustained by proofs. He approved the sentence of the court but decided to remit the penalty of dismissal from the service, instructing the Secretary of War to have JFC return to duty." Arguing he had nothing to merit the finding, Frémont announced he could not accept clemency and resigned his commission on February 19.[98]

* * *

Less than a month after Kearny and Frémont arrived at Fort Leavenworth, Mexico City fell, and the major fighting ended. Five months later, in February 1848, the treaty of Guadalupe Hidalgo ended the war and brought a huge land area officially into the US—all of the present states of California, Nevada, and Utah and portions of Arizona, New Mexico, Colorado, and Wyoming.

The Mormon Battalion and their guides had been faced with a severe challenge, but they had responded well—getting Cooke's wagon company to California a month faster than Carson thought possible and helping prevent a civil war from breaking out among American troops. These feats were genuinely appreciated by Philip St. George Cooke, who wrote:

> The lieutenant-colonel commanding congratulates the battalion on their safe arrival on the shore of the Pacific ocean, and the conclusion of the march of over two thousand miles. History may be searched in vain for an equal march of infantry. Nine-tenths of it has been through a wilderness where nothing but savages and wild beasts are found, or deserts where, for want of water, there is no living creature. There, with almost hopeless labor, we have dug deep wells which the future traveler will enjoy. Without a guide who had traversed them, we have ventured into trackless prairies where water was not found for several marches. With crowbar and pick and ax in hand we have worked our way over mountains which seemed to defy aught save the wild goat, and hewed a passage through a chasm of living rock more narrow than our wagons. . . . Thus, marching half naked and half fed, and living upon wild animals, we have discovered and made a road of great value to our country.[99]

* * *

Thomas Hart Benton never forgave James K. Polk for not taking stronger action in Frémont's defense. The two men continued to attend the same church every Sunday, but Polk said Benton "never speaks to me as he was in the habit of doing."[100]

It had been a different story with the man who had almost killed Benton in a gunfight. When Andrew Jackson was elected a US senator from Tennessee in 1823, writes Robert Remini, he and Benton sat in adjoining chairs and were frequently thrown together in meetings. One day Jackson asked about the health of Benton's wife. Not long after that, Benton stepped toward Jackson and bowed. "The General immediately shot out his hand, and the two men shook hands and wiped away the enmity of ten years."[101]

Much to his credit, Benton denounced slavery in the late 1840s: "If there were no slavery in Missouri today, I should oppose its coming in; if there was none in the United States, I should oppose it coming into the United States."[102]

Thomas Hart Benton died on April 10, 1858, at the age of seventy-six.

In 1856, when Ramsay Crooks read a newspaper article claiming that presidential candidate John C. Frémont had discovered South Pass (a claim Frémont himself never made), Crooks responded with a letter to the editor. "Even if the Colonel had discovered the 'South Pass,'" Crooks argued, "it does not show any more fitness for the exalted station he covets than the numerous beaver hunters and traders who passed and repassed through that noted place full twenty years before Col. Frémont had attained a legal right to vote."

To set the record straight, said Crooks, "I will tell you how it was." He briefly reviewed the history of the Pacific Fur Company and then told how the party that left Astoria toward the end of June of 1812, concluding it was too dangerous to take the route of 1811, "turned toward the southeast as soon as they had crossed the main chain of the Rocky Mountains, and, after several days' journey came through the celebrated 'South Pass,' in the month of November [actually October], 1812." He next named Robert McClellan, Joseph Miller, Robert Stuart,

Benjamin Jones, Francois LeClaire, and Andre Valee, listing himself last, "the only survivor of this small band of adventurers."[103]

Crooks called his large family "the only true solace of my existence." When he died on June 6, 1859, at age seventy-two, one obituary described him as an "upright and honorable man" who "endeared himself to all who knew him," concluding with the explanation that "Mr. Crooks had no particular disease; but had worn himself out by too close application to business. He died peacefully as a child going to sleep."[104]

NOTES

INTRODUCTION

1. Lewis's journal entry, June 29, 1806, Gary Moulton, *Journals*, 8:61–63.
2. Lewis's journal entry, June 30, 1806, Moulton, *Journals*, 8:68–69n8.
3. Lewis's journal entry, July 2, 1806, Moulton, *Journals*, 8:79.
4. Clark's journal entry, August 12, 1806, Moulton, *Journals*, 8:290.
5. Lewis's journal entry, August 12, 1806, Moulton, *Journals*, 8:158. Lewis's final words in his journal involved a description of a cherry, which Moulton explains was "the pin, or bird, cherry, *Prunus pensylvania* L. f." Ibid., 159n7.
6. Lewis's journal entry, August 12, 1806, Moulton, *Journals*, 8:157.
7. Tanis C. Thorne, s.v. "Crooks, Ramsay," in *Dictionary of Canadian Biography*, vol. 8, University of Toronto/Université Laval, 2003–, accessed May 30, 2018, http://www.biographi.ca/en/bio/crooks_ramsay_8E.html.
8. Letter, Meriwether Lewis to Thomas Jefferson, September 23, 1806, Donald Jackson, *Letters*, 1:319–20.
9. Larry Morris, *Fate of the Corps*, 1.
10. Albert Furtwangler, *Acts of Discovery*, 1.
11. Henry Nash Smith, *Virgin Land*, 17.

1. "WHAT WILL BE THE CONSEQUENCE?"

1. Mahlon Dickerson's diary, November 22, 1809, Jackson, *Letters*, 2:684.
2. Donald Jackson writes that "a faded clipping about Lewis's death from the *Democratic Press* of Philadelphia, 13 Nov. 1809" was found with Dickerson's papers after his death in 1853; *Letters*, 2:684. No copy of that paper was

located for the present study; background information was therefore compiled from two other newspapers: the *Evening Post* (New York, New York), November 15, 1809, and the *Pennsylvania Gazette* (Philadelphia), November 21, 1810.

3. *Evening Post*, November 15, 1809. This article also appeared in such newspapers as the *National Intelligencer* (Washington, DC) and the *Sentinel* (Gettysburg, PA) and was likely the same article seen by Dickerson. For more than two centuries, controversy has raged over Lewis's death: Did he perish by suicide or homicide? Many—but not all—twenty-first-century Lewis and Clark scholars argue for the suicide option (which itself has various options). For a good introduction to the voluminous literature on the controversy, see (in order of publication) Vardis Fisher, *Suicide or Murder: The Strange Death of Governor Meriwether Lewis*; John D. W. Guice, ed., *By His Own Hand? The Mysterious Death of Meriwether Lewis*; James E. Starr and Kira Gale, *The Death of Meriwether Lewis: A Historic Crime Scene Investigation*; Clay S. Jenkinson, *The Character of Meriwether Lewis: Explorer in the Wilderness*; and Thomas C. Danisi, *Uncovering the Truth about Meriwether Lewis*.

4. *Evening Post*, November 15, 1809. The editor eventually saw his hopes of Lewis's history of the Lewis and Clark Expedition being "ready for the press" dramatically dashed. Lewis indeed had made grand plans but never followed through. In the spring of 1807, six months after his and Clark's return from the West, Lewis published a prospectus promising three volumes "containing four to five hundred pages, each, printed on good paper." Rather than simply quoting journal entries from the expedition, Lewis planned to produce an original work by synthesizing and rewriting the raw entries. He had signed with C. and A. Conrad and Company, a Philadelphia publisher, and arranged for elaborate illustrations. However, on November 13, 1809, the very day the *Democratic Press* announced Lewis's death, John Conrad wrote to Thomas Jefferson: "Accounts received here . . . of his decease induce us to use the freedom to advise you of the contract. . . . Govr. Lewis never furnished us with a line of the M.S. nor indeed could we ever hear any thing from him respecting it tho frequent applications to that effect were made to him." Morris, *Fate of the Corps*, 56–57; letter, C. and A. Conrad and Co. to Thomas Jefferson, November 13, 1809, Jackson, *Letters*, 2:469.

5. Jefferson responded to the letter from C. and A. Conrad and Company (discussed above) on November 23 and strongly implied that he first learned of Lewis's death by reading Neelly's letter. Referring to Lewis's failure to send a manuscript to Conrad and Company, Jefferson wrote: "I had written to [Lewis] some time ago to know when he would have it ready & was expecting an answer when I received the news of his unfortunate end." He then discussed Neelly's letter. A prolific correspondent, Jefferson had written several letters in

the week prior to arriving back at Monticello, but none of them mentioned Lewis. Jefferson's letter to the Conrad company thus contained his first reference to Lewis's demise. (Neelly's letter had arrived at Monticello on November 21 and Conrad and Co.'s on November 22, the day of Jefferson's return.)

6. Letter, James Neelly to Thomas Jefferson, October 18, 1809, Jackson, *Letters*, 2:467–68, bracketed insertion added.

7. Letter, Thomas Jefferson to Paul Allen, August 18, 1813, Jackson, *Letters*, 2:589, 592. Jefferson wrote the letter—no doubt intentionally—on what would have been Lewis's thirty-ninth birthday.

8. Letter, Thomas Jefferson to C. and A. Conrad and Company, Jackson, *Letters*, 2:474–75.

9. Even though Clark expected to see Lewis in Washington, he was quite worried about his friend. "Several of [Lewis's] Bills have been protested and his Crediters all flocking in near the time of his Setting out distressed him much. Which he expressed to me in Such terms as to Cause a Cempothy [sympathy] which is not yet off," Clark wrote to his brother Jonathan. "Tho' I think all will be right and he will return with flying Colours to this Country." Letter, William Clark to Jonathan Clark, August 26, 1809, Holmberg, *Dear Brother*, 210. Lewis had made questionable investments in land speculation and, as Clark observed, the bills protested by the War Department alarmed his creditors. All of that was compounded by his unsuccessful attempt to marry, his failure to get started on the history of the expedition, and his increasing dependence on alcohol—as well as a possible predisposition to depression—giving Clark good reasons to worry. As to when Lewis departed for Washington, James Holmberg points out, "There is some confusion as to when Meriwether Lewis left St. Louis for the East. Clark clearly states it was 25 August. However, Frederick Bates stated that it was 4 September. The difference of ten days is significant because it would indicate a much longer travel time . . . and thus indicate the kinds of difficulties and illness mentioned by Lewis and [Gilbert] Russell." Holmberg, *Dear Brother*, 212.

10. Letter, William Clark to Jonathan Clark, October 28, 1809, Holmberg, *Dear Brother*, 216–17, bracketed insertions added.

11. Letter, William Clark to Jonathan Clark, October 30, 1809, Holmberg, *Dear Brother*, 224.

12. Letter, William Clark to Jonathan Clark, [November 8], 1809, Holmberg, *Dear Brother*, 225–26.

13. Morris, *Fate of the Corps*, 71.

14. William Clark 1809 Memorandum Book, cited in Landon Jones, *William Clark and the Shaping of the West*, 183.

15. Letter, William Clark to Jonathan Clark, November 26, 1809, Holmberg, *Dear Brother*, 228.

16. Letter, Thomas Jefferson to Conrad and Company, December 11, 1809, Jackson, *Letters*, 2:479.

17. "George Ticknor's Account of a Visit to Monticello," February 4–7, 1815, Founders Online, accessed on April 11, 2017, https://founders.archives. gov/documents/Jefferson/03-08-02-0190.

18. Letter, Thomas Jefferson to Meriwether Lewis, [June 20, 1803], Jackson, *Letters*, 1:62, bracketed insertions added.

19. Ibid., 64. Jefferson instructed Lewis to "carry some matter of the Kinepox" and encourage its use among the Indians. "Kinepox was cowpox," writes Bruce C. Patton, "a disease similar to smallpox, but much milder and not lethal. Scratching a small amount of secretion from a cowpox sore into the skin afforded protection against smallpox. . . . Jefferson had a strong personal interest in the prevention of smallpox, and he and his family had been vaccinated." Patton, *Lewis & Clark: Doctors in the Wilderness*, 36.

20. Clay Jenkinson, *Vast and Open Plain*, 427n230.

21. Moulton, *Journals*, 8:308–9n2, bracketed insertion added.

22. James Ronda, *Thomas Jefferson and the Changing West*, xiv.

23. Anthony F. C. Wallace, "'The Obtaining Lands': Thomas Jefferson and the Native Americans," in Ronda, *Jefferson and the Changing West*, 38–39.

24. Robert Miller, *Native America Discovered and Conquered*, 1. Miller subsequently concludes that "Lewis and Clark also emphasized America's power and sovereign authority by [performing] military maneuvers by parading and [demonstrating] American weapons, trade goods, and scientific instruments. This was part and parcel of Lewis's speech [to the Otoe and Missouri nations] that tried to cajole, threaten, and intimidate Indian Nations. In total, all of the efforts that Jefferson directed Lewis and Clark to undertake were meant to enforce the United States' Discovery sovereign and commercial authority against the Louisiana Territory Indian Nations." Ibid., 107. In his treatment of Jefferson and Lewis and Clark, Miller offers good reasons for his negative conclusions but tends to undercut his argument by failing to mention anything that could possibly cast any of the three men in a more positive light, such as Jefferson's concern about smallpox or Clark's reverence for Indian creation stories (both discussed above). Moreover, Miller is too quick to condemn Jefferson based on secondary evidence and his tone so cynical (calling him a "*rabid* proponent of American expansion," for example, emphasis added [p. 97]) that the reader can hardly expect him to treat Jefferson fairly.

25. Cited in Miller, *Native America Discovered and Conquered*, 46.

26. Ibid., 3.

27. Howard Lamar, *New Encyclopedia*, 537; Colin Calloway, *One Vast Winter Count*, 284.

28. John Mack Faragher, *Daniel Boone*, 111–12.

29. Ronda, *Jefferson and the Changing West*, xiv.

30. Letter, Thomas Jefferson to Randolph Jefferson, December 8, 1809, J. Jefferson Looney, *Papers of Thomas Jefferson*, 2:60.

31. Holmberg, *Dear Brother*, 239n4.

32. Looney, *Papers of Thomas Jefferson*, 2:72–75.

33. Jones, *William Clark*, 184.

34. Letter, William Clark to Jonathan Clark, January 12, 1810, Holmberg, *Dear Brother*, 233–34. Kentucky congressman Benjamin Howard was named to succeed Lewis, and he served until 1812, when he resigned to serve in the War of 1812. Howard died later that year of illness, and in 1813 he was succeeded by none other than William Clark.

35. Landon Jones believes Clark and Biddle met in Philadelphia (*William Clark*, 186); Paul Russell Cutright, on the other hand, concludes that Biddle was out of town at the time and that Clark left a note for him (*History of the Lewis and Clark Journals*, 57).

36. Letter, William D. Meriwether to William Clark, January 22, 1810, Jackson, *Letters*, 2:489. The Henry biography turned out to be a long-term project. Wirt first requested Jefferson's thoughts on Henry in July of 1805, bringing up the subject again a few days before Meriwether wrote his letter to Clark. The book, *Sketches of the Life and Character of Patrick Henry*, was published in 1817. Letter, William Wirt to Thomas Jefferson, January 18, 1810, Looney, *Papers of Thomas Jefferson*, 2:155–56.

37. Letter, William Clark to William D. Meriwether, February 2, 1810, Jackson, *Letters*, 2:491.

38. Letter, William Clark to Nicholas Biddle, February 20, 1810, Jackson, *Letters*, 2:494.

39. Letter, Nicholas Biddle to William Clark, March 3, 1810, Jackson, *Letters*, 2:495.

40. Letter, Nicholas Biddle to William Clark, March 17, 1810, Jackson, *Letters*, 2:496.

41. Cutright, *History of the Lewis and Clark Journals*, 53.

42. Letter, Nicholas Biddle to William Clark, July 7, 1810, Jackson, *Letters*, 2:550.

43. Sheheke and his family had gone east with Lewis and Clark as they returned to St. Louis in 1806. After meeting Jefferson in Washington, the chief had returned to St. Louis. The War Department instructed Clark to have Sheheke returned safely to his home, and Clark had ordered expedition veteran Nathaniel Pryor, by then an ensign in the First Infantry, to muster a group of soldiers to escort Sheheke and his family up the Missouri. George Gibson, another expedition member, was one of those soldiers; like Shannon, he was seriously wounded. A fourth expedition veteran, Joseph Field, was apparently

one of those killed. See William E. Foley and Charles David Rice, "Return of the Mandan Chief," 2–14; Holmberg, *Dear Brother*, 86, 93–95, 108–9, 115; and Morris, *Fate of the Corps*, 28, 29, 35–37, 76.

44. Andrés Reséndez, *National Identities*, 2. Austin, writes Reséndez, "gave up his American citizenship and became a Mexican national in order to validate a colonization contract awarded to his father. Furthermore, as Mexico's most successful colonization entrepreneur, Austin would encourage thousands of fellow Americans to settle in Texas, pledge allegiance to the Mexican constitution, and (at least on paper) convert to Catholicism." Ibid.

45. Cited in Alan Taylor, *Civil War of 1812*, 128.

46. Letter, William Clark to Nicholas Biddle, May 22, 1810, Jackson, *Letters*, 2:549.

47. Excerpted from an October 5, 1810, letter from Biddle to Edward Watts, cited in Jackson, *Letters*, 2:555n6.

48. Letter, Nicholas Biddle to William Clark, June 28, 1811, Jackson, *Letters*, 2:568.

49. Elliott Coues, *History of the Lewis and Clark Expedition*, 2:510.

50. Ibid.

51. Lewis's journal entry, August 17, 1805, Moulton, *Journals*, 5:109. Clark's entry was similarly brief.

52. Letters, William Clark to Nicholas Biddle, December 7, 1810, and Clark to Biddle, December 20, 1810, Jackson, *Letters*, 2:562 and 2:565, respectively.

53. Jones, *William Clark*, 192.

54. Thomas James, *Three Years among the Indians*, 23–24.

55. Richard Edward Oglesby, *Manuel Lisa*, 68–69.

56. James, *Three Years among the Indians*, 24.

57. Clark's journal entries, August 15, 16, and 17, 1806, Moulton, *Journals*, 8:302, 8:304, and 8:305, respectively.

58. John Ordway's journal entry, August 17, 1806, Moulton, *Journals*, 9:351.

59. Ibid.

60. Letter, Thomas Jefferson to Meriwether Lewis, [June 20, 1803], Jackson, *Letters*, 1:61.

61. Mark William Kelly, *Lost Voices on the Missouri*, 108.

62. James, *Three Years among the Indians*, 24.

63. Ibid., 24–25.

64. Lewis's journal entry, July 27, 1805, Moulton, *Journals*, 4:434.

65. Clark's journal entry, July 25, 1805, Moulton, *Journals*, 4:428.

66. One other expedition member had gone up the Missouri with Lisa in 1807—Baptiste Lepage. He had died late in 1809, apparently at the outpost at the confluence of the Bighorn and Yellowstone Rivers: Fort Raymond. See Morris, *Fate of the Corps*, 39, 77, 78, 195.

67. James, *Three Years among the Indians*, 36.

68. Ibid., 37–38.

69. Ibid., 38.

70. The poetry and songs of Robert Burns, who died in 1796 at age thirty-seven, were quite popular, both in his native Scotland and elsewhere. As Mark Kelly points out, it was not surprising that John Dougherty would quote him, especially given Dougherty's Scottish ancestry. Dougherty had probably read or even purchased *The Works of Robert Burns, with an Account of His Life and a Criticism of His Writings*, a four-volume work published in 1800. Kelly, *Lost Voices on the Missouri*, 714n56.

71. John Bradbury, *Travels in the Interior*, 44–45n18.

72. See Ronald M. Anglin and Larry E. Morris, *Mystery of John Colter*, 155–66, for the five different accounts of Colter's run.

73. Letters, Pierre Menard to Pierre Chouteau, April 21, 1810, and Pierre Menard to his wife, Angelique, April 21, 1810, in Jim Hardee, *Selected Papers of the 2010 Fur Trade Symposium*, 120 and 121, respectively.

74. Agreement for Return of the Mandan Chief, [February 24, 1809], Jackson, *Letters*, 2:446–50. See also Oglesby, *Manuel Lisa*, 74–77.

75. The military and trading parties traveled together after meeting at Fort Osage, in western Missouri. Lisa had pushed his men so hard that several had deserted by then. Oglesby, *Manuel Lisa*, 74–77; James, *Three Years among the Indians*, 2–5.

76. Letter, Reuben Lewis to Meriwether Lewis, April 21, 1810, in Hardee, *Selected Papers of the 2010 Fur Trade Symposium*, 121.

77. Ibid., 122.

78. Ibid. Reuben Lewis remained on the upper Missouri for another seventeen months, arriving back in St. Louis in October of 1811 with a party that included Manuel Lisa and Andrew Henry. He apparently learned of Meriwether's death when he saw Lisa at the Mandan Indian villages in June or July, but no details are known. Oglesby, *Manuel Lisa*, 114–16; Morris, *Perilous West*, 129.

79. James, *Three Years among the Indians*, 35. Of course, James's description of Colter and the others being attacked after leaving Three Forks means that he must have talked to Colter after that. That likely happened in St. Louis during the summer and fall of 1811, when Colter was called as a witness in the suits that James and the Missouri Fur Company filed against each other. See Anglin and Morris, *Mystery of John Colter*, 131–32.

80. Letter, William Clark to Jonathan Clark, July 3, 1810, Holmberg, *Dear Brother*, 245. The trip had been full of bad weather, carriage rides over rough or nonexistent roads, uncomfortable sleeping quarters, and sickness, with Julia and young Meriwether Lewis both returning to St. Louis covered with mosqui-

to bites, but one incident more than anything else had left Julia under a dark cloud: as the party reached the mouth of the Ohio River, Clark had written, "rachiel [presumably the young daughter of slaves Scott and Chloe] fell between the boats and Drowned." Ibid., bracketed insertion added.

81. As Gary Moulton states, "After some disciplinary difficulties during the winter at River Dubois, [Colter] proved useful to the expedition as a hunter." Moulton, *Journals*, 2:515. Colter and others visited a local whiskey shop without permission and were found drunk on duty. Ibid., 2:143, 179, 182, 183, 194, 200.

82. Clark's journal entry, August 15, 1806, Moulton, *Journals*, 8:302. Clark was essentially in command at this point because Lewis had been accidentally shot by Cruzatte (while the two were hunting) four days earlier and was still recovering.

83. Ralph Ehrenberg, "Mapping on the Trail," accessed on May 8, 2017, http://www.edgate.com/lewisandclark/mapping_on_trail.html. Clark had also obtained important information from Zebulon Pike. Jay H. Buckley, *William Clark: Indian Diplomat*, 84; Jones, *William Clark*, 193.

84. M. O. Skarsten, *George Drouillard*, 261. For more information on Drouillard's travels, see Skarsten, *George Drouillard*, 259–70, and Anglin and Morris, *Mystery of John Colter*, 79–81. Drouillard and Lisa had returned to St. Louis in August of 1808 to find themselves charged with murder for the killing of Antoine Bissonnet in May of 1807, a deserter from Lisa's expedition whom Drouillard had shot on Lisa's orders. Both men were acquitted. See Skarsten, *George Drouillard*, 271–79; Morris, *Fate of the Corps*, 49–53; and Melissa Tiffie, "The 1808 Murder Trial of George Drouillard," *Rocky Mountain Fur Trade Journal* 9 (2015): 38–63.

85. Letter, Thomas Jefferson to Meriwether Lewis, [June 20, 1803], Jackson, *Letters*, 1:61.

86. Clark's journal entry, July 26, 1806, Moulton, *Journals*, 8:232, italics in original, bracketed explanations added.

87. Clark's journal entry, August 11, 1806, Moulton, *Journals*, 8:288.

88. See John L. Allen, "The Forgotten Explorers," for a detailed discussion of Clark's master map; see the digitally remastered version of Clark's map at the website https://www.wdl.org/en/item/3057/view/1/1/, accessed on May 9, 2107.

89. Buckley, *Indian Diplomat*, 84. For more on the fascinating relationship between Clark's map and the legend of John Colter, see Allen, "The Forgotten Explorers," and Anglin and Morris, *Mystery of John Colter*, 75–98.

90. Anglin and Morris, *Mystery of John Colter*, 133.

91. *Missouri Gazette and Public Advertiser*, July 26, 1810. Thomas James was among those who discovered Drouillard's body about 150 yards beyond

the bodies of his two Indian companions, described as Shawnees by James. "We saw from the marks on the ground," wrote James, "that he must have fought in a circle on horseback, and probably killed some of his enemies, being a brave man, and well armed with a rifle, pistol, knife and tomahawk. We pursued the trail of the Indians till night, without overtaking them, and then returned, having buried our dead, with saddened hearts to Fort." James, *Three Years among the Indians*, 46.

92. Letter, Meriwether Lewis to Henry Dearborn, January 15, 1807, Jackson, *Letters*, 1:368.

93. "While it was true that Henry and his men could live off the land like the Indians, it was equally true that they would find it impossible to replenish their by now meager supply of powder and lead." Oglesby, *Manuel Lisa*, 103.

94. Letter, Thomas Jefferson to Meriwether Lewis, July 17, 1808, Jackson, *Letters*, 2:444–45.

2. "THE MOST DIRECT & PRACTICABLE WATER COMMUNICATION ACROSS THIS CONTINENT"

1. Clark's journal entry, September 20, 1806, and Ordway's journal entry, September 19, 1806, Moulton, *Journals*, 8:367 and 9:365, respectively.

2. Clark's journal entry, September 20, 1806, Moulton, *Journals*, 8:367, 8:368n4. Reed could well have been the John Reed who went west with the overland Astorians in 1811 and, along with Hoback, Reznor, and Robinson and Pierre Dorion Jr., was killed by Indians in present Idaho in 1814. Although Clark did not identify Ramsay Crooks by name, circumstantial evidence is quite persuasive that Crooks was indeed Reed's companion. See David Lavender, "Ramsay Crooks's Early Ventures"; Lavender, *Fist in the Wilderness*, 77–78; and Morris, *Perilous West*, 3–4.

3. Clark's journal entry, August 11, 1806, Moulton, *Journals*, 8:288, 8:289n1, bracketed insertion added.

4. Clark's journal entry, August 21, 1806, ibid., 8:311, 8:316n1, bracketed insertion added.

5. Clark's journal entry, September 3, 1806, ibid., 8:346, 8:347n3, bracketed insertions added.

6. Clark's journal entry, September 6, 1806, ibid., 8:351, 8:352nn3–4, and Ordway's journal entry, ibid., 9:359, bracketed insertions added.

7. Clark's journal entry, September 10, 1806, ibid., 8:355, bracketed insertions added.

8. Clark's journal entry, September 10, 1806, ibid., 8:355, 8:356n3, bracketed insertions added.

9. Clark's journal entry, September 12, 1806, ibid., 8:357, bracketed insertions added.

10. Clark's journal entry, September 12, 1806, ibid., 8:357, 8:358nn1–4, and Ordway's journal entry, September 12, 1806, ibid., 9:361, bracketed insertions added.

11. Clark's journal entry, September 14, 1806, ibid., 8:360, 8:360n3, bracketed insertions added.

12. Ordway's journal entry, September 16, 1806, ibid., 9:363.

13. Clark's journal entry, September 16, 1806, ibid., 8:362, 8:362n1, and Ordway's journal entry, September 16, 1806, ibid., 9:363, 9:363n1, bracketed insertions added.

14. Clark's journal entry, September 17, 1806, ibid., 8:363, 8:364n1, and Ordway's journal entry, September 17, 1806, ibid., 9:364, bracketed insertions added.

15. Clark's journal entry, September 20, 1806, ibid., 8:367, bracketed insertion added.

16. Ronda, "A Moment in Time," 77.

17. In 1536, after a journey of several years, the Spanish explorer Alvar Nunez Cabeza de Vaca and three others reached the Pacific Ocean at the Gulf of California from Florida.

18. Background information from Ronda, who also points out that Zebulon Pike had completed an expedition to the upper Mississippi in Lewis and Clark's absence and was now in Kansas (where he and his men would be taken prisoner by the Spanish) and that Thomas Freeman and Peter Curtis (under instructions from Thomas Jefferson) had explored the area between the Red and Arkansas Rivers, where they were stopped, but not imprisoned, by the Spanish. Ronda, "A Moment in Time," 82–86.

19. As Moulton notes, "What Lewis and Clark hoped to find was the 'pyramidal height of land,' the point from which, geographical theorists believed, the great rivers of the West flowed toward the Pacific, the Gulf of Mexico, and the Gulf of California . . . the closest thing still possible to the Northwest Passage that so many mariners had yearned and searched for." Moulton, *Journals*, 5:1.

20. Clark's journal entry, August 23, 1805, Moulton, *Journals*, 5:155–156, bracketed insertion added.

21. The town of Riggins, in western Idaho, is less than 120 miles from Salmon, Idaho, as the crow flies. Going west by car from Salmon, however (on highways generally open year-round), first requires avoiding the spectacular but rugged mountainous area now designated as the Frank Church–River of No Return Wilderness by going south to Highway 20 (south of Hailey, Idaho, and 160 miles from Salmon) or going north to Lolo, Montana (129 miles from

Salmon). The shortest route to Riggins is thus 328 miles (via Lolo). Nor is it possible to drive west from Riggins into Oregon because Hells Canyon blocks the way.

22. The Shoshone Indians helping Clark likely had little or no knowledge of the Snake River, far to the south, so there was no discussion of going that direction. Nor would a southern route have offered a solution because, as the overland Astorians would discover, deadly rapids in the Burley/Twin Falls area and the deepest river gorge in North America to the northwest (now called Hells Canyon) made navigating the Snake River impossible.

23. Background from Anglin and Morris, *Mystery of John Colter*, 41–42.

24. Patrick Gass's journal entry, September 16, 1805, Moulton, *Journals*, 10:143.

25. Lewis's journal entry, September 9, 1805, ibid., 5:192.

26. Elin Woodger and Brandon Toropov, *Encyclopedia*, 259. "Had Lewis and Clark not been set on their course of following the Missouri to its source and instead followed the Dearborn [a tributary of the Missouri briefly explored by Lewis on July 18, 1805], they would have come to what is now called Lewis and Clark Pass over the Continental Divide. This would have brought them to the Big Blackfoot River and then the Clark Fork River, which flows into the Columbia—a shorter journey than the one they ultimately took." Ibid., 112. As Gary Moulton points out, the Hidatsa nation had told Lewis and Clark about this road, but the captains had not recognized it as they ascended the Missouri. *Journals*, 5:195n7.

27. Letter, John Jacob Astor to Thomas Jefferson, February 27, 1808, cited in Ronda, *Astoria and Empire*, 40.

28. Lamar, *New Encyclopedia*, 65–66.

29. John D. Haeger, "Business Strategy and Practice," 189.

30. Letter, Meriwether Lewis to Thomas Jefferson, September 23, 1806, Jackson, *Letters*, 1:321.

31. Robert S. Allen, "Dickson, Robert," in *Dictionary of Canadian Biography*, vol. 6, University of Toronto/Université Laval, 2003–, accessed July 24, 2017, http://www.biographi.ca/en/bio/dickson_robert_6E.html.

32. Cited in Lavender, "Ramsay Crooks's Early Ventures," 95.

33. Ibid., 96; letter, James Wilkinson to Henry Dearborn, September 8, 1805, cited in Jones, *William Clark*.

34. Letter, George Hoffman to Frederick Bates, August 23, 1808, Thomas Marshall, *Life and Papers of Frederick Bates*, 2:18.

35. Marshall, *Life and Papers of Frederick Bates*, 1:202.

36. Ibid., 2:31; letter, Hoffman to Bates, August 23, 1808, ibid., 2:17, emphasis in original.

37. Lavender, *Fist in the Wilderness*, 108; James, *Three Years among the Indians*, 8. Lavender acknowledges that his account of interaction between Hunt and Crooks in the spring of 1809 is speculative but nevertheless makes a convincing case. See Lavender, *Fist in the Wilderness*, 108–13. Ronda notes that "because the Astor-Hunt correspondence is no longer extant, it is difficult to trace either Astor's intentions or Hunt's pursuit of his employer's instructions" and therefore cautions that whether Crooks and McClellan went up the Missouri in 1809 "as advance agents for Astor remains in doubt." Nevertheless, Ronda lists one other piece of evidence supporting Lavender's speculation: "Astor's St. Louis correspondent, Charles Gratiot, wrote him in June 1810 [and] reported that Hunt had been Crooks's supplier 'last fall.'" Ronda, *Astoria and Empire*, 53–54.

38. Washington Irving, *Astoria*, 135; Morris, *Perilous West*, 32.

39. Kenneth Porter, *John Jacob Astor*, 2:186.

40. Irving, *Astoria*, 129–35, 135n8.

41. Letter, William Clark to William Eustis, September 12, 1810, in Clarence Carter, *Territorial Papers*, 14:414.

42. Letter, John Jacob Astor to Albert Gallatin, May 26, 1810, cited in Lavender, *Fist in the Wilderness*, 444n10.

43. The Clark Fork flows northwest from its confluence with the Bitterroot into present Idaho and then into Lake Pend Oreille. The lake's outlet, the Pend Oreille River, flows into Washington, goes north, and dips into British Columbia before joining the Columbia River and flowing south back into Washington. Not surprisingly, the amazing Thompson had explored the area well before the Astorians—or any other American traders—could have reached it. In 1809 he reached Lake Pend Oreille and established Kullyspel House near the northeast shore. He also attempted to reach the Columbia River via the Pend Oreille River. As Jack Nisbet explains, the group was "stopped cold by the sudden drop of Metaline Falls, thirty miles from the spot where the Pend Oreille spills into the Columbia." Thompson's Kalispel guide attempted to explore the surrounding area on foot and found it "highly dangerous & passable only to light active men & they obliged to go on hands & Feet up the steep Crags." Thompson thus wrote: "Attentively surveying the country, and considering all the information I had collected from various Indians, I concluded that we must abandon all thoughts of a passage this way." Nisbet, *Sources of the River*, 160.

44. Ronda, *Finding the West*, 13.

45. Ronda, *Astoria and Empire*, 51. "Because almost all of Hunt's letters have been lost, it is difficult to know how much contact he had with Clark [in 1810]." Ibid., 191.

46. Bradbury, *Travels in the Interior*, 78. Bradbury was a naturalist who traveled with Hunt's party from St. Louis to the Arikara villages in present South Dakota.

47. Clark's journal entry, August 3, 1806, Moulton, *Journals*, 8:277.

48. James, *Three Years among the Indians*, 48.

49. Kelly, *Lost Voices on the Missouri*, 105, 185; letter, Major Thomas Biddle to Colonel Henry Atkinson, October 29, 1819, *American State Papers*, Senate, 16th Congress, 1st Session, Indian Affairs 2 No. 163, 202.

50. Letter, O'Fallon Dougherty to George Martin, January 3, 1907, cited in Kelly, *Lost Voices on the Missouri*, 120.

51. *Louisiana Gazette*, August 8, 1811. This article was written by Henry Marie Brackenridge, who had gone up the Missouri with Lisa, and by Bradbury. The two eventually united on the Missouri and returned to St. Louis together. The report had come from "some hunters who arrived at the [Missouri] Company's fort, at the Mandan villages, early in the spring [of 1811]" from Henry's camp on the "waters of the Columbia." Ibid. As explained later in this chapter, Henry's group spent the winter of 1810–1811 in present southeastern Idaho and built a fort on a tributary of the Snake River now called Henrys Fork.

52. In July 1810, after talking with Menard, who had just returned from Three Forks, Clark wrote a letter in which he claimed that "about 70 men of the [Missouri Fur Company] are yet in the upper Country. 60 went by way of the Madison River over to the heads of a south branch of the Columbia to hunt & trade with the Snake Indians." Letter, William Clark to William Eustis, July 20, 1810, cited in Kelly, *Lost Voices on the Missouri*, 118, bracketed insertion added. Since Thomas James makes it clear that Henry was still at Three Forks when Menard departed, the route described was the one Henry *planned* to take, which Clark assumed had happened by the time he wrote the letter. Reuben Lewis's letter to Meriwether, which Colter had carried with him on his return to St. Louis, offered solid evidence that Henry knew of such a route over the divide. "The upper branches of the Collubmbia are full of beavers," Reuben had written, "and the route by the middle fork of the Madisons River is almost without mountains. It is about 5 or 6 days Travel to an illegible place for a fort on that River where the Beaver (from the account of Peter Wisor) is as abundant as in our part of the Country." Letter, Reuben Lewis to Meriwether Lewis, April 21, 1810, Missouri History Museum, cited in Morris, *Perilous West*, 71–72. Lewis and Clark veteran Peter Weiser, who had enlisted with Lisa in 1807, had apparently explored the Madison River and the area to the south after being sent by Lisa as an emissary to the Absaroka Indians. See Morris, *Fate of the Corps*, 39–41.

53. See Adrian Heidenreich, "The Western Tipi Pole of Crow Territory: Tribes, Fur Trade and the Three Forks Area," particularly p. 85.

54. Kelly, *Lost Voices on the Missouri*, 118.

55. Kelly, *Lost Voices on the Missouri*, 104. Color photographs of the Dougherty Map and Dougherty Narrative are found in the section of illustrations between pages 346 and 347. As Mark Kelly explains, the document is "identified as Map No. 281, filed in the Cartographic Records of the Quartermaster General, Record Group: 92, Series: Post and Reservation File, and housed in the National Archives in College Park, Maryland." Ibid.

56. Dougherty Narrative, cited in Kelly, *Lost Voices on the Missouri*, 119, bracketed insertions in original.

57. At this point the men would have been in the Washakie Wilderness, southeast of the southeast corner of Yellowstone Park, with the headwaters of the Yellowstone River about five miles to the west (with the Continental Divide and headwaters of the Snake River only a few miles farther west).

58. Had Colter been present, he could have informed the men that this stream (now called the Wind River), which he had followed from Brooks Lake, was simply the upper part of the Bighorn. The Dougherty Narrative says the men mistook this river for Clark's Fork, but, as Kelly points out, "there is no Clark's Fork within reach of a *crossing over*" and concludes Dougherty's scribe may have "confused the names of the explorers Lewis and Clark, when demarcating the southerly-flowing subject river." Kelly, *Lost Voices on the Missouri*, 125, italics in original.

59. See Kelly, *Lost Voices on the Missouri*, 103–35, and Hardee, *Pierre's Hole!*, 69–82, for in-depth discussions of Henry's and Dougherty's passages in Idaho.

60. The Fall River, which originates in the southwest corner of Yellowstone Park, flows into Henrys Fork between St. Anthony and Ashton, and Henrys Fork flows into the Snake River near Menan. As Jim Hardee notes, "Fort Henry, built in 1810 and vacated the following spring, was the first American [fur trading] post built on the western side of the Continental Divide." Hardee, *Pierre's Hole!*, 75. Lewis and Clark had constructed the first military post west of the divide at Fort Clatsop. As for Henry's building the first trading post west of the divide, two groups of traders encountered by Lewis and Clark in September of 1806—those led by John McClallen and Charles Courtin—crossed the Continental Divide, apparently north of Three Forks, before Henry or Dougherty. However, there is no record of either group building a trading post. Nor did either group provide information that would prove meaningful in terms of westward expansion. Both McClallen and Courtin were killed by Blackfoot Indians in northwestern Montana in 1810. See Morris, "Mysterious Charles Courtin," for more information on both McClallen and Courtin.

61. Bradbury, *Travels in the Interior*, 77.

62. Ibid., 77–78.

63. Irving, *Astoria*, 176.

64. Kelly, *Lost Voices on the Missouri*, 131.

65. Ibid., 133.

66. Bradbury, *Travels in the Interior*, 78–79. William Clark and others believed the present northwest corner of Wyoming to be the source of virtually all the great rivers of the West, including the two mentioned by Bradbury—the Platte and the Yellowstone. Clark was half-right because the Madison, Gallatin, Yellowstone, Bighorn, Green, and Snake Rivers all have their headwaters in the area. However, several other important rivers, including the Platte, the Rio Grande, the Arkansas, and the Colorado, originate near the Continental Divide in present central Colorado.

67. Philip Rollins, *Discovery of the Oregon Trail*, 281. Hunt's diary is no longer extant; the earliest available document is the French translation, which begins with an interesting combination of first- and third-person accounts. It is reprinted in Rollins, *Discovery of the Oregon Trail*, 281–308. See Morris, *Perilous West*, 173–77, for information on the Dorion family.

68. Irving, *Astoria*, 306.

69. Rollins, *Discovery of the Oregon Trail*, 286.

70. A look at a current road map helps illuminate the different paths taken by Dougherty and Hunt across the Continental Divide. Dougherty ascended the Wind River past Dubois, crossed the Divide at Togwotee Pass, and then went west, descending the Buffalo Fork to its mouth at the Snake River (essentially following Wyoming Highway 26/287). Hunt took the same route initially, staying on the Wind River past Dubois but then followed "an Indian trail . . . southwesterly into the mountains," crossing the Divide at Union Pass, and reaching the "Spanish River," now called the Green River. He eventually picked up the Hoback River, descending it to its mouth at the Snake River (essentially following Highway 189/191 past Bondurant to Hoback Junction).

71. Ibid., 112.

72. Irving, *Astoria*, 276.

73. Rollins, *Discovery of the Oregon Trail*, 293.

74. Ibid., 299.

3. "WE COULD ALWAYS RELY UPON THEIR WORD!"

1. Letter, Franklin Wharton to James Barbour, February 28, 1826, Jackson, *Letters*, 2:640–41. Wharton got his information directly from Pryor.

2. Amy Greenberg, *Manifest Destiny*, 59; P. Richard Metcalf, "Tecumseh," in Lamar, *New Encyclopedia*, 1097.

3. "On [Thomas] Jefferson's orders, the territorial governors of Indiana and Michigan pressured natives to cede millions of acres for a mere penny or two per acre. William Henry Harrison of Indiana was especially relentless, resourceful, and ruthless. He negotiated land cession treaties with older chiefs representing smaller tribes or minorities, outraging most of the Indians, especially the younger warriors. They rallied to the leadership of two Shawnee brothers, Tenskwatawa, a religious prophet, and Tecumseh, a charismatic war chief." Taylor, *Civil War of 1812*, 126–27.

4. Thomas D. Clark, "Tippecanoe, Battle of," in Lamar, *New Encyclopedia*, 1115.

5. Karen Hall Moyars, *Battle of Tippecanoe*, 4; Richard J. Reid, *Battle of Tippecanoe*, 34; and Morris, *Fate of the Corps*, 118.

6. Taylor, *Civil War of 1812*, 127. Taylor also points out that on November 5, 1811, two days before the Battle of Tippecanoe, "Madison had urged Congress to prepare the nation for war against the British empire, which he accused of 'trampling on rights which no Independent Nation can relinquish.' . . . The new speaker of the House, Henry Clay, vigorously supported Madison's call to prepare for war." Ibid., 127, 128.

7. Letter, Franklin Wharton to James Barbour, Jackson, *Letters*, 2:641. Donald Jackson wrote that George Hunt, a trader who worked near Pryor, was taken prisoner the same time as Pryor (ibid., 642–43n1), a claim repeated in Morris, *Fate of the Corps*, 121. Pryor's biographer Lawrence R. Reno, however, has offered persuasive evidence that Hunt was attacked first and had escaped by the time Pryor was held captive. Reno also points out that the claim that Hunt and Pryor escaped with their Indian wives is not backed up by solid evidence. Nor is Pryor known to have had an Indian wife at the time. Reno, *Life and Times of Nathaniel Hale Pryor*, 83–85, 91.

8. Reno, *Nathaniel Hale Pryor*, 84. Blondeau, the son of a French father and Fox Indian mother, was well known as a trader and interpreter. At the time of Pryor's close call with the Winnebagos, he was serving under William Clark as subagent for the Sauk and Fox Indians. Blondeau had lived near the Dubuque mines for years and accompanied Zebulon Pike on part of his exploration of the Mississippi River. On June 27, 1825, Blondeau swore out an affidavit concerning the attack on Pryor's post and his subsequent financial losses. See Reno, *Nathaniel Hale Pryor*, 91n30; Lillian Ruth Colter-Frick, *Courageous Colter*, 486–88; Buckley, *Indian Diplomat*, 94, 118; and Lavender, *Fist in the Wilderness*, 60–61, 189, 191, 286.

9. Letter, William Clark to William Eustis, February 13, 1812, Clarence Carter, *Territorial Papers*, 14:518–20; Jones, *William Clark*, 204.

10. *New England Palladium* (Boston), March 6, 1812, cited in Reno, *Nathaniel Hale Pryor*, 85.

11. Letter, Governor Howard to the Secretary of War, March 19, 1812, Carter, *Territorial Papers*, 14:531–32.

12. A. Douglas Hurt, *Nathan Boone*, 86–87; background information from Anglin and Morris, *Mystery of John Colter*.

13. *Louisiana Gazette*, March 21, 1812, cited in Kate L. Gregg, "War of 1812," 12; Hurt, *Nathan Boone*, 87.

14. *Louisiana Gazette*, July 11, 1812, cited in Gregg, "War of 1812," 15.

15. James, *Three Years among the Indians*, 36.

16. Hurt, *Nathan Boone*, 87.

17. Irving, *Astoria*, 147; Bradbury, *Travels in the Interior*, 19–20.

18. Irving, *Astoria*, 323.

19. McKenzie, McClellan, and the others also discovered among the Nez Perce "a young American, who was deranged, but who sometimes recovered his reason." Gabriel Franchere, *Narrative of a Voyage*, 85. This was Archibald Pelton, who had been with Henry at Three Forks. See Larry E. Morris, "Archibald Pelton."

20. Alexander Ross, *Adventures of the First Settlers*, 53.

21. Ibid., 188–89.

22. Hunt, thirty men, and Marie Dorion and her two sons had reached Fort Astoria on February 15, almost a month after the group headed by McKenzie and McClellan.

23. Late in March, about two and a half weeks before meeting Crooks, the group that included Robert Stuart, McClellan, and Reed had been attacked by Indians near the falls, and McClellan had shot two Indians, definitely killing one and possibly both. Relatives of those men may well have been the Indians who robbed and threatened Crooks and Day.

24. Ross, *Adventures of the First Settlers*, 189–93.

25. Jones, *William Clark*, 206. In a letter to Clark, Secretary of War William Eustis reaffirmed the need to strengthen ties with Indian allies. "Your vigilance and attention are rendered peculiarly necessary . . . at this time, and no exertions or reasonable expenses will be spared to keep the Indians quiet and friendly." Letter, William Eustis to William Clark, June 19, 1812, cited in Buckley, *Indian Diplomat*, 97.

26. Taylor, *Civil War of 1812*, 133.

27. Jones, *William Clark*, 199; Thomas D. Clark, "War of 1812," in Lamar, *New Encyclopedia*, 1177–78. Alan Taylor notes that the long debate among historians over the primary cause of the declaration of war distorts the complex reality of the situation. Instead, he argues, the *interaction* of naval and frontier

concerns that produced "the profound alarm for the republic" ought to be thoroughly examined. Taylor, *Civil War of 1812*, 133–34.

28. Jones, *William Clark*, 85.

29. Letter, Nicholas Biddle to William Clark, July 4, 1812, Jackson, *Letters*, 2:577.

30. Letter, William Clark to Nicholas Biddle, August 6, 1812, ibid., 2:578.

31. Letter written by Christian Wilt, August 23, 1812, cited in Gregg, "War of 1812 ," 18; letter, William Hull to William Eustis, March 6, 1812, cited in Taylor, *Civil War of 1812*, 125. The Americans called Fort Amherstburg "Fort Malden," or "Mahldon" by Wilt's spelling. The British military post at Amherstburg included the fort itself (five miles south of the River aux Canards), a naval base (south of the fort), and the town of Amherstburg (south of the naval base), all lining the east side of the Detroit River not far from its mouth at Lake Erie. See the following website for an 1804 sketch of the post: http://www.warof1812.ca/fortambg.htm, accessed on July 14, 2017.

32. William Hull, "A Proclamation," July 12, 1812, accessed on July 11, 2017, http://www.whatwouldthefoundersthink.com/collossal-miscalculation.

33. Lewis Bond, Journal, cited in Taylor, *Civil War of 1812*, 159.

34. Ibid., 158, 162; Isaac Brock, "Proclamation," July 22, 1812, accessed on July 11, 2017, http://1812now.blogspot.com/2012/07/july-22-1812-brocks-proclamation.html.

35. Taylor, *Civil War of 1812*, 162.

36. Ibid., 162–63.

37. C. P. Stacey, "Brock, Sir Isaac," in *Dictionary of Canadian Biography*, vol. 5, University of Toronto/Université Laval, 2003–, accessed July 24, 2017, http://www.biographi.ca/en/bio/brock_isaac_5E.html; "On July 2, 1812," writes Bob Garcia, "the American schooner Cuyahoga sailed up the Detroit River loaded with supplies, a military band and numerous sick troops belonging to Brigadier-General William Hull's North-Western Army. The occupants of the vessel were unaware of Washington's declaration of war. As the Cuyahoga passed the fort a mixed force of soldiers, sailors and natives lead by Lieutenant Frederick Rolette of the Provincial Marine rowed out and forced the schooner to heave to. The startled Americans put up little resistance. Of vital interest to the British was the discovery of Hull's papers outlining scenarios for a campaign against Fort Amherstburg." Bob Garcia, "Fort Amherstburg in the War of 1812," accessed on July 14, 2017, http://www.warof1812.ca/fortambg.htm. The letters mentioned by Brock were also obtained at this time.

38. Taylor, *Civil War of 1812*, 164.

39. A court-martial trial was held for General William Hull from January to March, 1814, in Albany, New York. He was charged with treason, cowardice, neglect of duty, and un-officer-like conduct, all related to his surrender of Fort

Detroit. Martin Van Buren was one of the chief prosecutors. The court determined it had no jurisdiction to hear the treason charge but found Hull guilty of all the other charges and sentenced him to death, a sentence later remitted by President James Madison. Hull was dishonorably discharged, and his name was removed from army records. "General William Hull Court-Martial: 1814," accessed on July 11, 2017, http://www.encyclopedia.com/law/law-magazines/ general-william-hull-court-martial-1814.

40. Letter written by Christian Wilt on September 13, 1812, cited in Gregg, "War of 1812," 18.

41. Ibid.

42. Cited in E. A. Cruikshank, "Robert Dickson," 138.

43. Letter, William Clark to William Eustis, February 13, 1812, cited in Jones, *William Clark*, 203; underlining is Clark's, bracketed insertion Jones's. Clark's claim that Dickson had smuggled goods through Green Bay was accurate.

44. Robert S. Allen, "Dickson, Robert," in *Dictionary of Canadian Biography*, vol. 6, University of Toronto/Université Laval, 2003–, accessed July 24, 2017, http://www.biographi.ca/en/bio/dickson_robert_6E.html; letter, William Clark to Ninian Edwards, August 16, 1812, cited in Jones, *William Clark*, 207–8.

45. Letter, Captain Nathan Heald to General Thomas H. Cushing, October 23, 1812, Brannan, *Official Letters*, 85. On August 24, nine days after the massacre, Lieutenant T. Hamilton of Fort Madison heard a report from an Indian chief that "Fort Dearborn . . . was taken & burnt on the 16th by 200 Indians. 60 men were killed and 20 taken Prisoners, also 10 Women." This word-of-mouth account was surprisingly accurate. Letter, Lieutenant T. Hamilton to Lieutenant Colonel Daniel Bissell, August 24, 1812, cited in Gregg, "War of 1812," 18.

46. Louis A. Tohill, "Robert Dickson," 337; Robert S. Allen, "Dickson, Robert," in *Dictionary of Canadian Biography*, vol. 6, University of Toronto/Université Laval, 2003–, accessed July 24, 2017, http://www.biographi.ca/en/bio/ dickson_robert_6E.html. In February of 1812, with war looming, General Brock had sent a "Confidential Communication" to Dickson asking if his "friends" could help the British cause. Dickson soon responded by saying he had gathered 250 to 300 Indian allies and would lead them to the nearest British post immediately. Ibid.

47. Jones, *William Clark*, 209–10; Patrick Jung, *Black Hawk War*, 28, italics in original.

48. Cruikshank, "Robert Dickson," 138. See also Hardee, "Influence of the Red-Headed Chief," 8–18. Hardee notes that besides Clark and Dickson, one other person was known as "Red Head" during this period along the Missou-

ri—the Sauk chief Mess-con-de-bay. Thanks to Landon Jones for pointing out the parallels between Clark and Dickson. As Jones says, Dickson became both Clark's "antagonist and his real-life doppelganger." The perceptive Jones adds that when Zebulon Pike was on his expedition up the Mississippi in 1805 and met Dickson, Pike might as well have been depicting Clark when he said Dickson was "a gentleman of commercial knowledge and possessing much geographical knowledge of the western country and of open, frank manners." Jones, *William Clark*, 203–4. Cruikshank mentions another possible parallel between Clark and Dickson when he writes that Bradbury met Dickson and reported that Dickson had traveled the vast country lying between St. Louis and the source of the Missouri River. In this regard, however, Cruikshank has misread Bradbury because the latter makes clear that the Dickson he is talking about is Joseph Dickson, whom Colter joined (along with Forrest Hancock) to trap the Yellowstone River in 1806. See Bradbury, *Travels in the Interior*, 17n–21n.

49. Kelly, *Lost Voices on the Missouri*, 142; *Annals of Congress*, 11th Congress, 2d session, p. 580, Library of Congress website, accessed July 15, 2017, https://memory.loc.gov/cgi-bin/ampage?collId=llac&fileName=020/llac020.db&recNum=285.

50. Robert S. Allen, "Dickson, Robert," in *Dictionary of Canadian Biography*, vol. 6, University of Toronto/Université Laval, 2003–, accessed July 24, 2017, http://www.biographi.ca/en/bio/dickson_robert_6E.html; letter, Colonel Dickson to Jacob Franks, October 2, 1812, Dickson and Grignon Papers, 1812–1815, Library of Congress website, accessed on July 15, 2017, https://cdn.loc.gov/service/gdc/lhbum/7689a/7689a_0287_0331.pdf.

51. Rollins, *Discovery of the Oregon Trail*, 151.

52. Pacific Fur Company Minute Book, cited in Irving, *Astoria*, 355n2.

53. Ibid., 355.

54. Ibid., 355n5.

55. Rollins, *Discovery of the Oregon Trail*, 3, 31; see Morris, *Perilous West*, 146 and 172–73, for more information on Day and how he either quickly recovered from his madness or was feigning mental illness because he found McClellan's company intolerable.

56. Rollins, *Discovery of the Oregon Trail*, 86. The invaluable narratives of Robert Stuart compiled by Philip Ashton Rollins include both his contemporaneous journal entries and what Rollins calls "the travelling memoranda," a postscript commentary added by Stuart sometime before 1821. Rollins reprints the traveling memoranda in italics. See Rollins's foreword for more on the complex story of Stuart's narrative.

57. Ibid., 113.

58. See Morris, *Perilous West*, 155–60.

59. Rollins, *Discovery of the Oregon Trail*, 80, 128. As Dale Morgan has noted, when the Indian mentioned a shorter trace, "he was talking about South Pass, history's first intimation of that route across the Continental Divide." Morgan, *The West of William H. Ashley*, xxxix.

60. Rollins, *Discovery of the Oregon Trail*, 132, 131, 133. "To prevent an open rupture [with the Crow Indians]," wrote Stuart on September 13, "we gave them about twenty loads of Powder and left them happy at getting off on no worse terms." Ibid., 131.

61. Ibid., 137, 139.

62. Ibid., 152.

63. Irving, *Astoria*, 394; Rollins, *Discovery of the Oregon Trail*, 152.

64. Ibid.; Morris, *Perilous West*, 179–80.

65. Rollins, *Discovery of the Oregon Trail*, 153, 155.

66. Ibid., 156.

67. Ibid., 156–57.

68. Ibid., 157. See ibid., 155–58 and 173n73–175n74, for Rollins's extensive discussion of this episode.

69. Ibid., 161.

70. Ibid., 162. Rollins adds this explanation, which corrects Stuart but also shows how well he understood his position: "Although the Wind River Range of mountains was actually the watershed between (1) the waters, which, immediately east of that range, discharged into the Missouri River and (2) those which, immediately west of that range, were in the Green River's valley and thus flowed toward the Gulf of California, nevertheless the Wind River Range was not concerned with any streams which drained into the Columbia River basin. However, immediately northwest of Wind River Range and topographically tied to it, was the Gros Ventre Range, which did divide the waters destined for the Missouri from those destined for the Columbia." Ibid., 180n139–181n139.

71. Ibid., 164, 256; DeVoto, *Year of Decision*, 55; DeVoto, *The Wide Missouri*, 54. "Surely the most notable geographic accomplishment for the Astorians," writes Ronda, "came in 1812 when Robert Stuart and his eastbound party came upon South Pass in Wyoming's Wind River range." Ronda, *Astoria and Empire*, 323.

4. "LET THE NORTH AS WELL AS THE SOUTH BE JACKSONIZED!!!"

1. James Parton, *Life of Andrew Jackson*, 392; Certificate of James W. Sitler, September 5, 1813, Library of Congress website, accessed on July 20, 2017, https://cdn.loc.gov/service/mss/maj/01012/01012_0130_0131.pdf; and

Ken Mueller, *Senator Benton and the People*, 48. On their spring 1813 journey from Natchez, Mississippi, to Nashville, Tennessee, Jackson's company passed Grinder's Stand (southeast of Nashville), where Meriwether Lewis had died three and a half years earlier. The name of Talbot's Hotel and Tavern was later changed to the City Hotel.

2. Mueller, *Senator Benton and the People*, 48.

3. Letter, Thomas Hart Benton to Andrew Jackson, July 25, 1813, from Correspondence of Andrew Jackson, edited by John Spencer Bassett, Library of Congress website, accessed July 22, 2017, https://cdn.loc.gov/service/mss/maj/01012/01012_0061_0064.pdf.

4. Mueller, *Senator Benton and the People*, 49; Robert Remini, *Life of Andrew Jackson*, 69.

5. Certificate of James W. Sitler; Parton, *Life of Andrew Jackson*, 393–94; "Thomas H. Benton's Account of His Duel with General Jackson," September 10, 1813, *The Papers of Andrew Jackson Digital Edition*, Daniel Feller, editor; Charlottesville: University of Virginia Press, Rotunda, 2015–, accessed July 21, 2017, http://rotunda.upress.virginia.edu/founders/JKSN-01-02-02-0294.

6. Parton, *Life of Andrew Jackson*, 393.

7. "Thomas H. Benton's Account of His Duel with General Jackson." In the same published document, Benton offered his account of what happened: 1. That myself and my brother Jesse Benton arriving in Nashville on the morning of the affray, & knowing of Gen. Jackson's threats, went and took lodgings in a different house from the one in which he staid, on purpose to avoid him. 2. That the general and some of his friends came to the house where we had put up, and commenced the attack by levelling a pistol at me, when I had no weapon drawn, and advancing upon me at a quick pace, without giving me time to draw one. 3. That seeing this my brother fired upon Gen. Jackson when he had got within eight or ten feet of me. 4. That four other pistols were fired in quick succession: one by Genl. Jackson at me: two by me at the General: and one by Col. Coffee at me. In the course of this firing Gen. Jackson was brought to the ground; but I received no hurt. 5. That daggers were then drawn. Col. Coffee and Mr. Alexander Donelson made at me, and gave me five slight wounds. Capt. [Eli] Hammond and Mr. Stokley Hays engaged my brother, who being still weak from the effect of a severe wound he had lately received in a duel, was not able to resist two men. They got him down; and while Captain Hammond beat him on the head to make him lay still, Mr. Hays attempted to stab him, and wounded him in both arms, as he lay on his back parrying the thrusts with his naked hands. From this situation a generous hearted citizen of Nashville, Mr. [Thomas E.?] Sumner,

relieved him. Before he came to the ground my brother clapped a pistol to the body of Mr. Hays to blow him through, but it missed fire.

6. My own and my brothers pistols carried two balls each: for it was our intention, if driven to arms, to have no childs play. The pistols fired at me were so near that the blaze of the muzzle of one of them burnt the sleeve of my coat, and the other aimed at my head, at little more than arms length from it.

7. Capt. Carroll was to have taken part in the affray, but was absent by the permission of General Jackson, as he has since proved by the Generals certificate: a certificate which reflects I know not whether less honor upon the General or upon the Captain.

8. That this attack was made upon me in the house where the judge of the district Mr. [Bennett] Searcy, had his lodgings! So little are the laws and its ministers respected! Nor has the civil authority yet taken cognizance of this horrible outrage.

8. A. M. J. Hyatt, "Procter, Henry," in *Dictionary of Canadian Biography*, vol. 6, University of Toronto/Université Laval, 2003–, accessed July 24, 2017, http://www.biographi.ca/en/bio/procter_henry_6E.html; letter, Colonel Henry Procter to Major-General Sheaffe, January 25, 1813, Alexander Clark Casselman, *Richardson's War of 1812*, 141–42. The Indians had stripped Winchester of his uniform before taking him to Procter, leading Richardson to believe that the general had been so taken by surprise that he hadn't had time to dress.

9. Letter, Colonel Henry Procter to Major-General Sheaffe, January 25, 1813, Casselman.

10. A. M. J. Hyatt, "Procter, Henry," in *Dictionary of Canadian Biography*, vol. 6, University of Toronto/Université Laval, 2003–, accessed July 25, 2017, http://www.biographi.ca/en/bio/procter_henry_6E.html.

11. Casselman, *Richardson's War of 1812*, 134–35; David R. Beasley, "Richardson, John (1796–1852)," in *Dictionary of Canadian Biography*, vol. 8, University of Toronto/Université Laval, 2003–, accessed July 25, 2017, http://www.biographi.ca/en/bio/richardson_john_1796_1852_8E.html. John Richardson was the nephew, on his mother's side, of fur trader John Askin Jr., an associate of Robert Dickson.

12. William Atherton, *Narrative of the Suffering*, 42.

13. Casselman, *Richardson's War of 1812*, 135.

14. *Missouri Gazette*, February 20, 1813.

15. Letter, General William Henry Harrison to Governor Isaac Shelby, January 24, 1813, *Missouri Gazette*, February 20, 1813.

16. Letter, Major Martin D. Hardin to Governor Isaac Shelby, January 24, 1813, *Missouri Gazette*, February 20, 1813.

17. Letter written by Christian Wilt, February 20, 1813, cited in Gregg, "War of 1812," 186.

18. Gregg, "War of 1812," 187; Jones, *William Clark*, 211.

19. William Foley, *Wilderness Journey*, 37, 46, 175.

20. Letter, John O'Fallon to Fanny Fitzhugh, February 11, 1813, cited in Jones, *William Clark*, 210. Clark's biographers offer no information on John O'Fallon's release, but less than three months after the Battle of Frenchtown, he was at Fort Meigs serving as Harrison's acting assistant adjutant general. A year later he was in good health and operating a store in Kentucky. Benson Lossing, *Pictorial Fieldbook of the War of 1812*, 486n3; Jones, *William Clark*, 219. William Atherton, by contrast, was held prisoner by the Indians or British until June of 1814 when he was released in a prisoner exchange.

21. William Bratton's Discharge, October 6, 1806, Jackson, *Letters*, 1:347–48; *Heroes of 1812*, 17, 95–97.

22. "Captain Nathaniel Gray Smith Hart's Story," *Monroe Memories and More* (blog), November 26, 2016, accessed on July 28, 2017, https://monroemichigan.wordpress.com/2016/11/26/marker-memories-river-raisin-battlefield-perspectives.

23. Ibid., Taylor, *Civil War of 1812*, 211–12; Atherton, *Narrative*, 55.

24. Thomas Dudley, *Battle and Massacre at Frenchtown*, 2–3. Dudley believed Elliott was nervous because he "could not have forgotten the humiliation he had contracted in deceiving Hart's family, pecuniarily," a detail not explained (nor confirmed by Atherton). Ibid., 3.

25. Atherton, *Narrative*, 55–56. The most damaging testimony regarding Elliott came from John Todd, a surgeon with the Kentucky volunteer militia. He witnessed the meeting between Hart and Elliott on January 22 and was present the next morning when Captain Hickman was killed and the massacre began. Shortly thereafter, Todd was tied and taken by an Indian about four miles toward Malden to a British camp. "I informed [Elliott] what had taken place, and requested him to send back immediately," wrote Todd, "that some who were badly wounded might still be alive, and could be saved, and particularly named Captain Hart, for whom [Elliott] had manifested much friendship." Elliott was unmoved. "It is now too late," he said, "you may rest assured that those who are once taken up by the Indians are safe, and will be taken to Malden, and those who are badly wounded are killed 'ere this." When Todd continued to plead for Hart's rescue, Elliott responded with a platitude: "Charity begins at home; my own wounded are to be conveyed first, and if any sleighs remain they shall be sent back for your wounded." When Todd again reminded Elliott and a British surgeon of the outrage he had witnessed, "they appeared much exasperated, and declared it was impossible to restrain the savages." Statement of John Todd, M.D., before the Honorable Jesse Bledsoe, Lexington, Kentucky, May 2, 1813, *Debates and Proceedings in the Congress*, 2321–24.

26. Atherton, *Narrative*, 63.

27. Ibid., 62, 63. Atherton, who had risked his life to help the wounded and was eventually saved by Indians, added a memorable postscript: "The kindness and sympathy manifested toward me by the Indians, and particularly by the wife of the man who took me a prisoner, took off a part of the burthen [of sorrow and despair]. This poor heathen woman, who knew nothing of civilization, and the softening influences of the Gospel, nevertheless showed that the tenderness and affection which the Gospel requires were deeply imprinted upon her heart. I had another source of comfort: I found among the Indians a piece of a newspaper printed at Lexington, Kentucky, which I suppose had wrapped up the clothes of some of Captain Hart's men, and thus fell into the hands of the Indians at Raisin. This I read over and over, again and again." Ibid., 92. When he published his narrative in 1842, William Atherton had been an ordained minister of the Methodist Episcopal Church for almost twenty years.

28. Taylor, *Civil War of 1812*, 212.

29. Letter, Governor Isaac Shelby to General William Henry Harrison, February 9, 1813, "Correspondence between Shelby and Harrison," 131; letter, Shelby to Harrison, March 20, 1813, ibid., 132; letter, Shelby to Harrison, April 4, 1813, ibid., 136; and Larry Nelson, "Dudley's Defeat," 13–14.

30. General orders of Brigadier-General Green Clay, April 7, 1813, reprinted in Casselman, *Richardson's War of 1812*, 176.

31. Nelson, "Dudley's Defeat," 15–20.

32. Ibid., 20–21; diary of Major James Taylor Eubank in "Siege of Fort Meigs," 58–60.

33. Lossing, *Pictorial Fieldbook of the War of 1812*, 485; Nelson, "Dudley's Defeat," 23–24.

34. Lossing, *Pictorial Fieldbook of the War of 1812*, 485.

35. Nelson, "Dudley's Defeat," 25, 27.

36. Ibid., 28–29.

37. Ibid., 31–32.

38. Lossing, *Pictorial Fieldbook of the War of 1812*, 486.

39. Nelson, "Dudley's Defeat," 32, 33.

40. Casselman, *Richardson's War of 1812*, 151. Most contemporary observers estimated that approximately 70 of Dudley's men were killed, with 580 taken prisoner, and 150 escaping to either Fort Meigs or Fort Defiance. Nelson, "Dudley's Defeat," 39.

41. Casselman, *Richardson's War of 1812*, 153–54.

42. Cited in Nelson, "Dudley's Defeat," 38.

43. *New York Evening Post*, May 21, 1813.

44. *Missouri Gazette*, May 8, 1813. On April 13, in present southeastern Nebraska, Stuart and the others confirmed "the disagreeable intelligence of a war between America and Great Britain . . . but in such a confused manner was it related that we could comprehend but little." Rollins, *Discovery of the Oregon Trail*, 235. It had been ten months since the declaration of war.

45. *Missouri Gazette*, May 8, 1813.

46. *Debates and Proceedings in the Congress*, 2239. Besides the section on the treatment of prisoners at Frenchtown, the report presented evidence on eight other charges.

47. Ibid.

48. Ibid., 2321–22.

49. Ibid., 2241.

50. Letter, Harry Toulmin to the editor, September 7, 1813, *Raleigh (NC) Register*, October 8, 1813. Toulmin got his information from "a person of character and credibility who was present during the whole scene, and who escaped through the opening made in the pickets." Ibid.

51. Ibid.

52. Ibid. William C. Davis puts the total at "nearly five hundred." Davis, *Three Roads to the Alamo*, 26.

53. Remini, *Life of Andrew Jackson*, 71–72.

54. Ibid., 72.

55. Ibid.

56. David Crockett, *Life of Col. David Crockett*, 62; Davis, *Three Roads to the Alamo*, 225–27.

57. Remini, *Life of Andrew Jackson*, 72–73.

58. Crockett, *Life of Col. David Crockett*, 75–76.

59. Remini, *Life of Andrew Jackson*, 73.

60. *Missouri Gazette*, May 28, 1814. The Creek Wars essentially ruined Jackson's health for the rest of his life because of chronic dysentery brought on by wilderness life, a lack of essential food and medicine, and his own refusal to care for himself. Remini, *Life of Andrew Jackson*, 84.

61. Letter, William Clark to John Armstrong, January 6, 1814, cited in Jones, *William Clark*, 217. As Landon Jones notes, however, Sauk aggression generally happened *after* white settlers occupied territory the Sauk people considered their own. "The Sauks were still bitter over Harrison's 1804 treaty that had appropriated millions of acres of their land." Ibid., 217–18.

62. Carter, *Territorial Papers*, 14:746–47.

63. *Missouri Gazette*, April 9, 1814.

64. Henry Levens and Nathaniel Drake, *History of Cooper County*, 31–32.

65. *Missouri Gazette*, June 18, 1814.

66. Buckley, *Indian Diplomat*, 106.

5. "ENTERPRISING YOUNG MEN"

1. *Missouri Intelligencer* (Franklin), April 1, 1823. The article about the ball was separate from but on the same page as the announcement of the arrival of Ashley's keelboats. Ashley's exact birth date is unknown, but Dale Morgan writes that 1778 seems quite plausible. Morgan, *The West of William H. Ashley*, xv.

2. Ibid.

3. William E. Parrish, "Becknell, William," in Lamar, *New Encyclopedia*, 89.

4. Letter, Henry Atkinson to John C. Calhoun, January 25, 1822, in Morgan, *The West of William Ashley*, 1. Background from ibid., xvi.

5. *Missouri Gazette & Public Advertiser*, February 13, 1822. The advertisement also appeared in other newspapers in February and March. As Morgan points out, "Men were in demand for the fur trade as never before" because the Missouri Fur Company and various expeditions to Santa Fe were also recruiting hands. Ashley was the first trader to use the newspaper to enlist large numbers of employees. Morgan, *The West of William Ashley*, 228n18, 227n3.

6. Jedediah Smith, Journal, 1822, in Morgan, *The West of William Ashley*, 12.

7. Ibid.; Hiram Chittenden, *American Fur Trade of the Far West*, 1:262.

8. Jedediah Smith, Journal, 1822, in Morgan, *The West of William Ashley*, 12.

9. Ibid., 14.

10. Ibid.

11. Lewis's journal entry, April 25, 1805, Moulton, *Journals*, 4:66; letter, Daniel T. Potts to "Dear and Respected Brother," July 16, 1826, accessed on August 26, 2017, https://user.xmission.com/~drudy/mtman/html/potts2.html. The first post named after Henry was built in the spring of 1810 near Three Forks, the second on southeastern Idaho's Henrys Fork in the autumn of the same year. (A fourth would soon be constructed near the mouth of the Bighorn River.) A number of forts would be established near the confluence of the Yellowstone and the Missouri, most notably Fort Union. See Chittenden, *Fur Trade of the Far West*, 2:932–35.

12. Jedediah Smith, Journal, 1822, in Morgan, *The West of William Ashley*, 14. A pirogue was a large wooden boat usually measuring between thirty and forty feet long that could haul about eight tons of freight. Alan Hartley, *Lewis & Clark Lexicon of Discovery*, 128–29.

13. "Postexpeditionary Miscellany," Moulton, *Journals*, 8:381; *Missouri Saturday News* (St. Louis), April 14, 1838, in Morgan, *The West of William Ash-*

ley, 15; and letter, William Clark to John C. Calhoun, January 16, 1823, in Morgan, *The West of William Ashley*, 20.

14. *Missouri Republican*, January 15, 1823, in Morgan, *The West of William Ashley*, 19. As Morgan notes, the practice of offering the men a standard annual salary enlarged the recruiting pool by making it possible for some men to take advances and leave the money with their families.

15. *St. Louis Enquirer*, reprinted in *Missouri Intelligencer*, September 17, 1822, in Morgan, *The West of William Ashley*, 19; Reuben Holmes, "The Five Scalps," 6, 7; Morris, *Perilous West*, 115–16, 122; and Kelly, *Lost Voices on the Missouri*, 138–40.

16. "Letters from the West," 215.

17. Linda Hasselstrom, *James Clyman*, 1–2, 9.

18. John Sunder, *Bill Sublette*, 28–29, 35.

19. LeRoy R. Hafen, *Broken Hand: The Life of Thomas Fitzpatrick*, 7, 1.

20. *Missouri Intelligencer*, April 1, 1823.

21. *Missouri Republican*, March 12, 1823, in Morgan, *The West of William Ashley*, 22.

22. John Darby, *Personal Recollections*, 164; *Missouri Republican*, March 19, 1823, in Morgan, *The West of William Ashley*, 22.

23. Not surprisingly, Dale Morgan researched the gunpowder mishap meticulously. See *The West of William H. Ashley*, 22, 232n68. Elihu Shepard, one of the sources cited by Morgan, identified a "Mr. Lebarge" as one of the men who died in the accident; Shepard, *Autobiography*, 103. Ashley's biographer Richard M. Clokey goes further, stating that "the captain of the *Yellowstone* [one of Ashley's keelboats] was later reported to have been Joseph La Barge, a brother of the wagon driver who was killed in the gunpowder explosion." Clokey, *William H. Ashley*, 97n54, bracketed explanation added. But this seems to be a case of Shepard confusing La Barge, who was a keelboat captain for Ashley, with one of the victims, and Clokey compounding that mistake because no primary document claims that two men named *La Barge* were both Ashley employees—nor does any other primary document name any victims of the accident, while the best source simply says the men hauling the gunpowder stopped at "the tavern-house of Mr. Joseph Labarge." Darby, *Personal Recollections*, 261. Moreover, neither Dale Morgan (a William Ashley expert) nor Hiram Chittenden (both a fur trade and La Barge family expert) concludes that a Mr. La Barge was one of those killed. In a two-volume history of Joseph La Barge (1815–1899), the most illustrious captain in the history of Missouri steamboating, Chittenden confirms that the captain's father, also named Joseph La Barge (1787–1860), was with Ashley in 1823. Chittenden, *History of Early Steamboat Navigation*, 5. Finally, extensive genealogical research by the La Barge family acknowledges that Joseph Sr. indeed owned an inn (managed

by someone else during his travels with Ashley) but makes no mention of a family member perishing in the gunpowder misfortune. See, for example, the website https://www.geni.com/people/Joseph-LaBarge/6000000011601246711, accessed on September 2, 2017.

24. Clokey, *William H. Ashley*, 36.

25. Hasselstrom, *James Clyman*, 10.

26. Clark's journal entry, July 30, 1804, Moulton, *Journals*, 2:430; Sunder, *Bill Sublette*, 12.

27. Hasselstrom, *James Clyman*, 10; Holmes, "The Five Scalps," 4, 5n1.

28. Letter, William H. Ashley to the *Missouri Republican*, June 4, 1823, in Morgan, *The West of William Ashley*; ibid., 233n75; Morgan, *Jedediah Smith*, 50.

29. Deposition of Hugh Johnson, St. Louis, January 13, 1824, in Morgan, *The West of William Ashley*, 72; Account of Ashley & Henry for Property Lost to the Indians, 1822–1823, in ibid., 70.

30. *St. Louis Enquirer*, August 30, 1824, in Morgan, *The West of William Ashley*, 87. "After an absence of nearly three years [two years and five months]," read the article, "we are happy to announce the safe return of Maj. Henry, . . . with a part of his company, from the Rocky Mountains." See also Louis J. Clements, "Andrew Henry," in Hafen, *Mountain Men*, 6:173–84; and Linda Harper White and Fred Gowans, "Traders to Trappers," 58–65.

31. Hasselstrom, *James Clyman*, 11. As for the cause of the conflict between the Missouri Fur Company men and the Arikara, Morgan relates quite a different story, saying that in March a band of Arikara had robbed and assaulted six Missouri Company employees "who were out collecting furs and robes that had been traded from the Sioux." A few days later the post was again attacked by Arikara warriors, and Angus McDonald and several others held their ground, killing two Indians and wounding others in the process. Morgan, *Jedediah Smith*, 50–51.

32. Letter, William H. Ashley to the *Missouri Republican*, in Morgan, *The West of William Ashley*, 25–26.

33. Hasselstrom, *James Clyman*, 11.

34. Ibid., 26.

35. Pryor's letter to William Clark described how, in the midst of Pryor's intense and prolonged negotiations, "the chief to whom I had given the Medal [Grey Eyes], threw it to the ground, and . . . the Indians now raised a general Whoop, . . . as they retired to the willows [and] fired on the men." Letter, Nathaniel Pryor to William Clark, October 16, 1807, Jackson, *Letters*, 2:435, bracketed explanations added.

36. Hasselstrom, *James Clyman*, 11; letter, William H. Ashley to Benjamin O'Fallon, June 4, 1823, in Morgan, *The West of William Ashley*, 29, italics added.

37. Chittenden, *Fur Trade of the Far West*, 1:265.

38. James P. Ronda, foreword, in Chittenden, *Fur Trade of the Far West*, 1:xv.

39. Hasselstrom, *James Clyman*, 11.

40. Letter by one of Ashley's men to a friend in the District of Columbia, June 17, 1823, *National Intelligencer* (Washington, DC), September 3, 1823, in Morgan, *The West of William Ashley*, 32.

41. Ashley wrote three letters about his unfortunate encounter with the Arikara, two on June 4 and one on June 7. One of the June 4 letters includes the ambiguous description that he was informed of Stephens's death "just before day light"; the other June 4 letter agrees with his June 7 account, giving the time of "about ½ past 3 o'clock in the morning" (Morgan, *The West of William Ashley*, 26, 28, 30). Although Chittenden followed Ashley in listing the time "at half past three o'clock" (*Fur Trade of the Far West*, 1:265), other historians have hedged their bets—Sunder, *"before sunrise"* (*Bill Sublette*, 39), and Hafen and Morgan, "sometime after midnight" (*Broken Hand*, 15; *Jedediah Smith*, 53, respectively).

42. Hasselstrom, *James Clyman*, 11.

43. Letter by one of Ashley's men, in Morgan, *The West of William Ashley*, 32. This letter also reports that three Indians managed to get on Ashley's boat and reach his cabin, waking him when they opened the door. The Indians reportedly disappeared when Ashley drew his pistol. This story is suspect because it is not corroborated by any other source and because the writer did not claim to be an eyewitness, implying, to the contrary, that he was on the other boat. As Morgan says, "Ashley does not mention such an incident, and under the circumstances it challenges belief." (Ibid., 236n103.)

44. Letter by one of Ashley's men, in Morgan, *The West of William Ashley*, 32. Richard Graham, a respected Indian agent and former army officer, gave a similar report to the Senate Committee on Indian Affairs (chaired by Thomas Hart Benton) on February 10, 1824, noting that during the course of the evening of June 1, a chief warned Ashley "of the intention of the villages to attack him that night, or very early the next morning, and advised him to take his horses on the opposite bank of the river." Ashley reportedly concluded, however, that the chief actually wanted to steal the horses and therefore "strengthened his guard, and paid no further attention to the chief, who continued urging him to move to the opposite side." 18th Congress, 1st Session, Senate Document 56, Serial 91, in *American State Papers*, Class II, Indian Affairs [Washington: Gales and Seaton, 1834], 2:452. Earlier in his testimony,

Graham mentioned details included by Clyman but not by the Fort Kiowa letter, showing he collected information from a variety of sources.

45. Barton Barbour, *Jedediah Smith*, 41–42. Hugh Glass and the Fort Kiowa letter both mention the storm. Morgan, *The West of William Ashley*, 31, 32.

46. Letter, William Ashley to the *Missouri Republican*, in Morgan, *The West of William Ashley*, 26.

47. Letter by one of Ashley's men, in Morgan, *The West of William Ashley*, 32.

48. Hasselstrom, *James Clyman*, 12.

49. Ibid.

50. "Jedediah Strong Smith," *Illinois Monthly Magazine*, June 1832, cited in Morgan, *Jedediah Smith*, 54.

51. Holmes, "The Five Scalps," 44.

52. Ashley wrote that his "party consisted of ninety men, forty of whom were . . . encamped on the sand beach." That number was reduced to thirty-nine by the time of the attack because Aaron Stephens had been killed in one of the Arikara villages. David E. Jackson, later a partner with Smith and Sublette, had enlisted with Ashley in 1822 and, according to Morgan, "is said to have been with Jedediah on the beach before the Ree towns in 1823." No primary document, however, confirms Jackson's presence. Morgan, *The West of William Ashley*, 23, 30, 52; Morgan, *Jedediah Smith*, 189.

53. When Jedediah Smith first saw the Arikara towns early in September of 1822, he wrote that they were "situated about three hundred yards from the missouri [River]"; the Fort Kiowa letter adds: "In front of the town, at low water, a sand bar makes its appearance, and extends for about three hundred yards into the river." Morgan, *The West of William Ashley*, 13, 32. The distance, therefore, from where the men were camped on the sandbar to where the Indians were firing depended on how high the river was and how close to the water the men were camped (and, of course how accurate Smith and the other man were in their estimates). Given these details and Clyman's mention of "long range," 150 yards seems like the minimum distance between Ashley's men and their assailants. A good marksman could be accurate at two hundred yards or more with an 1800-era rifle, such as the M. 1803 rifles purchased by Meriwether Lewis for the expedition. As for the weapons used by the Arikara, Ashley contradicted himself when he wrote that most of the Arikara warriors were "armed with London Fuzils that carry a ball with great accuracy." Ibid., 27. *London fusil* was another name for the smooth-bore trade arm generally called the Northwest gun, the most widely distributed firearm in America during the eighteenth and nineteenth centuries. It was essentially a shotgun that was deadly at close range but ineffective at long range. The Arikara warri-

ors shooting accurately at long range must have been using rifles, certainly quite possible in 1823 or even before. See Carl Russell, *Firearms, Traps, & Tools*, 64–75.

54. Letter, William Ashley to a gentleman in Franklin, Missouri, June 7, 1823, in Morgan, *The West of William Ashley*, 30.

55. Hasselstrom, *James Clyman*, 12.

56. Letter, William Ashley to the *Missouri Republican*, in Morgan, *The West of William Ashley*, 26.

57. Letter by one of Ashley's men, in Morgan, *The West of William Ashley*, 32–33.

58. Hasselstrom, *James Clyman*, 12.

59. Ibid., 12–15. Ashley's final list of casualties was as follows: "KILLED: John Mathews, John Collins, Benjamin F. Sneed, Thully Piper, James M'Daniel, Joseph [John] S. Gardner, George Flages, David Howard, Aaron Stephens, James Penn, Jr., John Miller, Elliss Ogle. WOUNDED: John Larrison, Joseph Manso, Reed Gibson, (since dead), Joseph Thompson, Robert Tucker, James Davis, Aaron Ricketts, Jacob Miller, August Dufren, Hugh Glass, Daniel M'Clain, Thilless, (black man.)."

60. Will Bagley, *South Pass*, 54. Although Ashley sincerely mourned the loss of his men, he never acknowledged his failure to heed the continual signs of trouble, instead blaming the boatmen for not obeying his orders to rescue the riflemen after some of them had already been killed. This theme was picked up by Benjamin O'Fallon, Indian agent for the Upper Missouri Agency (and brother of John O'Fallon and nephew of William Clark). In a letter addressed to the forty-three men who by this time had deserted Ashley's expedition, O'Fallon praised Ashley, characterizing him as "amongst the greatest military chieftians of the State of Missouri," and reminded the men of their shame in leaving the "A'rickaras mangling the bodies and decorating themselves with the reeking sculps of 14 of your Comrads." Letter, Benjamin O'Fallon to Ashley's deserters, June 19, 1823, in Morgan, *The West of William Ashley*, 34.

61. *Missouri Gazette*, May 8, 1813.

62. The article, called "American Enterprize," ran for more than three thousand words and was published in the *Missouri Gazette* on May 15, 1813. It was apparently based on interviews with Stuart, Crooks, and McClellan. See Morris, *Perilous West*, 187–93, for a complete reprint.

63. McClallen and Courtin, however, along with the majority of their men, both perished at the hands of Blackfoot warriors in present northwest Montana. See Morris, "Mysterious Charles Courtin." The Astorians had little if any information on the two ill-fated traders but correctly concluded, based on reports of the troubles of Menard and Henry, that it was best to avoid Blackfoot territory on their way west.

64. According to David A. White, in 1811 Dr. Samuel Latham Mitchill, wrote of a west–east crossing of the Continental Divide. If true, this would have been the first crossing after Lewis and Clark. "The friend of a correspondent in Natchez claimed to have met Baptiste Lavall, Michael Connor, Jean Lozier, and Emanuel Silver, who had come overland to the Mississippi River from a point 200 miles south of the Columbia. Their ship, the *Sea Otter*, was wrecked there on August 22, 1808, and they made the trip 'with no other provision than their guns, with six pounds of powder, and twenty pounds of shot.' Bancroft (28:129) summarily rejected an entirely independent version of the same story from Henry Schoolcraft and George Gibbs, who got it from 'some ship's log.'" White, *News of the Plains and Rockies*, 123–24. Thus far, however, no primary document supporting this story has been found. See also the following websites, accessed on September 7, 2017: https://journals.lib. washington.edu/index.php/WHQ/article/viewFile/8574/7609 and http:// offbeatoregon.com/o1102b-shipwrecked-fur-traders-trekked-to-Louisiana. html.

65. Ross, *Adventures of the First Settlers*.

66. Morgan, *The West of William Ashley*, xli; Chittenden, *Fur Trade of the Far West*, 1:127–29.

67. Letter, Jules de Mun to William Clark, November 25, 1817, communicated to the House of Representatives on April 15, 1818, *American State Papers, Foreign Relations*, 4:211, 212.

68. Letter, John C. Calhoun to Thomas A. Smith, March 16, 1818, *Correspondence of John C. Calhoun*, accessed on September 8, 2017, https://archive. org/stream/correspondenceof00calhrich/correspondenceof00calhrich_djvu.txt.

69. William Lass, *Navigating the Missouri*, 36, 43.

70. Letter, John C. Calhoun to Andrew Jackson, August 18, 1818, cited in Lass, *Navigating the Missouri*, 35.

71. *St. Louis Enquirer*, June 23, 1819, cited in Kelly, *Lost Voices on the Missouri*, 169.

72. Foley, *Wilderness Journey*, 210; Mueller, *Senator Benton and the People*, 70–72. In a memoir written decades later, Benton, referring to himself in the third person, remembered that "a duel in St. Louis ended fatally, of which Colonel Benton has not been heard to speak of except among intimate friends, and to tell of the pang which went through his heart when he saw the young man fall, and would have given the world to see restored to life." *Senator Benton and the People*, 72.

73. Smith, *Virgin Land*, 24.

74. Ibid., 22.

75. Lass, *Navigating the Missouri*, 53; letter, Benjamin O'Fallon to John C. Calhoun, September 25, 1819, cited in Kelly, *Lost Voices on the Missouri*, 165.

76. Lass, *Navigating the Missouri*, 53; Kelly, *Lost Voices on the Missouri*, 171.

77. Kelly, *Lost Voices on the Missouri*, 175, 178.

78. Ibid., 172; Lass, *Navigating the Missouri*, 53.

79. Lass, *Navigating the Missouri*, 54.

80. Dwight Clarke, *Stephen Watts Kearny*, 25. In 1823, Long and Kearny would both be involved in determining whether the village of Pembina, in present North Dakota, lay in the US or Canada. Ibid., 67.

81. Ibid., 44, 55–56; *Missouri Gazette*, October 14, 1820. Several weeks after reaching Council Bluffs, on October 29, 1819, Major Thomas Biddle, after ample opportunities to interview and reinterview Dougherty, sat down and wrote a long letter to Colonel Henry Atkinson, giving a concise but detailed history of the fur trade that included information about Colter and Lisa, both of whom Dougherty knew well, and also told of Henry's troubles at Three Forks and his subsequent move to the western side of the Divide, which Dougherty had personally experienced. (See *American State Papers*, Senate, 16th Congress, 1st Session, Indian Affairs, 2:201–3, for the complete text of the letter used by countless fur trade historians.)

82. Hafen, *Broken Hand*, 16; Morgan, *Jedediah Smith*, 56–58.

83. Hafen, *Broken Hand*, 17; letter, Joshua Pilcher to Thomas Hempstead, July 23, 1823, in Morgan, *The West of William Ashley*, 50–51.

84. Hafen, *Broken Hand*, 18–19. For more on the Leavenworth/Arikara debacle, see Morgan, *Jedediah Smith*, 66–77, and Clokey, *William H. Ashley*, 101–21.

85. Clokey, *William H. Ashley*, 113.

86. Ibid; letter, William Ashley to John O'Fallon, July 19, 1823, in Morgan, *The West of William Ashley*, 48.

87. The Colorado River flows into the Gulf of California unless all of its water has been siphoned off for irrigation.

88. Foley, *Wilderness Journey*, 187. "My Dear Sir," Nicholas Biddle had written to Clark in March of 1814, "I have at last the pleasure of informing you that the Travels are published—that they have sold very well I understand, and have been well thought of by the readers." Letter, Nicholas Biddle to William Clark, March 23, 1814, Jackson, *Letters*, 2:598. Despite Biddle's optimism, the volume did not sell well. The passage of time and the appearance of Patrick Gass's journal, as well as several counterfeit histories—but most of all the War of 1812—had diminished interest in Lewis and Clark's tour of the Pacific. As for the magnanimous Biddle, he declined both payment and publication credit for the history, saying he wanted to be "recompensed *only by* the pleasure which attended" his many hours of labor. Clark expected to receive royalties from the history but that never developed. Worse yet, two years after publica-

tion he was still waiting to see a copy of the volume. Cutright, *History of the Lewis and Clark Journals*, 64–67.

89. Background for the entire discussion of Crooks in this chapter is from Lavender, *Fist in the Wilderness*, 192–208, 277–93.

90. Rollins, *Discovery of the Oregon Trail*, lxviii.

91. Thomas Hart Benton, *Thirty Years' View*, 1:13.

92. Ibid.

93. *Abridgement of Debates of Congress*, 79.

94. Benton, *Thirty Years' View*, 1:13.

95. Bagley, *South Pass*, 52. While Floyd's bill failed to gain support, writes David Dary, "Dr. Floyd introduced a substitute bill in 1822 stating that when the region reached a population of 2,000 it should become a territory of the United States. Dr. Floyd labeled the area 'Origon.' This was the first American use of the word. His bill lost by a vote of 100 to 61, probably because it was too visionary." Floyd did not give up, however, and eventually began working with Hall Jackson Kelley, who "organized the American Society for Encouraging the Settlement of the Oregon Territory, which grew rapidly in membership and was incorporated in 1831." Dary, *Oregon Trail*, 53–54.

96. Morgan, *The West of William Ashley*, 15–18.

97. Clyman said there were eleven men in the group; Solitaire (John S. Robb) said sixteen.

98. Hasselstrom, *James Clyman*, 21.

99. Ibid., 22.

100. "Letters from the West," 14. For Glass's letter to John Gardner's father, see Morgan, *The West of William Ashley*, 31.

101. See Morgan, *Jedediah Smith*, 96–114, for Glass's story, which inspired two well-known movies: *Man in the Wilderness* (1971), starring Richard Harris, and *The Revenant* (2015), starring Leonardo DiCaprio. See also the website for the Museum of the Mountain Man in Pinedale, Wyoming, accessed on September 18, 2017, http://hughglass.org/museum-of-mountain-man/.

102. Hasselstrom, *James Clyman*, 23–24.

103. Ibid., 24; Anglin and Morris, *Mystery of John Colter*, 96.

104. "Major Fitzpatrick, the Discoverer of the South Pass! By Solitaire," *Weekly Reveille* (St. Louis), March 1, 1847, in Hafen, *Broken Hand*, 339. This article was published under the name "Solitaire," a pseudonym of John S. Robb.

105. Hasselstrom, *James Clyman*, 37–38.

106. Ibid., 27–29, 29–30, 107.

107. Morgan, *Jedediah Smith*, 91; Hafen, *Broken Hand*, 34; Sunder, *Bill Sublette*, 52.

108. Morgan, *The West of William Ashley*, 76. The informant was Louis Vasquez, who had just returned from the upper Missouri. Vasquez was on the beach with Smith, Fitzpatrick, and the rest when the Arikara attacked on June 2, 1823, and had apparently gone with Henry to the mouth of the Yellowstone in September. The report that Glass had been killed by Arikara was premature—it would actually happen during the winter of 1832–1833. See Robert Betts, *In Search of York*, 138.

6. "THE MARCH OF OVER TWO THOUSAND MILES"

1. Letter, Oliver Cowdery to William Clark, February 14, 1831, in Leland Gentry, "Light on the 'Mission to the Lamanites,'" 233.

2. Letter, Richard Cummins to William Clark, February 15, 1831, in Gentry, "Mission to the Lamanites," 234. Cummins's letter thus includes the first mention of the Mormons' interest in going west to the Rocky Mountains.

3. Letter, Oliver Cowdery to "Our dearly beloved Brethren," May 7, 1831, in MacKay et al., *The Joseph Smith Papers*, 1:296.

4. Kaw Township, organized in 1827, was bordered on the north by the Missouri River, on the east and south by the Big Blue River, and on the west by the Missouri state line. Cowdery noted that his residence in Kaw Township was eleven miles from Independence. Jedediah Smith wrote that the company camped "near Big Blue"; Dale Morgan concluded they were "ten miles southwest of Independence." Morgan, *Jedediah Smith*, 362, 327.

5. Morgan, *Jedediah Smith*, 328.

6. Hafen, *Broken Hand*, 95.

7. J. J. Warner, "Reminiscences of Early California," 176. Warner became a naturalized Mexican citizen and changed his name to Juan Jose Warner.

8. Ibid. Smith's warning actually turned out to be a bad omen for himself rather than Warner. As the party headed over the Cimarron Desert, "Fitzpatrick and Smith went ahead of the wagons to look for water. While Fitzpatrick was scooping a shallow well in a dry stream bed, Smith pushed on toward the Cimarron. He found it dry. While digging into the wet sand he was pounced on by a band of Comanches and killed." Hafen, *Broken Hand*, 96; see also Morgan, *Jedediah Smith*, 364.

9. Richard Bennett, *We'll Find the Place*, 40.

10. James K. Polk's diary entry, June 3, 1846, cited in David Bigler and Will Bagley, *Army of Israel*, 36.

11. Ibid., 37–38.

12. Clarke, *Stephen Watts Kearny*, 43. Kearny's mother-in-law, Harriet Radford Clark—William Clark's second wife—died on Christmas Day, 1831. Kearny and his family were on military assignment frequently thereafter and probably saw Clark seldom if at all before his death on September 1, 1838, at age sixty-eight.

13. Order, Kearny to Allen, June 19, 1846, in Bigler and Bagley, *Army of Israel*, 41.

14. Hafen, *Broken Hand*, 233.

15. Erwin Gudde, *Bigler's Chronicle*, 19.

16. John E. Wickman, "Peter A. Sarpy," 292, 288.

17. *Jefferson Inquirer*, December 25, 1847, cited in Hafen, *Broken Hand*, 151–52. Hafen adds that Sarpy's supposed account has not been corroborated and that the journey that took Fitzpatrick into the area mentioned occurred in 1836 rather than in 1835. Dale Morgan, who discovered this article, was skeptical of its veracity and theorized that the accident took place "on Fitzpatrick's disastrous ride to rendezvous of 1832." Hafen, however, argues that "not one of the contemporaneous accounts of that ride, with all the details they give, mentions an accident that crippled his hand. Nor does any historical source tell of the accident before 1835." Quoting Hafen again, "The only item in Fitzpatrick's own writings that may refer to the accident to his hand and the loss of his horse is in his letter of March 18, 1836, to Pierre Chouteau: 'I need not undertake to give you a written account of our misfortunes, as you will too soon have a verbal one. . . . Our misfortunes in this expedition will be the cause of my making some extra expenses for horses.'" Hafen, *Broken Hand*, 150–51n15; 152. John C. Frémont simply wrote that "one of [Fitzpatrick's] hands [was] shattered by the bursting of his gun." LeRoy R. and Ann W. Hafen, "Thomas Fitzpatrick," in Hafen, *Mountain Men*, 7:87n1.

18. The account of Susan Shelby Magoffin, cited in Hafen, *Broken Hand*, 233, emphasis in original.

19. Letter, Thomas Fitzpatrick to Andrew Sublette, July 31, 1846, cited in Hafen, *Broken Hand*, 233.

20. *Democratic Review*, July 1845, cited in Lamar, *New Encyclopedia*, 676.

21. Frederick Merk, *Manifest Destiny*, 24. John Mack Faragher points out the flaw in assuming that "the United States was indeed united in a nationalist strategy of continentalism." Merk's research, he argues, "details division rather than unity. North and South were divided by fears over the future expansion of slavery into the territories and doubts about the wisdom of incorporating the mixed-race peoples of Mexico into a 'white man's democracy.' Moreover, many Americans worried that the nation was becoming too large." Faragher, foreword in Merk, *Manifest Destiny*, x.

22. Norma Ricketts, *Mormon Battalion*, 17, 20, 28; Bigler and Bagley, *Army of Israel*, 73.

23. Gudde, *Bigler's Chronicle*, 22.

24. Ibid.

25. Quoted excerpt from Ricketts, *Mormon Battalion*, 50; background from Ricketts, *Mormon Battalion*, 35–63.

26. Journal of Levi Hancock, cited in Bigler and Bagley, *Army of Israel*, 104.

27. John Zimmerman Brown, *Autobiography of Pioneer John Brown*, 67.

28. Hasselstrom, *James Clyman*, 262.

29. Brown, *Autobiography of John Brown*, 68.

30. Ibid.

31. Ibid.

32. Ibid., 69.

33. Ibid., 70.

34. John Yurtinus, "Colorado, Mormons, and the Mexican War," 111.

35. Francis Parkman, *The Oregon Trail*, 301–2.

36. Ricketts, *Mormon Battalion*, 56.

37. Gudde, *Bigler's Chronicles*, 25n15.

38. Ricketts, *Mormon Battalion*, 58.

39. Ibid., 61.

40. Ibid., 62–63.

41. Bigler and Bagley, *Army of Israel*, 135. Alexander Doniphan, who would become one of the great heroes of the Mexican War, and Philip St. George Cooke each had a close connection to John Dougherty. Doniphan was his good friend and attorney, and Cooke was his brother-in-law (Dougherty had married Mary Hertzog, and Cooke her sister Rachel).

42. Ralph Bieber, "Cooke's Journal," 69n144.

43. Yurtinus, "Colorado, Mormons, and the Mexican War," 118.

44. David Remley, *Kit Carson*, 165–66.

45. Ibid., 168.

46. Ibid., 166.

47. Ibid., 172.

48. Bigler and Bagley, *Army of Israel*, 135. The quoted section of Kearny's letter is taken from the diary of John D. Lee (later of Mountain Meadows massacre infamy) and is thus not a transcription of the letter itself.

49. According to Frémont's biographer, Ferol Egan, Frémont's description of the Great Salt Lake country was "quite accurate and became the deciding factor in Brigham Young's mind when he selected the Salt Lake Valley as the place of settlement for the Mormons." Egan, *Frémont*, 155.

50. Bieber, "Cooke's Journal," 70.

51. Ibid., 74.

52. W. Dale Nelson, *Interpreters with Lewis and Clark*, 82.

53. Ibid., 93.

54. Bieber, "Cooke's Journal," 74–75.

55. Ibid., 85–86.

56. Ibid., 86.

57. Ibid., 89.

58. Ibid.

59. Ibid., 94–95.

60. Ibid., 95.

61. Ricketts, *Mormon Battalion*, 240.

62. Ibid.

63. From the account of George Ruxton, cited in Ricketts, *Mormon Battalion*, 237.

64. Bieber, "Cooke's Journal," 101.

65. Ibid., 103, 104.

66. Ibid., 105, 106, 107. Cooke, who continually resented Kearny's taking all the best mules, added: "If I had been supplied with *good* fat mules, it might be safe to keep directly on in this wilderness" (106).

67. Ibid., 110.

68. Ibid.

69. Ibid., 111–12.

70. Ibid., 115–16.

71. Ricketts, *Mormon Battalion*, 136.

72. Ibid., 93.

73. Bieber, "Cooke's Journal," 140.

74. Ibid., 147, 146.

75. Ibid., 147.

76. Gudde, *Bigler's Chronicle*, 86–87.

77. Bieber, "Cooke's Journal," 200n205.

78. Ibid., 207.

79. Ibid., 213–14. This section is adapted from Larry Morris, "Mountain Men and the Taking of California, 1845–1847." See that same article for information on Frémont's activities in California prior to Kearny's arrival.

80. Sherman Fleek, "The Kearny/Stockton/Frémont Feud," 241–42. Some have blamed Kit Carson for the misfortunes at San Pasqual, claiming that Kearny intended to avoid the Californios and move on to San Diego but changed his mind when Carson assured him the lancers would not stand. (See Clarke, *Stephen Watts Kearny*, 204–7.) These claims are suspect because they generally come from late, hearsay reports, but, in any case, General Kearny was the commanding officer and the one responsible for the decision to attack.

81. W. H. Emory, *Notes*, 172–73.

82. Fleek, "Kearny/Stockton/Frémont Feud," 243.

83. Tom Chaffin, *Pathfinder*, 363–64.

84. Gudde, *Bigler's Chronicle*, 45.

85. Bieber, "Cooke's Journal," 227n224.

86. Gudde, *Bigler's Chronicle*, 45.

87. Carter, *Dear Old Kit*, 116.

88. At Frémont's court-martial, Kearny described his initial meeting with Carson thus:

> *Question. [from Frémont] Did the express [Carson] remonstrate against being turned back and did you insist and assert the right to order him back?*
> *Answer. [from Kearny] The express was Mr. Carson, who was at first very unwilling to return with me; he being desirous of proceeding to Washington, to convey letters and communications to that place, which he had received from Lieutenant Colonel Frémont and Commodore Stockton. He told me that he had pledged himself that they should be received in Washington. I at last persuaded him to return with me by telling him that I would send in his place, as bearer of those despatches Mr. Fitzpatrick, who was an old friend of Lieutenant Colonel Frémont, and had traveled a great deal with him. Mr. Carson, upon that, was perfectly satisfied, and told me so.* The Proceedings of the Court Martial in the Trial of Lieutenant Colonel Frémont, *Senate Journal*, p. 42.

Carson's account was brief and to the point: "On the 6th of October, '46, I met General Kearny on his march to California. He ordered me to join him as his guide. I done so, and Fitzpatrick continued on with the despatches." Kit Carson Memoirs, 112.

One of those present when Carson and his fifteen fellow horsemen arrived at Kearny's camp, Captain Abraham Johnston, offered this report in his journal:

> *The general told him [Carson] that he had just passed over the country which we were to traverse and he [Kearny] wanted him [Carson] to go back with him [Kearny] as a guide; he [Carson] replied that he [Carson] had pledged himself to go to Washington, and he could not think of not fulfilling his promise. The general told him [Carson] he [Kearny] would relieve him of all responsibility, and place the mail in the hands of a safe person to carry it; he [Carson] finally consented*

and turned his face to the west again, just as he was on the eve of
entering the settlements, after his arduous trip and when he had set
his hopes on seeing his family. Abraham R. Johnston, "Journal of the
March of the Army of the West, 1846," cited in Clarke, *Stephen*
Watts Kearny, 171.

Johnston, who was killed in battle two months later, looks to be an impartial
judge, making no apparent effort to favor one side over the other. If anything,
his account leans in Carson's favor because he closes it thus: "It requires a
brave man to give up his private feelings thus for the public good; but Carson is
one such! Honor to him for it."

The claim later made by Thomas Hart Benton that Kearny essentially
coerced Carson to return to California and told Carson many times that he
himself intended to appoint Frémont governor of California cannot be taken
seriously because it does not square with any other account, including Carson's
(quite significant when one considers that Carson did not testify at the court-
martial, even though he certainly would have done so if Frémont asked). In the
end, Frémont's effort to discredit Kearny by arguing over the details of what
exactly happened during Kearny and Carson's first meeting turned out to be
misguided and pointless.

89. Fleek, "Kearny/Stockton/Frémont Feud," 244.

90. Ibid., 246.

91. Letter, Henry Smith Turner to Julia Turner, March 16, 1847, in Dwight
Clarke, *The Original Journals of Henry Smith Turner*, 160. Benton indeed
took offense. During and after Frémont's court-martial, he went to great
lengths to destroy Kearny's reputation, despite their previous friendship.

92. Chaffin, *Pathfinder*, 370; Fleek, "Kearny/Stockton/Frémont Feud,"
246–47.

93. Fleek, "Kearny/Stockton/Frémont Feud," 229–30.

94. Bieber, "Cooke's Journal," 238.

95. Fleek, "Kearny/Stockton/Frémont Feud," 251.

96. Ibid., 252.

97. Ibid., 254.

98. Mary Lee Spence and Donald Jackson, *Expeditions of John Charles*
Fremont, xl, 468n–69n; Clarke, *Stephen Watts Kearny*, 369.

99. Bieber, "Cooke's Journal," 239–40.

100. Mueller, *Senator Benton*, 223.

101. Remini, *Life of Andrew Jackson*, 148.

102. Mueller, *Senator Benton*, 230.

103. Morris, *Perilous West*, 193–95.

104. Tanis C. Thorne, s.v. "Crooks, Ramsay," in *Dictionary of Canadian Biography*, vol. 8, University of Toronto/Université Laval, 2003–, accessed September 20, 2017, http://www.biographi.ca/en/bio/crooks_ramsay_8E.html; *Buffalo Daily Republic*, June 10, 1859.

BIBLIOGRAPHY

Abridgement of the Debates of Congress, from 1789 to 1856. Vol. 3. New York: D. Appleton, 1858.

Allen, John L. "The Forgotten Explorers." In *Selected Papers of the 2010 Fur Trade Symposium at the Three Forks*, edited by Jim Hardee, 26–39. Three Forks, MT: Three Forks Historical Society, 2011.

———. *Passage through the Garden: Lewis and Clark and the Image of the American Northwest.* Urbana: University of Illinois Press, 1975.

Alter, J. Cecil. *Jim Bridger.* Norman: University of Oklahoma Press, 1962.

Ambrose, Stephen E. *Undaunted Courage: Meriwether Lewis. Thomas Jefferson, and the Opening of the American West.* New York: Simon & Schuster, 1996.

American State Papers. 38 vols. Washington, DC: Gales and Seaton, 1834.

Anglin, Ronald M., and Larry E. Morris. *The Mystery of John Colter: The Man Who Discovered Yellowstone.* Lanham, MD: Rowman & Littlefield, 2016. (Originally titled *Gloomy Terrors and Hidden Fires: The Mystery of John Colter and Yellowstone.*)

Aron, Stephen. *American Confluence: The Missouri Frontier from Borderland to Border State.* Bloomington: Indiana University Press, 2006.

———. *How the West Was Lost: The Transformation of Kentucky from Daniel Boone to Henry Clay.* Baltimore: Johns Hopkins University Press, 1996.

Atherton, William. *Narrative of the Suffering & Defeat of the North-Western Army under General Winchester.* Frankfort, KY: A. G. Hodges, 1842.

Bagley, Will. *South Pass: Gateway to a Continent.* Norman: University of Oklahoma Press, 2014.

Barbour, Barton H. *Jedediah Smith: No Ordinary Mountain Man.* Norman: University of Oklahoma Press, 2009.

Bennett, Richard E. *We'll Find the Place: The Mormon Exodus, 1846–1848.* Salt Lake City, UT: Deseret, 1997.

Benton, Thomas Hart. *Thirty Years' View; or, A History of the Working of the American Government for Thirty Years, from 1820 to 1850.* New York: Appleton, 1858.

Betts, Robert B. *In Search of York: The Slave Who Went West to the Pacific with Lewis and Clark.* Rev. ed. Boulder: University Press of Colorado, 2000. (Originally published 1985.)

Bieber, Ralph P., ed. "Cooke's Journal of the March of the Mormon Battalion, 1846–47." In *Exploring Southwestern Trails, 1846–1854.* Glendale, CA: Arthur H. Clark, 1938.

Bigler, David L., and Will Bagley, eds. *Army of Israel: Mormon Battalion Narratives.* Glendale, CA: Arthur H. Clark, 2000.

Billington, Ray Allen. *Westward Expansion: A History of the American Frontier.* New York: Macmillan, 1974.

Billon, Frederick L. *Annals of St. Louis in Its Territorial Days from 1804 to 1821*. St. Louis, MO: Privately printed, 1888.

Brackenridge, Henry M. *Journal of a Voyage up the River Missouri; Performed in Eighteen Hundred and Eleven*. Baltimore: Coale and Maxwell, 1816.

Bradbury, John. *Travels in the Interior of America, in the Years 1809, 1810, and 1811*. Liverpool, UK: Smith and Galway, 1817.

Brannan, John, ed. *Official Letters of the Military and Naval Officers of the United States, During the War with Great Britain in the Years 1812, 13, 14, and 15*. Washington, DC: Way and Gideon, 1823. Reprint, Arno Press & the *New York Times*, 1971.

Brown, John Zimmerman, ed. *Autobiography of Pioneer John Brown*. Salt Lake City, UT: n.p., 1941.

Buckley, Jay H. *William Clark: Indian Diplomat*. Norman: University of Oklahoma Press, 2008.

Calloway, Colin G. *One Vast Winter Count: The Native American West before Lewis and Clark*. Lincoln: University of Nebraska Press, 2003.

Carter, Clarence, comp. and ed. *The Territorial Papers of the United States*. 25 vols. Washington, DC: Government Printing Office, 1943–1960.

Carter, Harvey Lewis. *"Dear Old Kit": The Historical Christopher Carson*. Norman: University of Oklahoma Press, 1968.

Casselman, Alexander Clark. *Richardson's War of 1812: With Notes and a Life of the Author*. Toronto, ON: Historical, 1902.

Chaffin, Tom. *Pathfinder: John Charles Fremont and the Course of American Empire*. New York: Hill and Wang, 2002.

Chittenden, Hiram M. *The American Fur Trade of the Far West*. 2 vols. New York: Press of the Pioneers, 1935. Reprint, Lincoln: University of Nebraska Press, 1986.

———. *History of Early Steamboat Navigation on the Missouri River: Life and Adventures of Joseph La Barge*. New York: Francis P. Harper, 1903.

Clarke, Charles G. *The Men of the Lewis and Clark Expedition*. Glendale, CA: Arthur H. Clark, 1970. Reprint, Lincoln: University of Nebraska Press, 2002.

Clarke, Dwight L., ed. *The Original Journals of Henry Smith Turner: With Stephen Watts Kearny to New Mexico and California, 1846–1847*. Norman: University of Oklahoma Press, 1966.

———. *Stephen Watts Kearny: Soldier of the West*. Norman: University of Oklahoma Press, 1961.

Clokey, Richard M. *William H. Ashley: Enterprise and Politics in the Trans-Mississippi West*. Norman: University of Oklahoma Press, 1980.

Collins, Ronald W. *Sergeant John Ordway: A History, with His Genealogy*. Hebron, NH: Collins, 2007.

Colter-Frick, Lillian Ruth. *Courageous Colter and Companions*. Washington, MO: Privately printed, 1997.

"Correspondence between Governor Isaac Shelby and General William Henry Harrison, during the War of 1812." *Register of the Kentucky State Historical Society* 20, no. 59 (May 1922): 130–44.

Coues, Elliott, ed. *The History of the Lewis and Clark Expedition*. 3 vols. New York: Dover, 1979. Republication of 1893 edition.

Crockett, David. *Life of Col. David Crocket, Written by Himself*. Philadelphia: G. G. Evans, 1859.

Cruikshank, Ernest Alexander. "Robert Dickson, the Indian Trader." *Wisconsin Historical Collections* 12 (1892): 133–53.

Cutright, Paul Russell. *A History of the Lewis and Clark Journals*. Norman: University of Oklahoma Press, 1976.

Danisi, Thomas C. *Uncovering the Truth about Meriwether Lewis*. Amherst, NY: Prometheus Press, 2012.

Darby, John F. *Personal Recollections*. St. Louis, MO: C. I. Jones, 1880.

Dary, David. *The Oregon Trail: An American Saga*. New York: Oxford University Press, 2004.

Davis, William C. *Three Roads to the Alamo: The Lives and Fortunes of David Crockett, James Bowie, and William Barret Travis.* New York: HarperCollins, 1998.

Debates and Proceedings in the Congress of the United States. Thirteenth Congress—First and Second Sessions. Washington, DC: Gales and Seaton, 1854.

DeVoto, Bernard. *Across the Wide Missouri.* Boston: Houghton Mifflin, 1998.

———. *The Year of Decision: 1846.* Boston: Houghton Mifflin, 1943.

Dudley, Thomas P. *Battle and Massacre at Frenchtown, Michigan, January, 1813.* Cleveland, OH: Western Reserve Historical Society, 1870.

Egan, Ferol. *Frémont: Explorer for a Restless Nation.* Reno: University of Nevada Press, 1977.

Eisenhower, John S. D. *So Far from God: The U.S. War with Mexico, 1846–1848.* New York: Random House, 1989.

Emory, W. H. *Notes of a Military Reconnoissance.* Reprint, *Lieutenant Emory Reports.* Introduction and Notes by Ross Calvin. Albuquerque: University of New Mexico Press, 1951.

Faragher, John Mack. *Daniel Boone: The Life and Legend of an American Pioneer.* New York: Henry Holt, 1992.

Fisher, Vardis. *Suicide or Murder: The Strange Death of Governor Meriwether Lewis.* Athens: First Swallow Press/Ohio University Press, 1962.

Fleek, Sherman L. *History May Be Searched in Vain: A Military History of the Mormon Battalion.* Spokane, WA: Arthur H. Clark, 2006.

———. "The Kearny/Stockton/Frémont Feud: The Mormon Battalion's Most Significant Contribution in California." *Journal of Mormon History* 37, no. 2 (Summer 2011): 229–57.

Foley, William E. *Wilderness Journey: The Life of William Clark.* Columbia: University of Missouri Press, 2004.

Foley, William E., and Charles David Rice. "The Return of the Mandan Chief." *Montana: The Magazine of Western History* 29, no. 3 (July 1979): 2–14.

Franchere, Gabriel. *Narrative of a Voyage to the Northwest Coast of America during the Years 1811, 1812, 1813, and 1814.* Translated and edited by J. V. Huntington, 1854. Charleston, SC: Bibliobazaar, 2007.

Furtwangler, Albert. *Acts of Discovery: Visions of America in the Lewis and Clark Journals.* Urbana: University of Illinois Press, 1993.

Gentry, Leland H. "Light on the 'Mission to the Lamanites.'" *BYU Studies* 36, no. 2 (1996–1997): 226–34.

Greenberg, Amy S. *Manifest Destiny and American Territorial Expansion: A Brief History with Documents.* Boston: Bedford/St. Martin's, 2012.

Gregg, Kate L. "The War of 1812 on the Missouri Frontier." *Missouri Historical Review* 33, no. 1–3 (1938): 3–22, 184–202, 236–48.

Groom, Winston. *Kearny's March: The Epic Creation of the American West, 1846–1847.* New York: Knopf, 2011.

Gudde, Erwin G. *Bigler's Chronicle of the West.* Berkeley: University of California Press, 1962.

Guice, John D. W., ed. *By His Own Hand: The Mysterious Death of Meriwether Lewis.* Norman: University of Oklahoma Press, 2011.

Haeger, John D. "Business Strategy and Practice in the Early Republic: John Jacob Astor and the American Fur Trade." *Western Historical Quarterly* 19, no. 2 (May 1988): 183–202.

Hafen, LeRoy R. *Broken Hand: The Life of Thomas Fitzpatrick; Mountain Man, Guide and Indian Agent.* Lincoln: University of Nebraska Press, 1973.

———, ed. *The Mountain Men and the Fur Trade of the Far West.* 10 vols. Glendale, CA: Arthur H. Clark, 1965–1972.

Hardee, Jim. "The Influence of the Red-Headed Chief: William Clark's Post-Expedition Interaction with Indian Nations." *We Proceeded On* (Lewis and Clark Heritage Foundation) 40, no. 2 (May 2014): 8–18.

———. *Pierre's Hole! The Fur Trade History of Teton Valley, Idaho.* Pinedale, WY: Museum of the Mountain Man and Sublette County Historical Society, 2010.

————, ed. *Selected Papers of the 2010 Fur Trade Symposium at the Three Forks*. Three Forks, MT: Three Forks Historical Society, 2011.

Hartley, Alan H. *Lewis & Clark Lexicon of Discovery*. Pullman: Washington State University Press, 2004.

Hasselstrom, Linda M. *Journal of a Mountain Man: James Clyman*. Boise, ID: Tamarack Books, 1998.

Heidenreich, C. Adrian. *Smoke Signals in the Crow (Apsáalooke) Country: Beyond the Capture of Horses from the Lewis and Clark Expedition*. Billings, MT: By the Author, 2006.

Heroes of 1812. National Society of United States Daughters of 1812, Nebraska. Omaha: Citizen, 1930.

Holmberg, James J., ed. *Dear Brother: Letters of William Clark to Jonathan Clark*. New Haven, CT: Yale University Press, 2002.

Holmes, Reuben. "The Five Scalps." *Missouri Historical Society, Glimpses of the Past* 5 (January–March 1938): 1–54.

Howe, Daniel Walker. *What Hath God Wrought: The Transformation of America, 1815–1848*. New York: Oxford University Press, 2007.

Hurt, R. Douglas. *Nathan Boone and the American Frontier*. Columbia: University of Missouri Press, 1998.

Irving, Washington. *The Adventures of Captain Bonneville, U.S.A., in the Rocky Mountains and the Far West*. Edited by Edgeley W. Todd. Norman: University of Oklahoma Press, 1961.

————. *Astoria*. 1836. Edited by Edgeley W. Todd. Norman: University of Oklahoma Press, 1964.

Jackson, Donald. *Letters of the Lewis and Clark Expedition, with Related Documents, 1783–1854*. 2 vols. Urbana and Chicago: University of Illinois Press, 1978.

James, Thomas. *Three Years among the Indians and Mexicans*. Philadelphia: J. B. Lippincott, 1962. Reprint of the 1846 edition.

Jenkinson, Clay S. *The Character of Meriwether Lewis: Explorer in the Wilderness*. Washburn, ND: The Dakota Institute Press, 2011.

————. *A Vast and Open Plain: The Writings of the Lewis and Clark Expedition in North Dakota, 1804–1806*. Bismarck: State Historical Society of North Dakota, 2003.

Jones, Landon Y. *William Clark and the Shaping of the West*. New York: Hill and Wang, 2004.

Josephy, Alvin M. Jr. *The Nez Perce Indians and the Opening of the Northwest*. Boston: Houghton Mifflin, 1965.

Jung, Patrick J. *The Black Hawk War of 1832*. Norman: University of Oklahoma Press, 2007.

Kelly, Mark William. *Lost Voices on the Missouri: John Dougherty and the Indian Frontier*. Leavenworth, KS: Sam Clark, 2013.

Kukla, Jon. *A Wilderness So Immense: The Louisiana Purchase and the Destiny of America*. New York: Knopf, 2003.

Lamar, Howard R., ed. *The New Encyclopedia of the American West*. New Haven, CT: Yale University Press, 1998.

Lass, William E. *Navigating the Missouri: Steamboating on Nature's Highway, 1819–1935*. Norman, OK: Arthur H. Clark, 2008.

Launius, Roger D. *Alexander William Doniphan: Portrait of a Missouri Moderate*. Columbia: University of Missouri Press, 1997.

Lavender, David. *The Fist in the Wilderness*. New York: Doubleday, 1964. Reprint, Lincoln: University of Nebraska Press, 1998.

————. "Ramsay Crooks's Early Ventures on the Missouri River: A Series of Conjectures." *Bulletin of the Missouri Historical Society* 20 (July 1964): 91–106.

"Letters from the West. No. XIV. The Missouri Trapper." *The Port Folio*, Philadelphia, March 1825.

Levens, Henry C., and Nathaniel M. Drake. *A History of Cooper County, Missouri*. St. Louis, MO: Perrin and Smith, 1876.

Looney, J. Jefferson, ed. *The Papers of Thomas Jefferson, Retirement Series*, vol. 2. Princeton, NJ: Princeton University Press, 2005.

Lossing, Benson J. *The Pictorial Fieldbook of the War of 1812*. New York: Harper & Brothers, 1868.

MacKay, Michael Hubbard, Gerrit J. Dirkmaat, Grant Underwood, Robert J. Woodford, and William G. Hartley, eds. *Documents, Volume 1: July 1828–June 1831*. Vol. 1 of the Documents series of *The Joseph Smith Papers*, edited by Dean C. Jessee, Ronald K. Esplin, Richard Lyman Bushman, and Matthew J. Grow. Salt Lake City, UT: Church Historian's Press, 2013.

Marshall, Thomas Maitland, ed. *The Life and Papers of Frederick Bates*. 2 vols. St. Louis: Missouri Historical Society, 1926.

Masur, Louis P. *1831: Year of Eclipse*. New York: Hill and Wang, 2001.

Merk, Frederick. *Manifest Destiny and Mission in American History: A Reinterpretation*. Cambridge, MA: Harvard University Press, 1963.

Miller, Robert J. *Native America Discovered and Conquered: Thomas Jefferson, Lewis and Clark, and Manifest Destiny*. Lincoln: University of Nebraska Press, 2008.

Morgan, Dale L. *Jedediah Smith and the Opening of the West*. Indianapolis, IN: Bobbs-Merrill, 1953. Reprint, Lincoln: University of Nebraska Press, 1964.

———, ed. *The West of William H. Ashley*. Denver, CO: Old West, 1964.

Morris, Larry E. "Archibald Pelton, Mad Man of the Mountains." *Rocky Mountain Fur Trade Journal* 9 (2015): 126–45.

———. *The Fate of the Corps: What Became of the Lewis and Clark Explorers after the Expedition*. New Haven, CT: Yale University Press, 2004.

———. "Mountain Men and the Taking of California, 1845–1847." *Rocky Mountain Fur Trade Journal* 10 (2016): 94–121.

———. "The Mysterious Charles Courtin and the Early Missouri Fur Trade." *Missouri Historical Review* 104, no. 1 (October 2009): 21–39.

———. *The Perilous West: Seven Amazing Explorers and the Founding of the Oregon Trail*. Lanham, MD: Rowman & Littlefield, 2013.

Moulton, Gary E., ed. *The Journals of the Lewis and Clark Expedition*. 13 vols. Lincoln: University of Nebraska Press, 1986–1997.

Mountjoy, Shane. *Manifest Destiny: Westward Expansion*. New York: Chelsea House, 2009.

Moyars, Karen Hall. *The Battle of Tippecanoe*. Lafayette, IN: Tippecanoe County Historical Association, 1999.

Mueller, Ken S. *Senator Benton and the People: Master Race Democracy on the Early American Frontiers*. DeKalb: Northern Illinois University Press, 2104.

Nagel, Paul C. *John Quincy Adams: A Public Life, A Private Life*. New York: Knopf, 1997.

Nelson, Larry L. "Dudley's Defeat and the Relief of Fort Meigs During the War of 1812." *Register of the Kentucky Historical Society* 104, no. 1 (Winter 2006): 5–42.

Nelson, W. Dale. *Interpreters with Lewis and Clark: The Story of Sacagawea and Toussaint Charbonneau*. Denton: University of North Texas Press, 2003.

Nisbet, Jack. *Sources of the River: Tracking David Thompson across Western North America*. Seattle, WA: Sasquatch Books, 1994.

Oglesby, Richard Edward. *Manuel Lisa and the Opening of the Missouri Fur Trade*. Norman: University of Oklahoma Press, 1963.

Parkman, Francis. *The Oregon Trail: Sketches of Prairie and Rocky-Mountain Life*. Boston: Little, Brown, 1900.

Parton, James. *Life of Andrew Jackson: In Three Volumes*. New York: Mason Brothers, 1860.

Patton, Bruce C. *Lewis & Clark: Doctors in the Wilderness*. Golden, CO: Fulcrum, 2001.

Porter, Kenneth W. *John Jacob Astor, Business Man*. 2 vols. Cambridge, MA: Harvard University Press, 1931.

Reid, Richard J. *The Battle of Tippecanoe*. Fordsville, KY: Privately printed, 1983.

Remini, Robert V. *Henry Clay: Statesman for the Union*. New York: Norton, 1991.

———. *The Life of Andrew Jackson*. New York: Harper Perennial Political Classics, 2009.

Remley, David. *Kit Carson: The Life of an American Border Man*. Norman: University of Oklahoma Press, reprint, 2011.

Reno, Lawrence R. *The Life and Times of Nathaniel Hale Pryor: Explorer, Soldier, Frontiersman and Spokesman for the Osage*. Denver, CO: Turkey Creek, 2006.

Reséndez, Andrés. *Changing National Identities at the Frontier: Texas and New Mexico, 1800–1850*. Cambridge, UK: Cambridge University Press, 2004.

Ricketts, Norma Baldwin. *The Mormon Battalion: US Army of the West*. Logan: Utah State University Press, 1996.

Rollins, Philip Ashton, ed. *The Discovery of the Oregon Trail: Robert Stuart's Narratives of the His Overland Trip Eastward from Astoria in 1812–13*. New York: Charles Scribner's Sons, 1935.

Ronda, James P. *Astoria and Empire*. Lincoln: University of Nebraska Press, 1990.

———. *Beyond Lewis and Clark: The Army Explores the West*. Tacoma: Washington Historical Society, 2003.

———. *Finding the West: Explorations with Lewis and Clark*. Albuquerque: University of New Mexico Press, 2001.

———. "A Moment in Time: The West—September 1806." In *Finding the West: Explorations with Lewis and Clark*, 77–95. Albuquerque: University of New Mexico Press, 2001.

———, ed. *Thomas Jefferson and the Changing West*. St. Louis: Missouri Historical Society Press, 1997.

———, ed. *Voyages of Discovery: Essays on the Lewis and Clark Expedition*. Helena: Montana Historical Society Press, 1998.

Ross, Alexander. *Adventures of the First Settlers on the Oregon or Columbia River, 1810–1813*. 1904. Reprint, Corvallis: Oregon State University Press, 2000.

Russell, Carl P. *Firearms, Traps, & Tools of the Mountain Men*. New York: Knopf, 1967. Reprint, Albuquerque: University of New Mexico Press, 1977.

Senate Journal. 30th Cong. 1st sess. April 7, 1848. Washington, DC: United States Senate, 1848.

Shepard, Elihu H. *The Autobiography of Elihu H. Shepard*. St. Louis, MO: George Knapp, 1869.

"The Siege of Fort Meigs." *Register of the Kentucky Historical Society* 19, no. 56 (May 1921): 54–62.

Skarsten, M. O. *George Drouillard: Hunter and Interpreter for Lewis and Clark & Fur Trader, 1807–1810*. Lincoln: University of Nebraska Press, 2005.

Smith, Henry Nash. *Virgin Land: The American West as Symbol and Myth*. Cambridge, MA: Harvard University Press, 1970.

Spence, Mary Lee, and Donald Jackson, eds. *The Expeditions of John Charles Fremont. Volume 2. The Bear Flag Revolt and the Court-Martial*. Urbana: University of Illinois Press, 1973.

Starrs, James E. and Kira Gale. *The Death of Meriwether Lewis: A Historic Crime Scene Investigation*. Omaha, NE: River Junction Press, 2009.

Sunder, John E. *Bill Sublette: Mountain Man*. Norman: University of Oklahoma Press, 1959.

Taylor, Alan. *The Civil War of 1812: American Citizens, British Subjects, Irish Rebels, and Indian Allies*. New York: Knopf, 2010.

Tiffie, Melissa. "The 1808 Murder Trial of George Drouillard." *Rocky Mountain Fur Trade Journal* 9 (2015): 38–63.

Tohill, Louis A. "Robert Dickson, the Fur Trade, and the Minnesota Boundary." *Minnesota History* 6, no. 4 (1925): 330–42.

Trafzer, Clifford E., ed. *American Indians/American Presidents: A History*. New York: HarperCollins, 2009.

Tubbs, Stephenie Ambrose, with Clay S. Jenkinson. *The Lewis and Clark Companion: An Encyclopedic Guide to the Voyage of Discovery*. New York: Henry Holt, 2003.

Utley, Robert M. *A Life Wild and Perilous: Mountain Men and the Paths to the Pacific*. New York: Henry Holt, 1997.

Warner, J. J. "Reminiscences of Early California from 1831 to 1846." *Annual Publication of the Historical Society of Southern California* 7, no. 2–3 (1907–1908): 176.

White, David A., ed. *News of the Plains and Rockies, 1803–1865*. Vol. 1. Spokane, WA: Arthur H. Clark, 1996.

White, Linda Harper, and Fred R. Gowans. "Traders to Trappers: Andrew Henry and the Rocky Mountain Fur Trade." *Montana: The Magazine of Western History* 43, no. 1 (Winter 1993): 58–65.

Wickman, John E. "Peter A. Sarpy." In Hafen, *Mountain Men and Fur Trade of Far West*, vol. 4.

Woodger, Elin, and Brandon Toropov. *Encyclopedia of the Lewis and Clark Expedition*. New York: Checkmark Books, 2004.

Woodworth, Steven E. *Manifest Destinies: America's Westward Expansion and the Road to the Civil War*. New York: Knopf, 2010.

Yurtinus, John F. "Colorado, Mormons, and the Mexican War." *Essays in Colorado History* 1 (1983): 109–45.

INDEX

ABOUT THE AUTHOR

Larry E. Morris is the author of *The Fate of the Corps: What Became of the Lewis and Clark Explorers after the Expedition*, a History Book Club selection, and *The Perilous West: Seven Amazing Explorers and the Founding of the Oregon Trail*, as well as coauthor of *The Mystery of John Colter: The Man Who Discovered Yellowstone*.